Please Protect Us

Also by Toni Maguire

Please Protect Us

The true story of twin boys,
their unbreakable bond and
a childhood of abuse

TONI MAGUIRE

with RYAN & PHIL FISHER

JB

Published by John Blake Publishing
An imprint of Bonnier Books UK
4th Floor, Victoria House
Bloomsbury Square
London WC1B 4DA
Owned by Bonnier Books
Sveavägen 56, Stockholm, Sweden

www.facebook.com/johnblakebooks
twitter.com/jblakebooks

Paperback: 978-1-78946-463-4
eBook: 978-1-78946-464-1
Audiobook: 978-1-78946-504-4

A CIP catalogue of this book is available from the British Library.

Design by www.envydesign.co.uk
Printed and bound in Great Britain by Clays Ltd, Elcograf S.p.A.

1 3 5 7 9 10 8 6 4 2

John Blake Publishing is an imprint of Bonnier Books UK
www.bonnierbooks.co.uk

For Helen,
who has been the most understanding, patient and
thoughtful human being since the day we met.

You have never judged us in anyway and never
thought any less of us as people. The road to where
we are now has been, at times, hard and very painful
but, somehow, you have always found the strength
to put your arms around us both and give us comfort
when we most needed it. We are and will always be
eternally grateful to you. You are very special and we
are lucky to have you in our lives.

Contents

Part Two: Abuse

Part Three: Survival

Author's Note
from Toni Maguire

Since writing my own story in *Don't Tell Mummy* and the sequel, *When Daddy Came Home*, both *Sunday Times* bestsellers, I have received many emails from readers who have also survived traumatic childhoods. Some of the stories have been so compelling that I have sought to turn them into books. The story of the Fisher twins, in *Please Protect Us*, was one such story.

It is only the second book that I have written about boys. After reading all the emails I received from Ryan and his brother Phil, I began to see that in some ways it is harder for men to accept the damage abuse has done to them when they were little boys; that years after it ends, there are still so many conflicting emotions left behind. It is only over the last few years that people have become aware of the abuse happening in various organisations, which has alerted me to how hard it is for men to come forward. And it was mainly that which made me want to get the twins' story out there.

Over the months I worked on their story, it became very much a team effort. I understand that reliving childhood horrors is never easy but Ryan and Phil, hugely supported by Helen, Ryan's wife, have guided me in how best to share their story. Telling it here has been cathartic for the relationship between the brothers and, as you will see within these pages, Ryan has taken a huge step forward as he and Helen now help other young people who have had traumatic beginnings.

Lockdown has been a time of reflection for many people and my inbox has never been so full with stories to write. Working with my wonderful editors, Beth Eynon, and Jane Donovan, I look forward to bringing some more of them to you in the near future.

Toni Maguire
August 2021

Part One

Grooming

1

Ryan

It must have been when Phil, my twin, and I were somewhere between the ages of four and five that I told our mother I didn't like her brother-in-law. I chose the time when she was in the kitchen, her hands in the sink, washing up the breakfast dishes, to blurt out that he smelt nasty, but then I didn't have the vocabulary to explain that it was the smell of stale cigarette smoke crawling up into my nostrils that made me feel sick that I was talking about.

I can remember her shoulders tightening with exasperation before she turned around to glare at me.

'Don't be so rude, Ryan. I don't want to hear those sort of words coming out of your mouth again. Do you understand?'

I did.

Still, those sharp words were not quite enough to make me hold my tongue. I was desperate to get everything out. For Mum to know just what was troubling Phil and me. And then I thought, *It would all stop, wouldn't it?* Small fists clenched, back straight, I used up the remnants of my courage to carry on. I had the words right there in my head that would have got her attention: *Mum, Phil and I don't like the games he plays with us. Can't you tell him to stop?* There, I'd said it. And I let my breath out in a long exhalation of relief.

We wouldn't have to see Clive ever again, I thought gleefully.

Maybe if I hadn't been standing just behind Mum, she might have read something in my expression that would have made her ask a few searching questions. Unfortunately, it was her back I had been grumbling to. A grumble that was enough to make her spin round, soapy hands in the air and a look of annoyance on her face.

'You ungrateful little boy,' she said angrily. 'Just look at all the lovely presents your Uncle Clive brings when he comes. Not to mention all those times he's taken you and Phil out in the car and treated you to ice cream. Now, if you can't think of anything nice to say about your family, make yourself scarce and get out from under my feet, will you?'

With that, she turned away, not seeing the tears forming in my eyes and then slowly running down my cheeks.

I know now it was my 4-year-old's lack of courage that prevented me from telling her just what the games were that Phil and I wanted her to stop. If only I had waited until I was a little older, then I could have told her all about the new game that he had invented, the one we particularly hated. He called it the 'Up and Down Game'. It consisted of him running his hands down our stomachs, before sliding his fingers under the elastic of our shorts. 'Ah, got them!' he would say each time his fingers wrapped firmly around our small penises. And we would look up at his face flushed with excitement and just pray for the game to be over. Not that he was in a hurry to end it. Once he held us both so tightly in his hands, we were scared of moving. He waited a few seconds until there was not so much as a wriggle stirring our bodies and then, those long, thin fingers of his would start rubbing the parts of our bodies we thought were just used for peeing.

'Oh, you're going to be big boys, alright,' he would mutter as he felt those small parts of us stiffening against his grasp. I wanted to say, 'Stop, I'll tell Mum,' but I was petrified and I knew by Phil's expression that he felt the same. I once tried to wriggle from his grip and he squeezed my penis so hard, it sent a fierce, stabbing pain through me.

No, I did not tell my mother about that. In fact, for twelve years, I refused to breathe a word about those games of Clive's. Instead, I tried to block out what was happening as though not talking about it stopped what he was doing to us being real and so the waves of shame playing with my mind had no place there, although for a long time I believed the anger coiled up inside me did. Over those years, I only allowed myself to remember what I had told my brother when I left the kitchen and went to our bedroom, where he was waiting anxiously for me.

'Did you tell her?' he asked.

And I, the older twin, said yes.

'And what did she say?'

'Not to be rude.'

Just uttering those few words planted the seed of belief

that I *had* told my mother, a belief that became stuck in my head for all of those twelve years. And with that belief came my increasing resentment and more anger towards the person I still loved.

It was not until I was made to see just how big a danger Clive was to children that I had to dig deep into those memories and bring them all to the surface.

2

Ryan

To understand Phil's and my story, I need to introduce you to a few of our family members that come in and out. Of course, there's Mum and Dad, and Dad's sons, Ian and Allen. Then there's Warren, my mother's first son, and finally, Leighton, Mum and Dad's son.

I'm going to let you see a little of their past as well as the present, for the foundations of our lives were laid over two decades before we were born. But then isn't that true of most people's families?

It is only since Mum's eldest son, Warren, sat Phil and me down and told us about another pandemic, the one in the fifties, that I thought I was finally getting to know our mother. I wonder whether, had I known about her early years much sooner, I would have become that difficult teenager who blamed her for not making our lives safer.

I'd like to think I wouldn't.

It was only when, with Warren's help, I was able to picture not the mother I knew, but the person she had once been, that I began to see her in a different light. I wished then that we could have stepped into a time machine, whirled ourselves back to the 1950s and met the girl he had finally managed to show us.

I had to brush away those embarrassing tears swimming in my eyes when Warren told me how, before she had celebrated her fifth birthday, Mum had woken with a blinding headache and a prickling in her legs. I should think she must have been terrified. Being young then did not protect children from hearing frightening stories about that fifties pandemic. During the years before a vaccine was discovered, polio instilled fear in many households. Between September and April of each year, it hibernated in winter's dark shadows. During those months, when people caught colds and flu, instead of looking forward to summer's warm days, parents dreaded its return. They knew that once the sun burst through the layers of grey clouds, the virus's tentacles would be ready to stretch across the country, wrapping its poison around children from the overcrowded city areas.

During that summer of 1955, my grandparents, like most families in the UK, turned on their radio to listen to the six o'clock news. The BBC commentators kept the public informed religiously on where the latest outbreaks had taken place as well as names of the schools that had to be closed. While parents did not wish their children to go to bed scared, they could not stop them from hearing about it. If it wasn't from their parents' conversation or the radio, their friends' older siblings told them scary stories about the virus. Outside in the streets, horror stories about polio had replaced the ones previously about bogeymen. The children who repeated them might have taken a delight in watching the smaller ones' eyes grow as big as saucers but no doubt at night, the storytellers' bravado completely disappeared: they knew it was a frightening illness and what could happen to them if they became infected.

I suspect my mother had heard some of those stories long before the morning when she woke up feeling unwell. And if she didn't understand what might have been causing the pain in her head, my gran would have. I can just imagine her trying not to show any alarm as she told her frightened daughter to stay put, before rushing downstairs to where the phone stood on the hall table. Her hands must have been shaking when she picked up the receiver and dialled the doctor's number. I do know, through my elder brother Warren, that almost as soon as she described Mum's symptoms, the doctor made another call to the hospital for an ambulance to be immediately dispatched.

'Why did she never tell Phil and me about that time?' I asked.

'Mum has never wanted pity,' Warren answered with a smile. An answer that explains why she never doled out much sympathy to Phil when he was being encouraged to try to walk. No cuddles for him when he sat down and cried.

'Try again, I know you want to,' was about the most comforting remark I heard her say then.

I'm sure she was just repeating the commands she received first from the nurses, then her physical therapist and lastly, my gran. Not that those thoughts stopped me from picturing my mother as a small, frightened child.

That morning, she must have wondered just who the strangers were who had come into her bedroom, and why they were rolling her onto that stretcher and carrying her down the stairs. And she certainly must have panicked when they placed her in the back of an ambulance and slammed the doors, leaving Gran outside it.

'It would not have only been Mum who was frightened then,' Warren observed. 'The whole neighbourhood would have been as well. I bet there was a lot of curtain-twitching the day she was carried out. Everyone would have wanted to know which member of the family the ambulance was for. If it was a child, they would know the virus had infiltrated their area. They would not have wanted their children to go anywhere near that house, that's for sure.'

He then went on to tell us about the times he had looked up old newspaper articles about the pandemic that ended in the fifties: 'I nearly cried when I saw the photographs,' he said. 'It was just awful. Imagine little kids on crutches, their legs in calipers.

'There were photos of the wards too. Rows of children in those metal beds and nurses in their starched hats doing their best, I'm sure. But still, they weren't family, were they? If you two want to know what she went through, have a look in the library's archives. Pretty upsetting, I can tell you.

'OK, if we go back in history, all pandemics had the same rules – like no one could travel in the ambulance with an infected patient or even visit them in hospital. But just think how awful those rules must have been for little tots to be in there without their mothers. They must have wondered just what they'd done to be taken from their families, mustn't they?'

'So what did the parents do?' I asked breathlessly, for all I knew then about polio was the vague memory of being injected against it.

'All they were allowed to do was stand at windows of the wards and wave at them. So, it wasn't just the children who suffered, was it? Those mothers would have had to squash down all their maternal instincts and force themselves to smile when all they wanted to do was to rush to their child's side.'

Warren paused, his forehead creasing as he pondered something else before adding, 'You know, I've often wondered just what damage was done by those enforced separations. Those kids would have transferred their trust for their parents to the nurses, wouldn't they? I think being in those wards might well have damaged them. I certainly believe that in our mother's case, it did. She was in there for over a month, with no one, apart from the doctors and nurses, allowed into the room to comfort her. She told me she felt so lonely, she didn't understand why our gran didn't come near her. And even when she was due to leave, it was not her mother who sat by her bed and told her about the treatment she was to receive, but a nurse. And all Mum understood was that she was going to be discharged and it was not going to be easy for her to learn to walk again. But if she did the exercises she was going to be shown, one day she would. Mum remembers the nurse said something about small improvements every day, but that's all.'

'You mean when she was little, she also couldn't walk?' asked Phil with a look of complete amazement on his face.

'No, she couldn't,' Warren replied before going on to explain how our mother had had physical therapy every day until she was eleven and after that, once a week for the next four years. In layman's terms, he explained to us that what polio does is that it makes the body's nerves go to sleep and only the right type of exercises can waken them again. However, what Mum wasn't told before she started was just how much pain these exercises were going to cause.

'But,' said Warren then with a grin, 'Mum being Mum, she gritted her teeth and did every exercise she was shown. She hated being seen as an invalid so you can imagine just how bad it was for her when she was taken to school in a pram. Mum told me she was frightened then that she would never walk again.'

'But she did! How long did it take?' I asked.

'The best part of three years. Yes, one leg was left shorter than the other – hence those shoes of hers. "They might be unsightly," she once told me, "but it's a lot better than crutches, isn't it?"'

It was not until Phil and I had listened incredulously to Warren's telling of her story that I realised not only the reason for our mother's limp but why she had to wear those ugly, thick-soled shoes.

I should have asked Warren earlier, I thought, as a blush

of shame stained my cheeks. Instead, I had allowed myself to feel embarrassed at my classmates seeing them.

'So that's why she still has a limp,' I said sadly. 'I never knew.'

If only I had known the second part of her story, then I might have understood even more. But that was not told to me until much later.

3

Phil

I'm the youngest twin by thirty-five minutes – not a very long wait, was it? But it was long enough for my brain to be starved of oxygen. Nor was I aware of my tiny body having a stroke within seconds of my entering the world. Dad told me that it happened so quickly, I hardly had a chance to make my first cry before a team of nurses and doctors rushed me into ICU.

I understand now just how hard those doctors had to work to save my life. While my mother lay in the hospital bed with one healthy baby nearby, she knew my survival would be touch and go. Clearly, I did recover eventually, but my body didn't. The stroke had affected the left side of my brain, which controls both movements and speech. The doctors had the distressing task of explaining to my parents that even with therapy, their youngest child might never walk or talk properly.

'Only time will tell,' was the answer to the question my mother asked: 'Will he be able to have some sort of normal life?' But then, they didn't know that she knew all about struggling to have a normal life of her own, a struggle that made her all the more determined that I too would overcome my disabilities. As a small child, I had no knowledge of my mother's past, nor did I ask why she had a limp. I don't think I even gave it a thought. Why would I? Wasn't mine far worse? It was not until Warren had told Ryan and me about her early life that I understood why she had been so tough on me. And tough, she certainly was. In fact, one of the good things about Warren showing us, through words and gestures, those details about Mum's fight to walk was that it removed some of the resentment I had previously felt – it had taken me up until then to see just why she had been so firm with me. It was not because she didn't care, nor was it because she found my – and I hate to use the word – 'disabilities' embarrassing, which I had always believed. It was because she knew that people who are different can often find the world a cruel and unaccepting place. Something that she herself knew only too well, I now realised.

It was always Mum who encouraged my elder brothers to take hold of my hands and pull me up. Once I was standing, she then told them to try and make me place one foot in front of the other. She was completely relentless in encouraging them to take turns in making me try to walk. Leighton, the brother closest to Phil and me in age by four years, told me that when I was still a toddler, Mum would announce firmly to whichever one of my three older brothers walked into the room, 'Your turn to try and get him to stand. Now take a firm grip of his hands and help him.' So, up I would go and within seconds, my treacherous left leg would start to buckle. 'Try and push that leg forward,' she instructed each time she noticed my leg collapsing beneath me. If I couldn't move it, she would tell them to pull it forward for me.

'Of course you let tears fall,' Leighton said with a grin. 'You knew how to make us feel bad, alright! There you were, tight fists rubbing your eyes, before glancing up through damp lashes, silently imploring us to leave you alone. You always found sitting on your behind far more comfortable than standing.'

I can laugh now about how those tears and snivels were a waste of time. How they never had any impact on my mother –well, not that I could see anyhow.

'If you really want to help him, don't take any notice of his crocodile tears,' she would snap at whoever was on the receiving end of my attempted emotional blackmail. Now, I'm grateful that I had a mother who did not believe in defeat, though maybe she could have relaxed her pushing me just a little. She even told my father to leave me where I was when I saw him smiling down at me as I raised my arms in the hope that he would lift me up into the air.

'He's got to learn, John.'

'Your father will pick you up when you are standing up,' she told me nearly every time. And so I would clutch whatever was nearest me and try my hardest to pull myself up. 'There, told you! You can do it if you set your mind to it,' she would say with a small smile when I succeeded.

Still, when she was not looking, or maybe she was just pretending not to notice, there were times when Dad would scoop me up, carry me over to the settee and perch me on his knee. I felt so safe then. The one good thing, if you can call it that, was my disability gave me the most of everyone's attention! Maybe that's one of the reasons why, unlike Ryan, who has little memory of those early years, I have vivid images locked firmly in my head. There are some I want to hold on to, others I simply wish I could make vanish. Over the years, I have tried hard enough to encourage the ugly ones to disappear into thin air, though over the twenty-five years since we escaped our uncle's clutches, time has only made them fade a little.

If, during the daylight hours, they float in my mind, I can usually push them aside. It's more difficult to do when they invade my dreams. I have learnt to accept what is happening – they're not as bad now as when they caused me to scream out in my sleep. When Ryan and I still shared a room at home, I can remember him padding over to my bed and shaking me gently awake – 'It's only a bad dream,' he would tell me each time.

I wonder if those nightmares still creep into my brother's dreams? I know he had them then. During those years he might have been unaware of the whimpers and protests he made in his sleep, but I wasn't – for didn't I recognise them as being the same as mine? Now, when they try and visit me, I force myself awake. I'm not going to let those dark images stay in my mind; I have other pictures in my head, ones that put a smile on my face. And it is those I pull down instead.

4

Ryan

Up until the moment when Clive came into our lives, I would have described both Phil and myself as being happy and trusting children. Not only did we have each other, but a family consisting of brothers and half-brothers who were always ready to play with us, a good-natured father and a mother who, although seemingly both distant and strict, always made sure there was food on the table. It must have been quite a task cooking for all of us, especially before my older brothers left home.

Regular meals, warm baths, clean clothes and comfortable, freshly made beds were all something we took for granted. In fact, right up to when we reached our early teens, we were unaware that money was scarce in our home. Oh, we never, ever went hungry or wore threadbare, secondhand clothes, my mother made sure of that, but there was little left over for luxuries. Naturally, there were always a few hand-me-downs as you'd expect in any household of boys. Not that we ever thought we were missing out on anything.

Dad's parents had given him an old cornflower-blue Bedford van and with seats in the back as well as the front, it was great for taking the whole family out. We all agreed that it was much nicer than our neighbours' shiny new cars that had to be washed and polished every weekend.

OK, it was not so easy as just piling into a car and taking off. First, the van had to be persuaded to start and then once it finally did and we were on our way, the motor protested with a high-pitched whine going up every hill we came across. I swear we hardly averaged more than five miles an hour on some of those journeys. But all of us loved going out in it, especially Leighton, who said it was the same shade of blue as Manchester City, his favourite team's colour. Football was an interest that he and Dad shared, as were the large air shows held at various RAF airfields.

Dad was a huge military and aviation fan. I still don't know where his interest in it came from as he was a sheet metal worker who had never been in the forces, but some of our best memories come from visiting those bases. Dad, Leighton and Ian simply loved those air shows and they could talk for hours about the different squadrons and their military history. But it didn't take long for the rest of us to become addicted to those outings as well. The noise, the anticipation and the sense of danger as the flyers appeared to dice with death during their acrobatics. The announcer on the loudspeaker always whipped up the excitement and had the crowds on their feet cheering as the flight formations appeared. Occasionally, a wartime Spitfire or a Hurricane would be put through its paces, though the pilots from the

Battle of Britain had long since hung up their flying goggles. Occasionally, these elderly heroes would be there, sat with ramrod-straight backs and signing autographs as they gazed at the sky longingly through rheumy eyes. If the Red Arrows were part of the show, they were always the grand finale.

For us, it was a really great day out. For my mother, it must just have represented a lot of hard work. She spent the whole of the previous day preparing and assembling all the food and drink for the outing. Mum was unquestionably ace at putting together enormous picnics for as many of the family who turned up. Usually Dad's brother, Uncle Barry, who was just as crazy about air shows as Dad was, and at least two of my half-brothers joined our van. Little wonder, with all of us and the huge hamper of food, that the van rumbled and groaned the minute the key went in the ignition.

I doubt the neighbours were as happy as we were when we made those trips, for depending on where the show was, our day started somewhere between five and six in the morning. Everyone helped carry the blankets and chairs into the van. Then the picnic hamper, full of cheese and ham sandwiches, salads, pickled onions and bunches of spring onions too, homemade meat pies and thick slabs of homemade cake, was lifted into the back. Lastly, a basket of soft drinks for us and Thermos flasks full of hot tea and coffee were packed in for the adults. One thing was for sure, no one was going to starve.

Dad nearly always got stressed – someone who was coming with us was running late, or Mum had forgotten something and had to go back into the house, or Phil still hadn't been put in his seat properly. He would often end up losing his rag at us younger ones: 'Stop messing about and get in the van!' he would yell. Without another word, we clambered in. Once we were all seated and everything we needed was definitely in the van, off we set. There were always sighs of relief when the engine decided to behave itself and Dad managed to drive off fairly smoothly.

As soon as we arrived at the base and found the best available parking, my elder brothers and Dad quickly unloaded everything we needed. Blankets were thrown onto the grass, two deckchairs for Mum and Dad and a small table were set up. Tea, coffee and sandwiches were passed around, people we knew from other air shows were waving to us and then we all settled down to wait for the show to begin. The sound system was playing military music, Dad and Uncle Barry recognised the theme music from war films such as *The Dam Busters* and would compete as to who could call out the title first.

Sitting in his deckchair, Dad put his binoculars up to his eyes, where they would pretty much remain until it was all over. The rest of us propped ourselves up against cushions or the hamper and gazed up at the sky, trying to be first to spot the planes approaching before they flew above our heads in formation. Phil and I always played a game to see which one of us could hold off putting our hands over our ears the longest. Which is easier said than done, for when those planes swooped down so low, we felt they were just above our heads. Let's just say there was no point even shouting until the last plane faded into the distance.

Once the final flypast ended, those days of fun continued for another couple of hours. We would walk around the grounds, where Dad and his brother always managed to bump into other enthusiasts they knew. Depending on the location there would be static displays of historic aircraft and planes used by the resident RAF Squadron. Also, stalls selling flying-related gifts and souvenirs.

Those outings were the ones my twin enjoyed the most. Phil would grin away to himself the moment he knew we were going. Our brothers had decided that there was no need for him to be in a buggy all day. They would help him manage a few steps by placing him in-between them and holding his hands. The second his left leg buckled, they would swing him backwards and forwards, making him giggle. And then it was piggyback time for us both. Sitting up on one of his older brother's shoulders, the smile never left Phil's face. Up there, no one could see his leg or hear how he spoke, they just saw two little boys having fun with their older brothers.

These outings were a big part of our childhood and more importantly, it is still a part we can enjoy looking back on, remembering lots of details as we do when we all meet up – something we still do to this day. Even on my own I revisit those days in my mind, see the shows that were so brilliant and wish I could go just once more with my brothers and all our children. Sadly, the Lincolnshire bases we spent so many days out in, RAF Binbrook and Coningsby, have been closed for several years.

Another time of the year that Phil and I looked forward to when we were little were the weeks running up to Christmas.

Over the autumn months, our mother made a huge Christmas cake and the plum puddings, and then the rest of her free time was spent knitting. Around then, we hardly ever saw her without a large ball of wool by her side, a pair of knitting needles in her hands. Watching her, we all knew what we were going to get for Christmas – thick, brightly coloured jumpers and scarves! The surprise element would be what colour yours would be.

While she busied herself with these tasks, a week or so before Christmas my father brought in the tree that was replanted in our garden on the Twelfth Night, each and every year. It was small when it started and as we grew older, it took more and more hands to manoeuvre it in and out of the house.

By Christmas Eve, Phil and I were really excited: we still believed in Father Christmas and knew that in the night hours he would be bringing us presents. Both of us hung our stocking at the bottom of our bed before Mum turned our light off. Of course, like many small children, we tried to stay awake to meet the plump, red-suited man with a white beard, but almost as soon as our heads touched our pillows, we were fast asleep. Then in the morning, there were our stockings filled with oranges and sweets, as well as other small presents. When it came to the Christmas meal, when all our elder brothers arrived, carrying parcels, the table was just about groaning with the weight of all of our mother's cooking.

Now I'm not sure if I can really remember those early Christmases so clearly, or if it's just my brothers talking about them when we are all together that stays in my memory. 'I've still got the scarf she knitted for me when I was twenty,' Warren once said and then more stories would come out. Like how Phil and I wanted to help put up the decorations and they gave him the job of hanging small things on the bottom branches of the tree – 'You should have seen how bright the pair of you's eyes were when we switched on the tree fairy lights,' Warren recalled with a chuckle.

One thing I do know is that we had no real reason not to be content with our lives then.

5

Ryan

During the months it took for me to turn from being a toddler to becoming a small boy, I was no different to others my age, I suppose. The day that I said goodbye to my potty, I was determined I was going to take myself to the bathroom. Something that to all of my elder brothers' amusement, I made very clear to them.

When they tried to help me with small things, such as putting on my shoes and socks or trying to put my arms into a coat, I would tell them I could do it myself. Not that I was always very good at it! Getting a jumper over my head and buttoning up a jacket proved a bit of a struggle, as did tying my shoelaces, but I was determined to manage on my own and not be treated like a baby any longer.

Phil, with his inability to walk unaided, hardly had any choice though. He knew where I was going when nature called and I strutted out the door. How he must have hated the fact that he could not follow. Even worse for him was his problem with speech. He tried so hard to form words, his face would turn bright red with his efforts. Mostly the words he formed sounded like gargling noises, or he would manage to run several together so that they were pretty unidentifiable. What was surprising was that when no one else could fathom out what he was trying to say, I could always understand him. It must have been something to do with a twin's ability to communicate with the other without words. Which meant that when we were little more than toddlers, I became the voice for us both.

Often, Mum would try and stop me. 'He needs to speak for himself,' she kept telling me when, as Phil was struggling to get a few words out, I piped up to explain what he wanted. I watched our mother when she made time every day to try and help him form words that were understandable. First, she would hold up an object, such as a clock, a pan or whatever was lying around the house. She would say its name very slowly, then ask him to repeat it. 'Come on, Phil, you can do it,' she would say after he struggled to get the word out several times. 'Just one more try, my boy.'

A smile of pure pleasure made his face light up each time he succeeded and I just wanted to cheer him on. As I'm sure did Mum. 'Well done, Phil,' she would tell him each time. 'See, I knew you could.' And another beaming smile so wide it almost split his face in two appeared again. 'Now, say it again.' She would say patiently and Phil would try, though often on the second time the word would get stuck in his throat.

Luckily, one of the most important words Phil learnt was the one that told everyone when he needed to be taken to the bathroom. 'Pee-pee!' he would shout, looking around for someone to help. On hearing him and noticing the look of distress on his face, one of my brothers or our father would quickly swoop down, pick him up and carry him upstairs – that was one time when Mum didn't say, 'Make him stand first'!

Phil told me years later that it was when I was beginning to show little bits of independence that he began to feel that we were growing apart. Seeing the look of triumph on my face the first time I managed to put on my shoes and socks was the start of him feeling lost and dejected. *Why can't I do that too?* was the question that began to spin round in his head. For not only could I dress myself and walk properly by the time I was three, I was able to hold reasonably intelligible short conversations with everyone I met. My twin said that was the beginning of people we met outside the house ignoring him.

6

Phil

Of course, I can't really remember Ryan taking his first steps or saying his first words, it's my brothers who have filled in those gaps. Though as they have talked about Ryan and my early days, pictures of our younger selves creep into my mind until I start to feel that they are my actual memories.

I asked Leighton what I did when Ryan began walking.

'You watched him holding my hand and tottering across the room and you thought you could do the same,' he told me. 'You looked up at me and put your hand out, and I pulled you up and your leg buckled, and down you fell. I felt really bad when I saw the tears welling in your eyes.

'You just didn't understand why Ryan could do it and not you.'

'Yes, I can still see you then,' Warren chimed in. 'Not only were you trying to stand, but you were also trying so hard to get some words out once Ryan began to talk. You knew what you meant and looked up at us expectantly, waiting for some sort of comment back. Trouble was, we hadn't a clue what you'd said. It was as though the words in your mind stayed stuck in your throat and only garbled sounds came out. When you saw us looking bemused, more tears would form.'

'That was when Ryan became my voice,' I explained. 'I know he understood what I was saying as far back as I can remember.'

'Maybe that's when you stopped trying for a while,' pondered Leighton. 'You got so agitated when you realised we couldn't understand you. I remember asking Mum why you couldn't do what Ryan did.'

'And what did she tell you?'

'Not much. I'm not sure if she really knew the answer, just that something had happened when you were just a small baby that had caused it. But she did tell me to keep pulling you up, that your leg was weak and everyone needed to help you strengthen it.'

And my brothers did help as much as they could, even taking me to the bathroom when I couldn't manage it for myself.

I can't remember when Ryan and I were both sat on our potties but I do have a picture of my brother taking himself off to the bathroom and me feeling, if not jealous, then upset because I couldn't follow him there.

Needing help to go to the bathroom wasn't so bad when my brothers or Dad were around to take me. But when it was just Mum and me in the house, I felt really embarrassed. It wasn't the embarrassment an older boy might feel about a woman taking him to the toilet, I was too young for that, but

I was old enough to know that she struggled and, with her limp, it was never going to be easy. She was a small woman and as I grew, she found picking me up and carrying me up the stairs difficult. I would hear her sigh, though she never once grumbled about it.

It was about that time that I became aware of the pitying looks coming in our direction whenever Mum took me with her to the shops. Other women in our town would greet her but they seldom spoke to me when they stopped for a chat. Did they think that because I couldn't walk or talk properly that I was deaf as well? I knew they were talking about me because my name was mentioned.

'How is he coming along?' was one of the questions I heard.

'A step at a time,' was Mum's stock answer.

Occasionally, one of them would bend a little so I could look up at their faces. I wanted to smile up at them, but I tried in vain. I could only feel the muscles in one side of my face and a dampness at the side of my mouth where a dribble had escaped. I felt them recoil slightly then and noticed just how quickly they straightened up and bade her farewell.

Soon I began to feel that the world outside our house was a silent one for me.

Everyone in our family tried to help me walk. Hands stretched towards me, pulled me up and then more often than not, my left leg gave way beneath me – it simply refused to obey the command to go forward.

When I was little, there was always one of my brothers who would try his best to help me, but it was always Ryan

I wanted to be close to. I understand now why that was: we had lain together and grown together in our mother's womb over those months before we entered the world. Warren told me that as soon as Ryan could sit up without support and I just toppled over backwards, he held my hand while I lay there like a gasping fish out of water until cushions were tucked behind me.

'And then you two sat shoulder to shoulder in your playpen.'

7

Ryan

Being the youngest in a large household did have advantages for both Phil and me. For a start, our brothers were only too happy to avoid a few household chores by offering to take us off to the park. But it was not only the brothers who were still at home but our older half-ones as well, who on visits back made a fuss of us both.

'How's the small fries then?' they would ask, putting their hands in their pockets and pulling out a bar of chocolate or a packet of sweets, much to Mum's disapproval.

'Too much sugar is bad for them,' she told them each time.

'Shall we take them out and let them work it off then?' was the question they nearly always asked.

Mum always seemed pretty happy to agree to this request though.

'Do you two want to come out with us to the park?' one or other of them would ask.

'Yes, please,' was my answer and Phil's was an enthusiastic nodding of his head.

'Mind you, get them back for their tea and don't be buying them any more sweets or ice cream,' was all Mum said before leaving my brothers to sort out our outdoor clothes and get Phil's pram out of the cupboard under the stairs.

I know that Phil's enthusiasm for going out with our brothers began to wane when he became more aware of some of the stares coming in our direction. This began when I was seen walking and he was still being pushed in his pram. And if the adults only looked pityingly towards him, children were more forthright in expressing their curiosity: 'What's wrong with him?' they would say, coming up close to the pram.

'Nothing! Now run along and mind your own business,' was the only answer they got. Not that it stopped the remarks, which they called out to their friends – 'Hey, look at that spastic in the pram!' Of course, 'spastic' is a word few would use today, but forty years ago, it was different. These comments might have angered my brothers, but I knew they made Phil feel such an outcast. I'm sure now that Leighton running off as soon as we reached the park gates added to my twin's anguish. At eight, Leighton wanted to let off steam once we were through the gates and now four, I did my best to follow him. A noisy little pair we would have been then as we chased each other, kicked a ball around and jumped up onto the swings, although whichever of our brothers was in charge of the 'small fries' as they called us did not allow us to get into too much mischief. At that age, we didn't spare a moment's thought for Phil, who had nothing to do but sit in his pram and watch us. I'm sure he knew, even back then, that he was never going to able to run, kick a ball or join Leighton and me when we played leapfrog.

Luckily, our older brothers were aware of that and quickly pushed Phil to his favourite place – the swings. They made sure that the safety bar was firmly in place before they took turns in pushing it. Up he went, his face pink with pleasure, feeling just for that short time as he swung high in the air that he was the same as other boys.

A feeling that was soon due to be taken from him. By the time Mum's brother-in-law Clive entered our lives, Phil knew he was different to the rest of the family. He just didn't understand why. And that difference had already begun to make him feel inferior. But it was when he met the man whose aim was to remove any confidence he had left that his life took a major downward trajectory.

8

Phil

I have a very clear picture in my mind of the day Clive came on the scene. I can see him now as he walked into our living room, his well-dressed wife just a foot or so behind him. He was a tall man with freshly barbered, thick, dark hair, a loud, commanding voice, a wide smile and, that first time, clutching an armful of presents. If his image had been taken by a camera or drawn by a deft hand onto paper, I would tear it into the tiniest of scraps and give them to the wind to blow far away. But it is not a photograph or a drawing, it is a memory that still lives deep inside my head.

So, what made me take more notice than I usually did when told we were expecting guests? Mum's sister Elaine and her husband Martin were always visiting, but why was all this fuss being made? From the moment Mum received the phone call from her sister Maureen accepting her invitation, we could tell she was really excited. In fact, she was like a whirlwind, tidying everything up, clearing out the spare room which had belonged to my older brothers before they moved out into their own places. Everything that had been left behind was packed into boxes and carried up to the attic. Fresh bedding and extra pillows were put on the beds. Bags of shopping hung from the back of my buggy when she shopped for new bath towels and a bedside lamp.

Yes, my brothers' old room was completely transformed that week.

Not that she stopped there. Over the couple of days before their arrival, my mother worked as fast as she could: every picture frame was dusted, every piece of silver polished. And then came the day they were due to arrive. We had been bathed, our hair newly washed and we were dressed in our best clothes, the moment we finished our breakfast. Instructions were given as to their names. 'It's Auntie Maureen and Uncle Clive, make sure you remember that,' she told us before saying that our toys were to remain in the toy box where they were put each evening. 'You can choose one each,' she added. 'The rest can stay where they are.'

Next, she dragged the vacuum cleaner out into the room and we had to suffer that noise. Once she was satisfied there was not a speck of dust anywhere, she told Leighton to keep an eye on Ryan and me while she went upstairs to change.

I can remember us sitting quietly when the bell rang and she rushed to answer the door. I could hear voices in the hall, Mum's higher than usual, and then the three of them entered the sitting room.

9

Ryan

When asked how old I was when the abuse started, I always give the truthful answer: 'I don't know really, because I can hardly remember much before it.'

'And how did it begin?'

'With Clive playing his games with us' is the answer to that question.

He linked them to nursery rhymes so that they seemed like those innocent games that parents with small children play with them. In actual fact, now I have more understanding of the sort of man my uncle was, I would say he began grooming us the moment he walked through the door. A hand ruffling our hair, those presents he bought Phil and me: two wooden trucks wrapped in brightly coloured paper. Oh, he had brought flowers for Mum and a book for Leighton and paid my parents compliments on how well behaved we were too. But, according to Leighton years later, it was us his eyes kept wandering towards.

'I've got a pretty clear picture of that day,' Leighton said when I asked. 'He was certainly taken by you two. Seemed to love the fact that you were twins, even though you weren't identical.'

Not with my dark hair and Phil's bright red mop.

'Though,' Leighton continued, 'he made sure to be very friendly to Dad.'

I remembered that bit then. When Mum and her sister Maureen had disappeared into the kitchen, Clive had engaged not only Dad, but Leighton as well, in a discussion about football.

That first visit was the beginning of Clive and Maureen appearing on a regular basis. Something that seemed to make our parents happy.

*　*　*

I can't remember exactly how long it took for Clive to start touching us. I know now what a patient predator he was, one who almost certainly formed his plan before he even met us. First, it was just a warm hand resting on our knees, then a hand sliding down to run its fingers over our calves. The next few times when he and his wife Maureen arrived, he would make a point of greeting us with the words, 'How's our little men then?' Of course, I liked him calling us that – those words made me straighten up, puff out my chest and beam up at him.

Mum said he was the ideal guest, especially when he gave Leighton a lift to where he was playing football and took Phil and me along for the drive. For my twin and me, it was a real treat to be sitting on those comfortable leather seats of his dark green Rover and feeling the breeze coming in the windows when he pressed the button to open them.

He stopped to buy ice cream. 'I hear it's your favourite thing,' he said with a wink, bringing us over two huge cones, ice cream sliding over the edges. I remember our knees being patted and when I sat beside him after Leighton got out of the car, his hand slid down to my calf.

'Just seeing if you're warm enough with the window open,' was his excuse.

There were times when my mother and Maureen were preoccupied in the kitchen, sharing a cup of tea and a gossip, when Clive's fingers very slowly started to change direction and began to move upwards. We didn't see straight away that what he was doing was wrong. Phil and I were used to our brothers playing pretty tactile games with us. Either they would tickle us until we screamed at them to stop, or spin us up in the air, making us whoop with laughter. So, when Clive's games included a lot of touching to begin with, we thought he must be doing the same. Which didn't mean that his hand inching its way up our legs didn't make me feel uncomfortable and I knew by the expression on Phil's face that he felt the same. But as we began to wriggle away, out would come a packet of sweets, which he placed just under our noses. Into it our hands would go, making us forget about his sliding hands.

Well, it did then.

His next steps were to introduce a few games that involved a lot of tickling and touching. The first one he recited was all about a spider called 'Incy Wincy' that crawled up a waterspout into the rain. That was one where his hands climbed up our bodies until he came to the bit called 'Tickle you under there'. The trouble was tickling made us scream with laughter, not scream out protests and he used this to full advantage.

At first, the next game that Clive introduced us to looked as though it was going to be fun. He arrived, holding a pink felt dinosaur. 'For you two to share,' he explained, dropping it neatly between us. Now what little boy doesn't like dinosaurs, even pink ones? So, with Mum and her sister watching, we both grinned happily up at him. 'Later, we're going to play a new game,' he promised. Which we did after he had drunk a couple of cups of tea and devoured a few sandwiches. 'Ready now, you two?' he asked, picking up Phil and walking into our garden with me following. The new game was called 'Round and round the garden goes the teddy bear', only in our case this was changed to the pink dinosaur – 'Teddy bears are too babyish for little men, aren't they?' said Clive, jiggling our hair. 'Big boys like things like this, don't they?'

Of course we did.

Not that we liked the game as much as our squeals of laughter would have led anyone to believe. There was hardly a part of us, hands, arms and the backs of our knees, that was not tickled. All the adults saw when we were out in the garden with Clive were two little boys who were enjoying playing his games.

Clever man, that Clive. What could we say to the older

members of our family, that we didn't like the way he was touching us? For they did not see his hand running further up our trousers, touching us in a place so swiftly we almost thought we had imagined his hand on the tips of our penises.

After all, it was just a game.

'He's so good with children,' I heard Auntie Maureen more than once tell our mother. Though once I had seen an expression on her face that told us something else.

'She doesn't like any of us,' Phil said to me in our special language. 'I can tell.'

And he was right.

10

Ryan

I knew from the phone call that Uncle Clive and Auntie Maureen were on their way down to visit us. 'No, they're not staying,' Mum said when Leighton asked. 'They're coming here for a business meeting tomorrow so they've booked into a hotel.'

Business meetings in Lincolnshire seemed to happen on a regular basis for Clive and his wife. Not that I knew what the term actually meant, though I did see how much my parents liked the sound of them. Especially as on the night before the meeting, they were nearly always invited to join them for dinner at the hotel and, for Mum and Dad, that was a real treat. One of my older brothers would be summoned to babysit at short notice.

'Audrey, you do enough cooking for your brood,' Clive would say jovially each time Mum suggested they ate with us. 'No, dinner is on me tonight, it's all down to expenses. So, no arguments about the bill when it comes, John,' he would tell Dad firmly before his face creased into a disarming smile.

Clive always rang from his car to let Mum know how far away there were. No one in our family had a mobile phone, but he had one the size of a brick, as well as another in his car. On the one visit I remember so vividly, our mother did her usual thing and rushed up the stairs as soon as she put the phone down to change her clothes and smarten herself up before his car drew up. But this time almost as soon as he walked through the door, all smiles and charm, he announced that he had a surprise for her.

'You've been so hospitable to us so I thought you deserved a treat. I've booked you and Maureen into a really nice restaurant for lunch. You can have a good old chat with no one else there to interrupt you. And don't worry about the boys, I'll look after them for you. I've even brought some lunch for us all, so apart from yourselves, you don't need to get anything ready. And there's no hurry about getting back. The boys are never any trouble now, are they?'

From the wry smile Mum gave him, I could see she did not entirely agree.

One of the reasons I can remember that day so clearly is not just because of my uncle introducing Phil and me to a different game, but the wave of uneasiness I felt at us being left on our own with him. Not that I understood then just why that was – maybe it was a slight hint of an early developing sixth sense.

When the cab arrived and after Mum had told us to be good and not give Clive any trouble for the third time, she and her sister were off. Once Clive heard the rumbling sound of the taxi's engine starting up as it pulled away, he leant against the part of the wall furthest from where Phil was sitting.

'Now, boys, come over here,' he said, beckoning to us in a gesture that somehow made him look different. 'I've got something for both of you.' His smile was not the warm one he normally showed all of us. I would say in retrospect it was more of a smirk, one that managed to send another twinge of uneasiness down my spine. It stayed firmly on his face while he watched Phil struggle to get to where he stood. That picture of my little brother, his leg dragging behind him, cheeks flushed a bright pink, his expression a mixture of grim determination and apprehension, has stayed in my mind for all these years. I felt even then, when I saw his unblinking gaze fixed on Phil, that making my twin almost crawl across the room gave Clive a curious sense of pleasure.

'Sorry! Forgot about it being difficult for you, Phil. But you managed, didn't you? That's good! The more exercise you have, the stronger that leg of yours will become.' I saw that the smirk had disappeared to be replaced by his normal smile. Later, I wondered if I had imagined that unsettling expression on his face. But then children don't look for the worst in adults, do they?

'The good thing is that you tried and that deserves a reward, don't you think?' said Clive, moving his hands into his pockets and coming out with two large sweets wrapped in cellophane.

Phil smiled at what he saw as praise and obediently stretched out his hand to receive his reward.

'And here's one for you too, Ryan,' he added, still with

that warm, friendly smile. Trustingly, I took it from him and, like Phil, undid the wrapping.

Inside was the biggest brown and cream sweet I had ever seen. One that would certainly fill our mouths. Not that it stopped us popping them greedily straight into them. My cheeks literally bulged, sugar-sweetened saliva slid down my throat.

Within a few seconds, I wished I had just held it in my hand. There was no way I could utter a word. It was just so big, I was scared that if I didn't get rid of it, I would choke. Catching Phil's eye, I saw from his expression that he was feeling the same.

'Now, boys,' said Clive, ignoring the worried looks on our faces, 'time to play a new game, don't you think?'

Playing any sort of game was not in my thoughts then. All I wanted was to get rid of that huge ball of sickly hardness that filled every corner of my mouth. Could I spit it out as hard as I could? No doubt if I had been older, I would have done exactly that, but spitting out a present would be considered rude, wouldn't it? And being rude to adults was not allowed in our home, something Mum had drilled into all of us for as long as I could remember.

Of course, looking back, Clive knew the pair of us were far from happy. But then, wasn't that his intention? Not that we understood this was another way of controlling us. Which was most likely the reason he carried on talking about his new game as though we had already agreed to participate.

'Now, this one is a little different,' he told us. Not that we could ask him why it was, while our mouths were still so full. 'It's called the Up and Down Game. I really think you're going to like it.'

Somehow, I didn't think any such thing.

'Just enjoy your sweets for a few more minutes first.'

Now, I can understand why my uncle gave us a few minutes' respite. He might have wanted to be in complete control, but he hardly wanted us choking to death. Which must have been why he placed a cushion under our heads when he told us to lie down flat.

There are nights when I can still hear that voice of his, so calm and smooth, telling us to lie down, reverberating in my head. 'That's right, on your back, hands down beside you. Good boys,' he said as we did as we were told. I'm sure it amused him not only for us to be so compliant, but also how we were wanting those gobstoppers, as I later learnt they were called, to be finished. Meanwhile, both of us were sucking as hard as we could, desperate to reduce the sweets down to a point where we could crunch them into tiny pieces and swallow them.

What's he going to do next? This was the question running around my head as I waited for Clive to say something about this new game. I could hear him breathing and then felt the weight of his large hand covering my stomach. 'Now,' he said, 'this is called the Up and Down Game and you're in charge. So, which way do you want my hand to go? You choose.'

Well, I knew where I *didn't* want it venturing, so still keeping my mouth firmly closed, I pointed upwards.

Oh, please, don't let him tickle me, was the thought that came into my head then.

He didn't, perhaps because he knew that if we started to laugh, we might choke. Instead, those long-fingered hands of his moved up our bodies while we lay there, hardly daring to breathe. And then he stopped, patted us on our stomachs and laughed.

'That will do for now, so up you both get.'

Not needing any further encouragement, I jumped to my feet and pulled Phil up beside me. Both relieved and bewildered as well as suspicious, I wondered was he still playing a game? I had a feeling that he had something else in mind that he was about to spring on us, but all I saw when I looked up at him was the smiling, friendly uncle I was used to.

One who remained that way for the rest of the day. In fact, by the time Mum and Maureen returned, we had almost forgotten that Clive had shown us the darkness of his other side.

'Let's get you both some lunch, shall we? Your mum and aunt will be enjoying theirs by now, so we might as well too. I think you both heard me telling them I brought it with me. And I know it's something you like.' Then, giving us one of his wide, warm smiles, he opened up a small box to show us the three chicken pies nestling inside.

He was right, they were one of our favourite things, and no sooner were they heated up than we were sat at the kitchen table, tucking into them.

'Time to get the Lego out,' he announced as soon as the table was cleared and our plates washed up and back in the cupboard.

For the rest of the day until Mum and Maureen returned, with Clive giving us directions and helping a little, wc fitted together those tiny blocks as though nothing untoward had happened.

'That looks wonderful, Clive,' Mum said when she saw the large red, white and blue aeroplane we had made together.

'I wondered what you would all be doing to pass the time,' Maureen said, placing a hand on her husband's shoulder. An action that no doubt Mum saw as affection. But if neither she nor Clive noticed the frosty glance my aunt gave us both, I did. Maybe she was anticipating something that Mum hadn't been expecting or perhaps she had picked up on the fact that neither Phil nor I were as relaxed and cheerful as we should have been. For there was something about this new game that had frightened us. And something remained unexplained: why had he stopped so quickly?

But then we didn't know that this was merely a brief dress rehearsal for what our uncle had planned for the future.

11

Ryan

It's funny, isn't it, how the memories we have packed away can suddenly fly into our adult heads, and in a flash take us back to our childhood? It was seeing my neighbour's pretty tabby cat in our garden that made me travel back to a part of my life I would have preferred not to visit. There was the tabby, head up and fluffy tail quivering, striding across our garden as though he owned it. Not one glance in my direction. Oh no, tabby cat had something far more interesting to focus its gaze on: a small bird, perched contentedly on a branch of my apple tree, completely unaware it had been spotted by a predator. A quick clap of my hands made the bird flap its wings and take off towards the sky, while tabby cat, giving me a disdainful glare after deciding I was no longer a friend, shot through our hedge and back into its own garden.

As it disappeared, a picture from my childhood of another cat flashed into my mind. Why did I find that disturbing? Because all those years ago, I learnt something I hadn't wanted to: that there are those whose desire to commit acts we hate is embedded so deep in their nature, there's little that can be done to stop them.

Phil and I could not have been more than four or five years old when we were introduced to that. Not that then we were old enough to understand it, that came much later.

Our next door neighbour's cat, a fluffy cream one with huge blue eyes, treated our garden as though it was hers – something that both of us encouraged. Titbits were smuggled out and taken delicately from our small hands. We loved the feel of her soft muzzle and those long whiskers tickled our fingers. Thanks came in the form of her furry body rubbing up against our legs. When we tickled her under the chin, her eyes would almost close with ecstasy as she purred away; a rumbling sound which seemed to vibrate throughout her body. We just loved it, as we also did when she curled up on our laps while we stroked her soft fur. To us, she was our gentle feline friend.

At least that was until we saw the other side of her nature.

It was only a small mouse, one that lived in the fields surrounding our village. We were in the garden when we spotted the tiny grey creature at almost the same time as our feline friend had. Her purrs ceased as she flew off my lap. Her back arched, her eyes fixed unblinkingly on her prey as within seconds she turned into a creature we hardly recognised. The mouse, recognising it had made a mistake – in this case, a fatal one – froze for a second and then tried to run as fast as it could. Too late! The cat caught it easily, swung it around in her mouth just long enough to terrify the poor creature before dropping it on the ground.

Little grey mouse must have believed for a second that it was free and once more attempted to make a run for it. It had hardly moved more than an inch when down came the cat's paw on its back. I never knew, until that day, that a mouse could squeal so loudly. Though not so loudly as I did, when I yelled at the cat to let it go. Not that she took any notice, her mind was made up. Her coat bristled, her back arched again and without blinking, she picked the mouse up one more time, shook it vigorously and then dropped it. We could hear more squeals, but fainter this time, a noise that clearly irritated the cat. *Time to put an end to that*, she must have thought, as picking it up by the neck, she quickly bit its head off. And then perhaps thinking we would appreciate a present, she dropped the decapitated corpse by our feet. If that was her idea of a gift, our screams must have told her we were far from grateful.

My mother, hearing us, came rushing outside to see what the noise was about.

'Look what the cat did,' I told her as I pointed tearfully to the mouse's remains.

'It's what cats do,' she told me. 'It's in their nature.'

Of course, I forgave the cat when it visited again and I was sad when, at the age of fifteen, my white fluffy friend passed away. But I never quite forgot seeing her torture that mouse. If I had learnt one thing from that episode, it was that while I might have seen a pretty feline friend, the mouse saw a dangerous enemy.

Not so long ago, I remembered that cat. It had no need to kill the mouse, it just enjoyed the game. And it was remembering that incident that brought Clive back into my mind. Not surprising, I suppose, when you look at the similarities of how most of our family saw him and how Phil and I came to see him.

I have never worked out exactly how much his wife Maureen knew about his other side, the one that for a long time remained unseen by so many. When she married, did she believe it was to the man my parents saw? Surely, over the years she was with him, she must have caught glimpses of the darkness that lived inside him? Perhaps she had and, as I had done when small, pushed those thoughts aside. I have never found out if she was shocked when she could no longer deny just who her husband really was, but I do know that right up to when they had no choice, my parents never doubted him.

With his smart clothes, large car and beaming smile, they believed him to be a hardworking man who had done well in his business and was both generous and kind. Phil and I, however, grew to see someone quite different; a man who took pleasure in both controlling and abusing us, a man who during our childhood became our worst nightmare. But then, at four, I had seen that man, hadn't I? The picture of him standing in our lounge, a cold smirk on his face as he watched a child with a disability crawl across the floor, dragging his leg, was one I pushed aside too.

I realise now he was a very patient man. One who bided his time while studying his prey. He took mental notes of our weak points so he could work out which ones he could use to his advantage. The fact that we were close to our older brothers must have been a concern, so it was not just Phil and me he was watching.

12

Ryan

It can't have been many weeks after that visit when we were unnerved by Clive's latest game that he invited us to visit him and his wife in Cambridge. It was Mum who picked up the phone and my sharp little ears heard him saying, 'Come down for the weekend.' She passed it over to Dad, repeating what he had said. And I heard the delighted tones of my father's voice thanking him.

Although we had lots of days out and there were visits to Dad's parents, which Phil and I always looked forward to, Clive's invitation must have sounded a lot different. Both Mum and Dad were beaming with pleasure once they got off the phone.

'You two are going to have a really nice weekend,' Dad told us once he had informed us that we were to spend the weekend at Clive's house. 'It will be good for both of you and Leighton. And he has arranged something for you,' he added.

Of course, we asked what, only to be told that it was going to be a surprise. We perked up at the sound of that word. Surprises always turned out to be good. In fact, our brains were filled with so much curiosity, we pushed aside the memory of Clive frightening us on his last visit.

Going away for a whole weekend, apart from when we stayed with Nan and Grandad, was not something we often did. Then it was just a case of Mum packing a change of clothes for us and a couple of our favourite toys. This time she spent a lot longer going through her wardrobe and without saying why, she sorted out our best clothes as well. The day before, overnight bags were packed, as were a couple of small suitcases. After all, there were five of us going.

Although us three children might have been pretty young then, it's surprising that we can all remember quite a few things about that weekend.

* * *

The journey from our small town, Cherry Willingham in Lincolnshire, to where my uncle and auntie lived was just under one hundred miles. In Clive's car, this would have been nothing, but in our van, we knew it would take all morning.

Tucked in the back, Leighton got us to play the game Spot – like, how many blue cars can you spot? – until Mum yelled, 'We're nearly there, so stop your noise back there, will you? I'm concentrating on map-reading for Dad.'

Knowing a command when Mum uttered one, we all sat dutifully in silence with our lips sealed shut, listening to her giving Dad directions. Once we heard her say that we were nearly there, and 'Yes, this is his road,' we craned our necks to try and see where he lived. And then 'It's here, this is it,' as Dad slowed right down and turned into a long, tree-lined gravel drive.

Tucked away at the end was Clive's sprawling, five-bedroom, redbrick house. Parked in front of the double doors to the garage was that dark green Rover of his, which I instantly recognised. And there he was, standing in the doorway, a wide smile on his face and his arms stretched out to greet us. Hugs all round and then, grabbing our biggest case, he ushered us all in.

Inside, there seemed to be so many rooms that it almost took my breath away. A separate dining room, a room he called 'the drawing room' furnished with two long, pale grey settees, several small tables and some comfy-looking chairs. I heard Mum saying how pretty it looked.

It was when we entered the kitchen where Auntie Maureen was preparing our lunch that I heard my mother gasp. I'd never seen a kitchen like it and nor, clearly, had she. With its black granite worktops, high black stools with the same shiny steel bases as the large fridge and the oven were made of, the room looked like something featured in a magazine. Well, that's what I heard my parents say on the drive home. I remember Mum laughing as she said, 'Goodness, talk about being big! Half a dozen chefs could have worked in that space.'

'Doubt they would have wanted those cream marble tiles under their feet all day. Imagine having to clean them every night,' Dad replied with a grin.

After the first part of our tour, Clive showed us our

bedrooms. My parents were on one side of the house and us three children were in two adjoining rooms with their own bathroom on the opposite side.

'Cor, just look at that!' exclaimed Leighton when he saw the shower with its sliding glass door.

Clive quickly told us that this was not to be touched unless an adult was in the room. In fact, only the toilet and the washbasin were to be used when we were alone. 'Just until you are all a little older,' he said with one of his avuncular smiles, 'then you can have all the power showers you want.'

Once the tour was finished, we made our way into the garden, where a long wooden table was already laid. 'Loads of salad, healthy stuff and good for children,' Maureen told us when she noticed lettuce leaves being pushed around our plates.

The absolute best part of the day came after we had finished lunch. Clive and Dad glanced at each other, Dad gave a nod and the two of them disappeared for a few moments before they made their way back, carrying that very large box that had taken up so much room in the back of the van. 'Something Clive wanted us to bring for him,' Dad had told us at the start of our journey, and although we'd had to manoeuvre around it a bit, we were too engrossed in our journey to give it much thought.

'I think your mum mentioned a little surprise, didn't she?' asked Clive. 'Well, the surprise is in here! Can you guess what it is?'

Both of us were wide-eyed, looking at that box. I wondered if it could be the one thing I had wanted for ages.

Not that I wanted to blurt it out, in case it was something completely different.

'No guesses then?' asked Dad.

We shook our heads.

'Well then, we'd better open it, hadn't we?'

Neither of us could take our eyes off that box as Clive and Dad pulled away all the cardboard to reveal what was hidden inside: two three-wheeled tricycles.

'A present from all of us,' Clive explained.

I could see from the grin on Leighton's face that he already knew about them. That explained why his own two-wheeler had come with us as well.

'I think you'd better practise a bit on these,' said Dad.

Not needing any encouragement, we shot off our seats.

'You can ride them up the drive, but not into the road,' Clive told us.

I can still remember the fun we had that day and how learning to ride those bikes was easy, even for Phil. I have a photo of us sitting on them. Both Phil and I in our bright blue, zip-up tops. I was wearing shorts, while my twin had on a pair of Leighton's cast-off blue trousers. Even then, Phil was self-conscious about his leg and insisted it was covered. Looking at that photo now still makes me smile. Phil looked so happy sitting on his bike – finally, he was able to do the same thing as his brothers.

I can't tell you just how excited the pair of us were at receiving those tricycles. We thought we were little racing drivers as we rode up and down that drive. The bike was fantastic for Phil as it helped make the muscles in his legs work more. In fact, after a couple of weeks of riding them nearly every day, we could all see his coordination improving.

For Phil, riding alongside both his brothers gave him such a sense of freedom.

Those small misgivings I originally had about Clive began to disappear as soon as I sat on my bike. And by the end of the weekend, they had gone completely. But then that was the idea, wasn't it? What I have learnt about grooming children is that it's not done overnight. The predator's aim is to gain trust and to a certain extent, loyalty, from the ones he has selected. That weekend certainly enforced my parents' belief that Clive was a sensitive and caring man. It even began to make me feel the same and accept that his feeling and touching was because he cared for us. But then, I was too young to understand that two different characters can coexist comfortably in a certain type of person's head. There was the man who put his hand in his pocket to help Dad buy the bicycles. And then there was the effort he made to make sure we all enjoyed going to the restaurant he was taking us to.

'It's my favourite place,' he told us. 'I've booked a table for the first sitting. Can't have the boys falling asleep before the ice cream now, can we?'

'Never known such a generous tipper as Clive,' I heard my father say a few days later. 'No wonder the waiters hardly left our table! And that fancy maître d' … well, he just about bowed when we entered. Mind you, Clive's certainly popular in the town, isn't he? Look how many people came up to say hello.'

I think all of us were a bit impressed by that evening. We felt we were dining out with someone pretty important and we were flattered by the way he introduced us.

'My nephews,' he said, naming each of us with a tinge of pride in his voice. Phil, who would normally have found strangers coming up to him an ordeal, felt confident enough to smile up at them and even once or twice managed to say a hello.

That spurt of confidence was, Mum and Dad knew, down to Clive.

Leighton and I found out later that Clive had phoned the restaurant in advance and explained about Phil's special needs. A table near the door had been arranged, which meant, by holding on to Dad's hand, Phil could manage to walk that short distance. Not having to be pushed through the restaurant in his buggy and then being helped onto a chair had made all the difference. Not only that, but there were cushions arranged on two of the seats for Phil and me, so we were on the same level as Leighton. I have to say my twin looked rather smug about being considered big enough to sit at the table without any props.

The careful choice of table and how we were treated explained what Mum had meant when just before we left, I heard her thank Clive and tell him how thoughtful he was. She was practically beaming at him and this from a woman who was not a big smiler, nor in fact was she the least bit demonstrative. No hugs and kisses from her if we fell over, just a cleaning of the graze and a plaster stuck on. To some, she must have seemed rather cold and distant, I suppose, but then she had the house to run, Phil to deal with and her own growing problems with her polio-damaged leg. Something she tried her utmost to hide. So, this smile of gratitude did surprise me a little, as I think it did Clive. I saw him touch her arm briefly as he smiled back at her – 'I just want these boys to be happy, Audrey.'

Well, all of that certainly scored him loads of brownie points for sensitivity. They must have been added to the ones he had already notched up for generosity when he had helped out with the majority of the cost of the tricycles. If he hadn't managed before, by the end of the weekend my uncle had moved himself firmly into the space titled 'The Man Who Can Do No Wrong'!

13

Ryan

Eavesdropping was something that, like most small children, I was pretty good at. There were trigger words that made my ears prick up the moment I heard them, 'school' being one. I knew I would be going to the same one as Leighton and from the bits I had heard, it sounded a fun sort of place. Leighton didn't talk much about his lessons, or the homework he brought back with him. His conversation was more about the friends he had there and the sports they played. Football was the one he raved about the most. I can still picture his face flushed with excitement when he burst through the door to tell us that he had been chosen to play in the school's junior team.

Dad made sure he was there to watch those matches and cheer his son on. I can remember the times they came back together from a match, my father with his arm draped round Leighton's shoulder, while my brother, muddier than I had ever seen him, grinned up at him happily.

'You should have seen him,' Dad said proudly to everyone

in earshot. 'He's going to be a real sportsman. It was his goal that won the match.'

Leighton looked as though he was going to burst with pride at those words. All I could think was that it would not be long before I could also play football as well.

'Good for you, Leighton,' said Mum before firmly telling him to go upstairs and get all those muddy clothes off.

So far, I had only kicked a ball around the park with Leighton but that didn't stop me from wanting to play the real game. Mum did mention that there was more to school than the playground and the football pitch, remarks that went straight over my head.

To me, going to school was the first stepping stone towards being a grown-up. And then my brothers wouldn't treat Phil and I as babies any longer, would they? What I didn't know was how Phil felt about starting school. It was not until we reached our teens that he confided in me what his real fears had been then. He was simply dreading it, he told me, aware of how children looked at him when he was wheeled around in his pram. I had also heard the sniggers and the remarks. But unlike me, my brother was able to bottle up his thoughts and pretend stoically he had not heard anything.

What made his fears even greater was his problem with speech. Although Mum and most of our family could understand quite a lot of what he was saying, I was the only one who could interpret more or less everything he said. He was also scared that once at school, I would be making my own friends and no one would want to play with him. If the children in the park had poked fun at him, what would a whole classroom of them do? But at nearly five, I didn't give that much thought. By then, I might have experienced some touching from Clive which had made me want to push his hand away, and some of the firmness of my mother towards us, but I had not yet learnt what cruelty was.

That was something I had to wait a couple of years for.

14

Phil

Even at four, I understood why the word 'school' excited Ryan. He'd wanted to join Leighton there as soon as he was old enough and do the same things he heard his brother talking about. I'd seen the look of envy on his face almost every time Leighton left in the morning. And as soon as he returned, blond hair tousled, satchel hanging off his shoulder, there was my twin, bright-eyed with curiosity, waiting to hear what his brother had got up to that day.

To me, the word 'school' was one I pushed as far back in my mind as I could. It was not something I wanted to think about until I had no other choice. Wasn't it a word only to be considered in the future? I was able to tell myself that anyway, until it suddenly dawned on me that school was just around the corner.

Our grey skies had turned into blue ones, clouds had scuttled away and the sun's bright yellow globe cast its warm rays high above our heads. Summer had arrived, the school holidays were beginning and Leighton was free to spend time with us. It was then that I realised that the day he had to return would be the same day that Ryan and I would be going with him. That was the beginning of the word 'school' becoming a frightening one. I just knew that I would never fit in. Hadn't I witnessed enough pitying glances when Mum was pushing me in my buggy to realise that it was her people felt sorry for, not me? Some adults made efforts to be kind, but they were the ones who knew her. On the other hand, most children we met showed little of that quality.

It was usually a Saturday when my brothers took us to the park. Unlike the weekdays when it was fairly quiet, it was full of children and their parents. Of course, I was aware of some of the older ones sniggering and pointing their fingers at me. They all saw that I was too old to be in a buggy. Then I heard my older brothers telling some of the ones who acted as though I was deaf and asked questions about me to mind their own business. The children might have scampered off when Warren glared at them, but that didn't stop me from hearing the words they had uttered.

'What's a spazzy?' I wanted to know.

'Oh nothing, just a silly, made-up word,' was my brother's answer.

But I knew it was a nasty one that had been aimed at me. Being placed on the swings with a safety bar firmly in place took the bad taste of those words away. I turned my face up towards the sky, where I could watch the birds circling high above me. On those swings, I always felt a sense of freedom, no longer trapped in a body that did not work like other people's. Up there, I was able to push aside the sting of those children's comments. My brothers believed that either I didn't always hear them, or the meaning didn't sink in. The thing is though that they could only believe that because I stopped myself showing any reaction.

There were other conversations too that penetrated my mind while I sat silently, like when I heard Leighton talking about his gym classes and what he did in them. They seemed to be all about climbing frames and jumping over something called a 'horse'. These were things I would never be able to do, which was another reason for me not wanting to go to school. The worst was knowing that I could never play football – a subject that Leighton, Dad and Ian (when he came round) seemed to talk about all the time. When they watched a match on TV, I could hear them cheering on one side. Of course, no one seemed to consider that for me, watching something I could never participate in might be upsetting.

It was not so much knowing there were games I would never be able to play, it was seeing how proud Dad was of Leighton when he got into the junior team and how close they looked when he had been to the matches. No doubt in a few years it would be Ryan's turn to receive the same type of praise. But Dad was never going to have a reason to be proud of me, was he?

Another worry that kept niggling away in my head was who would I sit next to in the classroom? I'd heard Leighton telling Ryan that it was a great place and he would soon make friends there. So, would he choose to sit with them? In all honesty, this was probably my biggest worry. I'd seen how good Ryan was at chatting to other boys. He knew all those who lived near us, and in the park there were ones who called out his name, but never mine. And what about in the playground? He would hardly stay at my side now, would he?

However good my older brothers were to me, it was still Ryan I wanted to be close to. Now I understand why. When he was not at my side I felt a part of me was missing. Twins feel that bond much more than other siblings, I have been told – 'You lay together for nine months before you entered the world,' Warren told me when I found the courage to confide in him about my fears. Of course, I can't recall exactly word for word what was said, but I do remember how he tried his best to both understand what I was saying and to reassure me that everything would be alright. I suppose some of it is still quite clear in my head because that conversation was so important to me.

Warren pointed out that of course I felt dependant on Ryan – 'After all, he was the one who, from the moment you started trying to form words, understood what you meant. He even seemed to read your thoughts before you managed to get them out.'

He chuckled then, before adding, 'You two looked so sweet when you were little. I can just picture you now. You always tried to do the same as him. When Ryan began to sit up, you did your best to copy him.'

'And then I fell over!'

'Yes, over you went, little legs in the air, and I had to lean over to straighten you up. I did try giving you my hand to hold on to, but the moment I let go, there you were, back down like a little fish out of water. So, then we got some cushions off the sofa to prop you up and there the two of you sat, shoulder to shoulder, grinning away happily at us. So, don't get all worked up about school. Your leg is improving all the time and so's your speech. Of course, you and Ryan will be in the same class. And you've got Leighton there to keep an eye on you as well. You're going to be alright, Phil, I promise you.'

He gave me a brotherly pat on the shoulder, believing that he had reassured me enough. Truth was, he hadn't. I fretted and fretted right up to the day I went. The thought of being in a classroom full of people I didn't know was very frightening.

Unlike me, Ryan hardly stopped talking about it. I tried to think of an excuse not to go. Pretend to be sick or something. But I knew that was pointless; there was no getting round my mother.

'It's not all games, you know, Ryan,' Leighton said impatiently when he had been asked the same questions about sport for the tenth time. 'Wait till you have to learn your times tables and spelling, the teacher will want you to listen then.'

Not that those remarks made Ryan stop, he just laughed before telling my mother that he too wanted a satchel like the one Leighton used. Not that he had much idea exactly what he was going to put in it. A plea Mum took no notice of then. Instead, she surprised us a couple of days before school opened by telling both Ryan and me that she was taking us shopping: 'You are not going to start school wearing Leighton's hand-me-downs,' she said. 'They might be alright for playing in, but your brothers have clubbed together to give me enough money to buy you both new ones. And some decent shoes as well. Warren said that yours were looking a bit worn. And they're coming over later to see your new outfits, so you can thank them then.'

Even I was pleased by that bit of good news.

On hearing the words 'new clothes', Ryan was of course jumping around all over the place. Wanting to go as soon as he could, he simply gobbled down his breakfast. Even I felt a little excited. We had never been taken out to buy new clothes before. Mum had always been very good at altering those hand-me-downs and darning the holes in them.

I could see that Ryan thought it was going to be a fun outing, but the prospect did not excite me. Once again, I was going to be seen in my too-small buggy. And how was I going to manage trying anything on in the shops? But I needn't have worried. Mum had carefully taken all our measurements so that she would not have to struggle with helping two little boys try on clothes. I might have hated the journey there, but once in the shop, I began to feel more relaxed because the lady serving us was so friendly and kind, chattering away to both Ryan and me as though she hadn't noticed the buggy. She helped Mum find the white shirts, grey trousers and blue jumpers she wanted, as well as two navy-blue duffle coats. Then came the new school shoes, brown lace-ups from Clarks, and the specified grey socks.

On the way back, I was too busy sniffing the aroma of

our new outfits from the bags on my lap that I barely noticed if anyone was looking in my direction.

* * *

It was not much longer after we got home than true to their word, Warren, his girlfriend Vicky, Ian and Allen all turned up.

'Hey, small fries! Let's have a look at your new clothes then,' said Warren, his face creasing into a wide smile as he pointed to the bags.

Ryan, not needing any more encouragement, dived into the bags and pulled everything out before Mum could stop him.

'We've both got the same,' he told Warren excitedly as he held his new coat up against his chest.

'My, you two are going to look very smart now, aren't you?' said Warren, looking in my direction.

If Ryan didn't notice the flash of concern on his face, I did. And I knew it was me he was thinking about then.

'So, we'll all be going together next week, won't we?' Leighton piped up cheerfully and everyone smiled and nodded. I too smiled until he asked Mum the question that I had not been able to. Because I didn't want to hear the answer, did I?

'How's Phil going to get there?'

The room fell silent.

'I'll be taking them, of course. Well, I would hardly not on their first day now, would I?'

We all knew that even though my leg was improving, it was still not strong enough for me to walk all the way there.

'I could come with you, if you like,' Warren told Mum and I knew what he meant was that he could give me a piggyback.

'Thanks, Warren, but you won't be able to do that every day now, will you?'

There was no answer to that. Because with a full-time job, he could hardly take me to and from school. I would just have to put up with being wheeled there.

Already I had experienced some of the reactions of children and I silently wondered if the teachers would feel the same.

* * *

So, when I say I have memories about days that Ryan has forgotten, my first day at school is one. There I was, wearing my new clothes, sitting in the buggy, a cold sinking feeling in my stomach that, with every step our mother took towards the school, became colder still.

I could hear Leighton and Phil chatting away as they walked behind us, right up until we reached the school gates. At the sight of the other children standing there with their parents I just wished a hole would appear in the ground and swallow both me and the buggy up. I could feel the stares coming in my direction burning into my neck. My mother must have done as well. But then over thirty years earlier, she had felt exactly what I was feeling, the day she returned to school after contracting polio. Her shoulders went back and with her head held high, she wheeled me through the groups of children saying goodbye to their mothers. A teacher who had clearly been waiting for us moved swiftly to our side.

A young man with floppy light brown hair and bright blue eyes, he had a smile that was both warm and caring. He bent down and took my hand.

'Hello, Phil, I'm Mr James, your teacher,' he informed me.

I wanted to say hello back, but my throat was closed and my lips frozen. I could neither speak nor smile, instead I just looked blankly up at him.

'Don't worry, Mrs Fisher,' I heard him saying to Mum. 'I'll look after him. And you,' he said, turning to Leighton, 'can come along with Ryan this time.

'Now, Phil, I'm going to give you a lift on three. One, two and ...' Warm hands swiftly lifted me from the buggy and gently placed me on the ground. 'Now hold my hand, we'll walk very slowly together. Alright?'

I nodded and with my eyes looking straight ahead, I hung tightly on to his hand as he led me down the corridor leading to our classroom. And all the time I concentrated on placing one foot in front of the other, conscious of that left leg of mine dragging behind me.

I breathed a sigh of relief once we entered the classroom and he told me that being twins, he was sure Ryan would want us to sit together. I wanted to say something to him. Wanted to say thank you. I felt him waiting for some words to come out of me but during those first days at school, I felt too scared to talk. Only Ryan could understand me. None of the other children would be able to. I was not even sure if Mr James would, and that would be even worse. So, I nodded when spoken to, but hardly one syllable managed to leave my mouth.

All these years later, I can still remember what I felt then because it is how I have felt for much of my life. *Was it always going to be like this?* That was the question that sprang into my head then and so many times since. *Were my thoughts always going to remain trapped inside my head?*

15

Ryan

Even now, eleven years after his death, Clive still manages to invade so many of my childhood memories. Before he arrived in our lives I was one of those children who fell asleep hearing the voices of my parents in the downstairs rooms, the padding of feet as Mum went into the kitchen and the creak of the stairs when my brother Leighton made his way to bed. All familiar sounds that, as Phil and I lay drifting off to sleep under our blankets, made us feel safe and secure.

Every detail of how Clive somehow managed to infiltrate our family until my parents were simply beguiled by him still remains firmly etched on my mind. Just how did he manage to do it, to make himself seem as if he was a man without a flaw in his character? Well, everyone likes flattery and attention, don't they? And this was something that he was a master at subtly doling out. Within a few months, he had stepped easily into the role of 'caring uncle', a supporter of my mother and a friend to my father – a man I would have thought he had little in common with. Like a black widow spider, he laid his sugar-coated trail and then watched as one by one, we fell unsuspectingly into his web.

Once there, my parents failed to see the time when Phil and I began struggling to escape his control. They ignored the odd complaint we made, the fact that we had nightmares and that I had begun to wet the bed. Nor did they say anything to Leighton when he made excuses not to visit Clive in Cambridge. Football practice was the reason he gave each time, before adding that he would be fine staying with Warren.

They put the bedwetting down to me finding school harder than I had thought. The nightmares Phil and I both had were most likely caused by us looking at comics too old for us. Oh, Clive was clever, alright. By the time we were in our seventh year, he was able to do whatever he liked with us almost under Mum and Dad's noses. I can just imagine how happy that must have made him feel. He must have whooped with joy when he heard his wife's sister had just produced twin boys – talk about two for the price of one!

His main aim to have not just Phil and me under his control but our parents as well looked as though it had succeeded. He had made sure that we heard his praises being sung by both Mum and Dad so can you imagine just how difficult a child would find telling tales about him then? Especially as he had taken his time pulling out all the stops to ensure that Phil and I came to enjoy his company. There were our frequent visits to Cambridge, where he spoilt us all with dinners out and trips to the ice-cream cafe. Visits that for two years I looked forward to and I thought then that Phil did as well.

Clive had such a knack of making all of us feel special.

It was on one such visit that he invited me to help him in his shop – 'Just to keep an eye open, let me know if a customer comes in when I'm doing paperwork in the back,' he said, giving me a pat on the shoulder.

I glanced out of the window for a moment. Outside, there was a faint mist that hinted at rain to come; not that it had stopped Phil getting out his bike. There he was, blue windcheater zipped up, pummelling away at that bike like crazy. He knew it was strengthening his leg and he was determined to walk unaided into the school. Leighton was with us that time and had brought his bike to be encouraging. I had just been about to join them when Clive brought up his invitation.

Did I wonder a little why it was me he was asking and not Leighton, who was four years older? Maybe a little, but I was too puffed up with pride to give it much thought. Clive really was treating me as though I was grown-up. And what little boy doesn't like that? Even better, no one had asked him if I was not a bit young for the job. Well, if he didn't think so then Mum wasn't going to either. Auntie Maureen, I noticed, said nothing; there was just a tight little smile with zero warmth in it when she glanced at me.

'You make sure you do your best to be helpful,' was all my mother said as she straightened my jumper. I could tell she was pleased that he was taking me with him. No wonder I simply strutted out to his car, where he held the door open until I had climbed in happily. From that first weekend we had spent at Clive's house I had forgotten all about not wanting to spend time alone with him. Phil, though, was still cautious around him: 'Wonder why he's being so nice?' he said more than once. But then, not that I realised it when I was younger, he was always much better at reading people than I was.

There had been none of the 'it's better if you sit in the back because you're small'. Oh no, he continued to treat me as though I was quite grown-up. I was in the passenger seat in the front. He leant over to make sure my seat belt was firmly locked and pressed a couple of buttons to warm both the car and our seats.

'Are you warm enough, Ryan?' he asked, although it was hardly a cold morning. Not waiting for me to reply, he started giving my leg one of his gentle strokes. 'Feel warm enough to me,' he said, flashing me a smile.

Still, I was too busy feeling grown-up as we drove to his business to be really bothered by a little stroke. He had only gone a bit above my knee, so nothing to worry about. Instead, I tried my best to understand what Clive was telling me about his business. The fact that he was talking about it to me as he drove made me feel even more flattered. He explained that his shop was never really busy because his firm did electrical installations – 'It's more the building companies we work with than the man in the street,' he said as though I was an equal who was capable of understanding every word that came out of his mouth. 'But we still stock a few essentials needed in the house so we do get some people popping in.' I can remember that conversation almost word for word because over the years, I heard it being repeated smugly to his admirers enough times.

When we reached the shop, which had a fairly unassuming frontage, tucked into a row of similar buildings, he seemed to take pride in showing me some of the objects that he was selling. Not that I was able to grasp what they were for, but I tried to look as interested as I could. After all, wasn't I his assistant for the day? Before boredom could creep in, a few people who clearly knew Clive well, or at least they thought they did, arrived in the shop, asking for the odd plug or fuse.

'Got to introduce you to my nephew,' he said each time, placing an arm around my shoulders. 'He's learning the trade already.' And each time I heard that sentence, I felt so proud to be standing next to him. My hand was shaken and friendly comments like, 'See you again, son' were offered as they left. His arm remained around my shoulder as he gave me a quick squeeze. 'Well, they certainly liked you, Ryan. I think you're a natural.' Not that he explained what I was a natural at. But at not quite seven years old, I took it as a compliment and beamed back at him. I was becoming used to him being rather tactile. It was just the way he showed his affection for me, I thought then.

He did try again to explain what some of the stock piled up neatly on grey steel shelves was for, but seeing it was going over my head, he came up with another idea, one I liked more.

'As you are my assistant today, you can take yourself off to the cafe we passed, the one just up the road. Get me some takeaway coffee, yourself a cola and whatever cake takes your fancy. You alright doing that?'

Of course, I said yes to that.

'Oh, and when you come back, I'll ask you to guard the shop just while I make some phone calls. Alright?'

'Yes, sure,' was my quick reply. That was a request that made me feel even more important.

'Just tell Agnes, she's the woman at the shop, that it's for me and she'll put it on my tab. OK?'

Certainly, it was. I'd never gone into a shop on my own before, far less ordered something for someone else.

I can't say that during the next couple of hours I did not begin to become a little bored. I could hear Clive's voice, the jovial one speaking into the phone, and a few times the phone ringing for him as I sat eating my cake. Once every crumb had been swallowed and my fingers licked clean, I wondered what was going to happen next. I thought of Phil and Leighton having a good time on their bikes and began to wish I was with them.

As though sensing that I had had enough of the shop, Clive appeared from his office. 'Time to go home,' he said. He chatted to me on the way back, asked if I had enjoyed myself and then slipped a ten-shilling note into my hand.

'Wages,' he told me. 'You've been really helpful, so put it aside for a rainy day.'

No sooner were we back than Maureen suggested that Clive took Dad out for a drink while she and Mum organised supper. A suggestion that was enough to make my father's face light up.

'Come on then, John, you heard the missus' instructions, didn't you?' Clive said to Dad with a chuckle, and within seconds the two of them had made their way to the front door.

That was the start of Clive and Dad visiting the pub together nearly every time we met up. There was no doubt that Dad enjoyed his company. It didn't take long for them to look as though they had been friends for years.

Yes, Clive had purposely manoeuvred himself into our family. And in it, he firmly stayed for another ten years.

Part Two

Abuse

16

Ryan

Clive had waited until we were just a few months shy of turning seven before he decided to adjust those games that we had come to see as harmless. Or maybe only I had, I suspect Phil sensed something that I didn't. When we visited him in Cambridge, I was too absorbed in enjoying helping in the shop to question the fact that Leighton nearly always had an excuse not to come with us.

My chest just about puffed out with pride as far as it would go whenever he introduced me, not only as his nephew but his assistant, who was already learning the trade. Of course, his friends encouraged him and also paid me compliments. Well, haven't I said that flattery works wonders? And in my case, it did.

I even liked the way he spoke to us: 'Hello, little men,' he would say each time we met before tousling our hair and giving us a grin. Something I knew Phil shied away from whereas I took it as a compliment.

Yes, Clive made me feel important.

And of course, what did my family see? Exactly what they were meant to: a kind uncle, whom their twins enjoyed being with.

Clive's grooming had not just been aimed at Phil and me, had it? He'd groomed Mum and Dad as well.

'So generous, so kind,' were the words I heard my mother repeating after each visit.

'Yes, he's a good bloke, alright,' Dad would say whenever Mum brought his name up. Which for him was high praise.

Tact was another thing Clive seemed to possess in abundance. He always made an excuse for his generosity so as not to embarrass my parents: a tax write-off covered the meals out, a holiday home that needed more people in it than just him and his wife was another. While on one of his visits to our house, he invited us to join him and Maureen in Scotland for a holiday.

'The place is just too big for us now the family has grown up and left the nest,' he told our parents as he pulled out some photos from a folder. 'But, Maureen and I have so many lovely memories of being there, don't we, darling?' he added, glancing over at his wife.

A tight smile came onto her face as she answered, 'Yes, we certainly do.'

'And that's the reason we just can't bring ourselves to give it up, so we would both love it if you and the boys came over for the Easter holidays.'

My mother, who had looked at a few of the photos showing a large whitewashed house set near woodlands, passed them over to Dad. I noticed the wistful expression on her face as she glanced over at him – I guessed she was crossing her fingers in the hope that he would agree.

'Oh, say yes, John,' Clive said with a light laugh. 'You know you'll enjoy it and it won't be the same for Maureen and I if you don't come,' he added persuasively, the moment he heard my dad gasp as he studied the photos of the house.

'What can I say?' said Dad. 'It's really good of you, Clive.'

Mum's face just lit up. It was to be the first proper holiday our family had ever had. I too felt excited, because this was going to be something I could talk about at school. Up until then, our breaks had been days out and visits to our grandparents. This was going to be different, I just knew it.

I certainly got that bit right: it was in Scotland that Clive's real game began and our safe world was forever changed.

Phil told me later that he thought Auntie Maureen was none too pleased that we had been invited on that holiday – 'She doesn't like us, Ryan. I know that,' an assessment I ignored. For when Clive had spread out more photos of the town and the house and told us all about the ancient prison he was going to take us to, I could hardly wait.

For once, I blocked my ears to what my twin was telling me. I turned my back on the edges of concern I could hear in his voice as, stuttering badly, he tried to tell me that he wished we weren't going. All I could think of were the plans Clive was making when he had showed us more photos and a big map of the area. One was of a place called Dumbarton Rock and in the photo, the sun glinting on the volcanic rock made it look as though it was rising out of the river.

'Looks like a sentinel on the banks of the river, doesn't

it? Well, in a way it was. Long ago, when we dressed in bearskins and lived in caves, the Romans began to invade us. And this,' my uncle said, stabbing the photo with his finger, 'was one of the Picts' and Celts' strongholds when they were invaded first by the Romans and then by the Vikings.

'Tough lives our ancestors had,' he told us. 'But you know what's really interesting about it, boys?'

A question we could hardly answer.

'You've heard of Merlin the wizard, haven't you?'

'Yes,' we replied in unison as we had been read stories about him by Warren.

'Well, he lived there a long time ago. And I bet you'll want to see that, won't you?'

The answer to that was another resounding yes.

The fact that Mary Queen of Scots had been held there was less exciting to us, even though Dad did express an interest. But then we didn't have a clue as to who she was. Seeing where a wizard had lived was the thing that grabbed my attention.

Clive was going to show us a really old prison, Inveraray Jail, as well as the Rock and there were loads more places we could visit. And we had to go on a ferry to get to where we were staying ...

'So much to see there,' he kept repeating. 'I can take the boys out, John, let them blow off some steam, give you and Audrey a little rest. There's some lovely tearooms I'm sure you would enjoy.'

That was more of his tact. Mum's leg had got worse and walking on anything but a smooth pavement was becoming more and more challenging for her. He knew how much she must have disliked using a stick so he was carefully making plans for places they could go to that she would enjoy.

'The journey from Greenock to Port Glasgow is a bit boring except for Inchgreen's Dry Dock. It's the biggest one in the world. I bet you would find that interesting, John.'

'Oh, I would,' Dad enthused.

'It will mean getting a ferry back over, but for a day trip, I think it will be worthwhile. We can all squash up in my car. The girls might prefer a bit of shopping and we lads can go to Dry Dock. We might be lucky and see a ship waiting there for repairs, I'll find out once we're there.'

There was no doubt by then that both my parents were totally hooked on taking up Clive's offer to join them on that holiday.

'Well then, we'll go. There's a great fish and chip shop near the ferry, where we can all have a late lunch or an early tea. What do you think, boys?'

I gave a wide grin back for although the part about a dry dock didn't interest me much, eating fish and chips definitely did.

By the end of the day, it was all arranged. We could take our bikes, we were told. Which was good, as Phil hardly liked to be separated from his. He was still determined to improve his leg, which to some extent he had. It had now been nearly a year since he had managed, albeit very slowly, to walk to school. I can remember that day really well. He had looked so pleased with himself and some of our classmates gave him the thumbs up.

We were due to leave the moment school broke up. Leighton again pleaded that the football team had an Easter training clinic and so he arranged to stay with Warren. My mother seemed to spend all her time shopping and packing. There was certainly an undercurrent of excitement running through the house.

The day we were waiting for eventually came. Dad loaded up the van in the middle of the night. As usual, he was hell-bent on leaving before dawn broke so that we would miss some of the traffic. 'After all, it's over three hundred miles and we want to get there before supper time, don't we?' he said more than once when Mum muttered that four o'clock in the morning was really a bit too early. He told us that he had arranged to meet Clive near to where the ferry left, once we were in the port town of Gourock. We would then follow him the rest of the way.

Phil and I were lucky enough to sleep through the sound of cases being taken down the stairs. We were still half-asleep when we were pulled from our beds before dawn broke. Mum, as always, had filled up the hamper with food, hot drinks for her and Dad and cold ones for us – 'We'll stop for a break and our breakfast in a while,' she told us once we climbed in.

Phil and I fell back to sleep almost as soon as the van started and had to be woken up once we had stopped. Dad certainly didn't waste any time on that break. Once we had all eaten a sandwich and had a drink, we were on our way again. Phil and I, in between napping, spent our time flicking through comics and looking out of the window.

It was not until the scenery grew more rugged and a sign

announced that we were now in Scotland that we began to feel our holiday had started. Especially when we pulled into a lay-by off the A76 and walked down to the broad River Clyde's bank to have our picnic. It might not sound too exciting, but to us this was an adventure and a sign that our holiday had just begun. It was hard to believe that this huge expanse of water was a river. There were waves on it, and to us it looked just like the sea. Even Phil cheered up as we munched away on our sandwiches.

Driving along the road to Gourock towards the ferry, Phil and I gazed out of the window at the river that Dad had told us was tidal and flowed out into the North Atlantic Ocean.

'Smooth today,' said Dad with a tinge of relief in his voice, no doubt thinking that he had to get the van on that ferry pretty soon.

The moment we saw the sign for the ferry and pulled in, we spotted Clive's car. I saw him coming towards us, not dressed in one of his usual dark suits, but in cream chinos, a pale blue shirt and with a jumper of a deeper shade tied around his shoulders.

'Bang on time, John,' he said with his usual wide smile, when he bounded over. 'I've already got the tickets, so let's get in the queue.'

From a boy's point of view, who had pictured in his head standing on the deck watching the waves, it was not so big a thrill as Phil and I had thought. Not only was standing on the deck not allowed, but it seemed we had hardly got on before it was time to get off again.

'Follow me, John,' Clive told Dad once we had embarked.

On from Dunoon, where we drove into Glendaruel, the smallest village I had ever seen. A few miles further and we had reached Maymore holiday cottages that I saw were on the edge of a farm.

'Forgot to tell you about the farm here,' Clive said nonchalantly as we climbed out of our vehicles. 'I'll take you there to have a look at the animals later on this week. Think you'd like that?'

I certainly would and even Phil nodded his head in agreement.

The whitewashed building we were to stay in might have been called a cottage, but to me it looked more like a mansion. It was simply massive and once inside, Clive showed us around.

'It's even better than the photos,' I heard my mother saying as she admired the wooden beams and the big open fireplace. There must have been at least six bedrooms, a couple with their own bathrooms. Three or four upstairs and two on the ground floor. One of those bedrooms was for Phil and me.

The first thing we noticed about our room was the view from the windows. One of the farmer's fields came nearly up to it and we had a clear view of spring lambs gambolling outside.

'That's a nice sight to wake up to, isn't it?' Clive said, pointing to the window, and we both agreed enthusiastically.

That first evening, the men brought in all the luggage, including our bikes, while Mum and Maureen sorted out a supper of meatballs in tomato sauce with pasta and a salad. I thought then that this was going to be a simply awesome holiday.

Ryan

He waited until the second night we were there to come into our room. I was fast asleep and it was the sound of Phil's voice stuttering with anxiety that woke me. Looking over to his bed, I then saw Clive, a dark figure leaning over my brother.

He must have sensed that I was looking at him for he turned around.

'Oh, awake are you now, Ryan?'

He moved over to where I was and sat down on the end of my bed. I rubbed my eyes and squinted at him, still not fully awake.

'So, Ryan, my little assistant, are you enjoying yourself here?'

'Yes,' I managed to mumble, feeling unease at his presence for the first time in the last couple of years.

What was he doing in our room in the middle of the night? I asked myself.

'You like this house, do you? Think it's quite grand, no doubt?'

What else could I say but yes? I was feeling more and more uncomfortable and there was only a dim night light in the room, but even its faint glow showed the coldness in his eyes. This was not the uncle I had grown so fond of, it was as though a completely different person had invaded his body.

With a faint shiver, I was reminded of the time he had made us suck those sweets.

'Not somewhere you would normally holiday, is it?' he asked in a curiously expressionless voice.

I had no answer to that. True, I had never been in a place like this, but my mind was too busy trying to grab hold of what he really meant to think of a suitable answer other than no.

'Well, I'm sure you've noticed how much your parents like it, haven't you? Especially your dad. He's very grateful to Maureen and I, told me he could never have afforded anywhere like this. I mean, your family never really has holidays, does it? It's just not in their budget – expensive things, children. But your dad's such a good man. He's prepared to go without to make sure you and Phil have everything you need, so you two owe it to him to make sure he really enjoys himself, don't you?'

What was he going on about now? It was the question that I wasn't prepared to ask out loud. Somehow I knew he was really telling me something else in the form of questions.

'But that's what families are about, aren't they? They look out for one another. And since I've become part of yours, that's what I've done, isn't it?'

'Yes,' was all I could manage.

Did he want thanks?

Whatever he wanted, he hadn't finished making it clear.

'And you, Ryan, I've looked out for you and your brother, haven't I? Made sure you got both got those bikes. And just look at how good that has been for Phil. That leg of his is so much better, isn't it?'

Again, I agreed with a yes and tried to smile at him, but I was conscious of my brother in the other bed watching us and I felt his fear. I knew it was because Clive was there.

'So,' he said finally, 'I thought as I can't sleep, you two could show a little gratitude and play some games with me. Just so as I can go back to bed and get a good night's sleep. I'll need it as I'm taking you all out to the largest dry dock tomorrow and your dad can't wait to go. Now you know what the Up and Down Game is, don't you? So, up you get,' he said, turning his gaze towards Phil. 'I know you're still awake, so you get up as well. Then the two of you can lie down over there,' he told us, pointing to a large sheepskin rug. 'That will be more comfortable for you, won't it?'

I sensed then what was coming and walked hesitatingly over to it as Phil crawled out of his bed and did the same.

'Lie down on your backs now,' he instructed us. Without saying a word, we did as he told us. 'Now, boys, you remember the Up and Down Game, don't you? Well, we're going to play it again, only a little more grown-up version than the one we played before. You'll like that, won't you?'

Neither of us replied. Phil was just about incapable of speech and I was not much better. I already knew that whatever he had in mind, we were not going to like it. I remember my body was completely stiff with fear once I was on that rug. As he had done over two years ago, Clive placed his hands on our stomachs.

'Now, boys, which way shall I go, up or down?'

'Up,' I said, praying silently that this was all he wanted to do.

Up went his hands, stroking us.

'Now, it's my turn to choose,' he whispered, 'and I say down.' And his hands snaked quickly under our pyjamas and landed on our penises. I felt his cold finger stretching mine in his hand before his grip tightened and he moved his fingers backwards and forward until I felt that part of my body growing stiff.

Stop, please stop, my mind was screaming to him and to my body, but still, I lay motionless. I felt a tingling going up my spine, a dizziness in my head.

'See, you liked it, Ryan,' he told me mockingly when he finally let go. 'I felt you wriggle and saw your eyes glaze, that's all the proof I need. You can't fool me! Can't say the same for Phil, though, need to work a bit harder on him.'

I wanted to tell him to leave Phil alone. We might have been twins but I was the elder, wasn't I? And I was taller and I didn't have a bad leg. It was my job to look out for him, wasn't it? Mum had always said it was. Instead, I just sat there saying nothing, waiting for the night to be over.

Phil was so completely helpless. I knew he wanted to push Clive's hands away, but he couldn't. Clive made sure of that – when he crouched over him, it was Phil's left side he positioned himself over. I looked away; I couldn't bear to see the expression in Phil's eyes begging me to do something to help him. But even when I shut mine, I could feel his silent pleas ringing in my head. Twins I had learnt by then can sense each other's emotions. I wonder if he also felt my shame? I heard my little brother trying to form words so that he could beg Clive to stop, something he never managed to do when agitated. My eyes refused to stay shut when I heard him and, with a sick feeling, I looked over, only to see Phil's arms jerking.

Clive must have realised that he had almost gone too far for he rose up and patted Phil on the head.

'Don't worry, little man, you'll soon grow to like it. All boys do, you know.'

And then as though nothing untoward had happened in the room, he gave us one of his 'nice uncle' smiles.

'Now, boys, you remember what I said about tomorrow? We're going to have a nice day out. Your father's really looking forward to it so I want you two to be on your best behaviour. Be a pity, wouldn't it, if anything went wrong and your dad was disappointed, don't you agree?'

We both nodded – it was all we could bring ourselves to do.

There was no mistaking a firm threat was implied: we were not to cause trouble because if we did, it would ruin our parents' holiday and they would be angry.

And then with his usual white smile, Clive said goodnight and was gone.

Phil and I looked at each other without saying a word – it was just too difficult to talk. Then we climbed back into our beds.

As I pulled the blanket over my head, I wanted to block the world out. *What was that feeling I had felt in my stomach?* I hadn't enjoyed it, he had lied about that. But then I still had to learn that lying was something else that Clive was exceptionally skilled at.

*   *   *

The next day, Mum came into our room and despite it being early, the sun was already up. Clive had explained the night before that in Scotland, summer evenings are longer and dawn is earlier than where we lived.

'Lovely day,' she announced brightly. 'Time for you two to get out of bed. And look,' she added as she drew the curtains, 'there's a sheep saying good morning to you.'

Sure enough, there was a woolly white head with those long-lashed, yellow eyes just outside our window. At least the sight of it managed to make me smile. After instructing us to wash our faces and hands before we got dressed, she left us.

'Breakfast will be ready in the kitchen,' she told us before closing the door.

Phil and I looked at each other but neither of us could bring ourselves to say anything about what had happened in the night. Instead, we did as Mum had told us to do, then pulled on our clothes and still without saying a word, we made our way downstairs.

'Ah, here are my two little men,' said Clive as we walked in. 'Looking forward to our day out? Your dad certainly is.'

And what could we do but agree?

I suppose what I should have felt then was anger, I should have had the courage to speak up. What I felt instead was shame, a deep penetrating shame.

This feeling was not going to leave me for a very long time. There were times when I could see it in my eyes when I looked in the mirror, making me clench my fists in anger. Many times, I felt such an urge to smash the glass into a thousand little pieces. Instead, I bottled it up inside me and tried to tell myself that everything was going to be alright. Not that I believed that.

I can't recall much about that trip to the Dry Dock, nor the crossing on the ferry or actually going around the dock. I just remember that my father enjoyed it. Mum had not wanted to go – 'Too much walking,' she said – so she and Auntie Maureen took themselves off to a cafe and for a bit of shopping.

After we had walked round for what seemed like hours, we collected Mum and our aunt and we all went to the fish and chip cafe near the ferry. The smell of our lunch cooking should have made my mouth water, but it didn't. And once the food was placed in front of me, I had to force it down. At one point, Phil caught my eye and I did my best to smile at him.

The pair of us must have put on some sort of a reasonable act or Mum and Dad just thought we were tired from our early start, for neither of them asked why we were being so quiet. But then Dad and Clive were busy talking about what they had seen at the dock, while Mum was doing her best to appear interested. I felt the chill of Auntie Maureen's gaze directed towards us and, glancing up, I saw that there was no smile coming in our direction.

That night, I sat in my bed, drew my knees up to my chin and rested my head on them. I was too scared to close my eyes. Fearful that Clive would come into our room once he was sure that everyone was asleep. I prayed he wouldn't right up to when I could no longer fight it off and lay down and fell fast asleep.

He didn't that time. And having slept through the night, I felt a little brighter. Maybe that night was a one-off and he was sorry, was the hopeful thought running through my head as I brushed my teeth.

Once we were in the kitchen, where the aroma of grilling bacon brought saliva to my mouth, Clive suggested that everyone should take it easy for a bit and he would take both Phil and me to the farm.

'You'll see the animals up close then,' he told us. 'How would you like that?'

'Sounds good,' was my reply.

After all, there was not much he could do to us on a farm was there? And as soon as breakfast was over, we left.

His arm, which grew heavier with each step we took, was lying across my shoulders on the walk there. While Phil, not wanting to come close to him, determinedly rode his bike. He didn't want to have a fall and be picked up by Clive, that was for sure.

Clive's presence might have overshadowed most of the enjoyment we could have had on that holiday, but the one good memory that still stays with me is those visits to the farm. Acres of green fields provided the grass to feed the animals. The fields were being mown the first day we visited and that intoxicating smell of freshly cut grass was enough to make me want to bury my nose in it – the scent remains in my childhood memories to this day.

The farmer, a big blond man with twinkling blue eyes, came out of the house to greet us. He shook Clive by the hand and said it was good to see him again. Then Clive, still with an arm thrown over my shoulders, introduced us as his nephews. He even managed to place a tinge of pride in his voice when he said the word 'nephew'.

He was back to being the good-natured and benevolent uncle, or so it seemed.

'You'll have to bring them back again and I'll give them a ride on my tractor. Would you like that, boys?'

Now that received two resounding yes responses and I felt myself beginning to relax a little. We might have seen the sheep with their lambs in the fields from our bedroom window but seeing them close up was just so much better. I noticed how the newest ones hardly left the ewes' sides, nor did the smallest of the pale brown long-legged calves nestling close to their mothers.

'That one was born yesterday,' the farmer told us, pointing to a deep cream calf. 'Look, bairns, her legs are still a bit shaky.'

I leant over the fence to see better and a pair of huge, thick-fringed brown eyes looked back at me.

'She's beautiful!' I exclaimed, wishing I could go over and stroke her.

'Aye, that she is.'

When I asked the farmer if I could go into the field, he just laughed.

'She and her mother would run off if you tried,' he said with a grin. 'That's if she didn't toss you in the air with those wee horns of hers.'

Then he took my arm and my eyes followed the direction he was pointing to.

'Now, what do you think of that then, laddies?'

Following the direction of his finger, my eyes landed on the biggest animal I had ever seen.

'He's a handsome creature, my bull. Won loads of prizes. And he's father to all those calves you can see. Not that he shows much interest in them, leaves it to the cows to look after them.'

I was pretty enthralled by the bull but there was no way I would ask to go anywhere near him.

We must have stayed at the farm for well over an hour. The farmer's wife brought out coffee for Clive and milk for us. It tasted far better than any we had poured from the bottle.

'It will do,' the farmer said laughing when he saw us smacking our lips. 'It was in the cow till last night! Can't get fresher than that, can you?'

When we left the farm, we were in high spirits – that was until Clive stopped walking when we reached the woods. As the trees closed in around us, he roughly pushed me against a tree.

'Get off your bike, Phil,' he ordered, 'and sit down. And don't worry, you'll have your turn next.'

And before I could form the words 'Please don't', his hand went down my trousers, grabbing my penis with a really hard grip. His fingers moved so fast, it began to hurt. I felt as though the skin was being ripped, and whimpering with fear, I put my hands somewhere below his chest and tried as hard as I could to push him off.

He stopped.

'You hurt me,' I protested loudly, doing my best not to cry. Being weak would not make him respect me. I remembered seeing the contempt on his face when he had watched Phil struggling across the room to him.

'I'm so sorry, Ryan, I didn't mean to,' he said, and to me, he sounded sincere. Of course, what he really meant was that he didn't want to return a boy to his parents with tear tracks on his face.

On the other hand, he didn't want me hating him either.

In his fantasy world, him pulling away at my private parts was something I would learn to really enjoy. I wonder now if he even thought there was a real bond between us, the one he had tried so hard to form. Did he not realise that while it had taken the best part of two years to completely win me over, it had taken less than an hour to shatter my illusions? He must have been aware in one part of his brain that I hated what he did, otherwise he would not have blackmailed the two of us into keeping quiet. The word 'abuse' it seemed was not in his vocabulary any more than it was in mine, not then.

Hurting me that morning might have won me an apology, but what it did not do was stop him coming into our rooms. Not every night, but often enough for the pair of us to be sitting up in bed, listening with dread for his footsteps. Ones we never heard, for he waited until everyone in the house was deep in their slumbers before he came to us, wearing soft slippers to muffle his footsteps.

It took him a few more days before he appeared. This time it was earlier in the night and he came straight over to my bed.

'Have to be quick, Ryan,' he told me as though the news would come as a disappointment. 'Maureen's having a bath, she'll be up to her chin in it.'

Not an image I wanted in my mind.

It was the same as the first night except this time he just pulled back the bedclothes and shot his hand down the front of my pyjamas before I could move. I knew Phil was watching, thinking it would be his turn next.

Not removing those fingers of his from that part of my body that still felt so tender, he glanced over his shoulder at my twin.

'You'll have to wait for your turn,' he said mockingly. 'But don't worry, I'll start with you the next time.'

A few minutes later, he gave a sigh and stood up. 'That will have to do for tonight,' he said, shooting us a grin of satisfaction as he opened the door and to my relief, walked through it.

I prayed each time that he would not return, but to no avail. Those visits marked what I was always to think of as the holiday from hell.

18

Ryan

It took scarcely more than a day or two before Clive was back in our room. Again, it was my bed he made his way to first.

'Your brother will have to wait a bit, I've not got much time.'

He laughed then, a hollow sound that made me tremble.

My whole body clenched as he leant over me. I felt his hand on my stomach sliding down to that small part of my body, my 'willie' as I called it then, that he was so determined to hold. I could feel every one of his long fingers grasping it. This time his grip was tighter, his rubbing faster. There was an urgency in him I had not seen earlier. Before I shut my eyes to block out his face, I saw that it was flushed and his eyes, which once looked at me with warmth, were dark, glittering and unseeing.

I just hoped that he meant what he had said, that he didn't have much time. Then he would have to leave Phil alone, wouldn't he? But he didn't. As soon as he was satisfied with what he had been doing with me, he sprang up while my body was still throbbing and shot over to where Phil lay. I could see him bending over my brother's small body and this time, as much as I wanted to hide under the bedclothes, I was unable to take my eyes off them. I saw his hand disappearing and knew that he was doing to Phil what he had done to me.

This was so much worse than the Up and Down Game. Mainly because there was no way I could think of this act as any sort of game, for Clive had stopped disguising it as anything other than what he wished to do. And having seen the side of him that had little feeling for our distress, I had already felt that any protests on my part wouldn't stop him and somehow I knew they would only make him angry.

At the back of my mind, I couldn't help but wonder just what would be the next thing he would think to do to us.

19

Phil

The past, I have learnt, never leaves us. However hard we try to hide it under layers of alternative pleasant memories, it somehow manages to push its way into our minds and dreams. Which must have been the reason I had such negative feelings when we returned from Scotland, feelings which have never left me. The shame I felt stayed with me for many years, as did the darkness of deep black loneliness. As a child, there was no one I could run to and tell about what had happened with Clive, was there? Or so I believed. One part of me wanted Ryan to go back to Mum again and tell her exactly what Clive had done, not just to me, but to both of us. But then I worried just what might happen if he did.

Would Clive find a way to punish us so that no one would know?

I had felt the cruelty that lived inside him ever since I was small. A cruelty that frightened me. It shone out of his eyes when his 'nice person' mask slipped. And when there was no one near he wished to impress, it also echoed in his voice.

I was aware, even then, that his smile and charm hid something rotten deep down in the core of his being. Yes, I knew that alright, same as I knew the day we left Scotland that we were far from free of him. What had happened there was going to be repeated. I felt so desperately aware that there was little we could do about it. Our parents liked him so much; it was as though he had woven a spell over them and they were incapable of seeing his flaws. Whose side would they take if Ryan spoke up? I hardly wanted to know the answer.

And our older brothers? They came to the house less often now, they were busy getting married and having children of their own. And when we did see them, their wives or girlfriends were usually with them. And what would they say anyhow? Why had we let it happen, we hadn't told Mum and Dad the first time, so why tell them now?

It was Warren's reaction that I was most worried about. Wouldn't he be angry if we caused trouble? Being Mum's first child, he was close to her and I knew how pleased he was for her when she and her sister Maureen became such good friends after so long. It was something I had heard him express more than once.

I had a pretty good idea that there was a reason they had not seen each other until the day Maureen arrived with Clive. Though no one had explained why that was and to be fair, I had never asked. But I had heard Warren praising Clive for bringing his wife back into the family fold and I had seen how overjoyed he looked when Mum told him that we were going on holiday with them.

'Brilliant, Mum! I'm sure you will all have a wonderful time,' I heard him saying when she told him about it.

So how could I bring myself to ask Ryan to tell Mum about Clive? The answer was that I couldn't. Nor did I confide in him about my concerns, for I guessed that he had the same ones as me.

Two days after our return, we were off to school again.

'What are we going to say about our holiday?' I asked Ryan.

'That we had a good time. What else can we say?' he answered. 'Wouldn't want anyone to think we didn't, would we?'

'I suppose not,' I said, though I didn't know how I was going to pretend that I had enjoyed our time there. But then no one expected me to talk much. For once, my difficulty in talking coherently was working to my advantage.

Ryan, I have to admit, was pretty good at telling tales about what we had done on our holiday. He talked about the farm and received wide-eyed interest when he told the class he had seen a place where a wizard once lived.

Clive had lived up to all his promises and taken us out on the trips he had told us about. And yes, we had seen the prison and a lot of the beauty spots in the area, as well as exploring the Isle of Bute, where we had spent a couple of hours going around a huge house called Mount Stuart. I heard him telling Mum and Dad that its blend of Georgian and Victorian made it unique, whatever that meant. But they had looked impressed. There was one really sunny room with a glass roof. Clive explained that during the war, it had been used as an operating room for wounded soldiers. I struggled up and down the large staircase. Everyone said it was so impressive, but I just found it a huge challenge. I must say, Ryan and I were pretty bored with walking around that vast building while the adults kept exclaiming how wonderful everything was. The only things I enjoyed were looking up at the ceiling studded with stars and the tea with cream cakes that we had outside. Not that any of this eased my thoughts about how Clive had made us both suffer on those nights when he slid into our room.

If there were any good memories of our holiday that we could have stored in our minds, Clive had wiped them out and replaced them with bad ones. Not that anyone would have guessed that we had not enjoyed ourselves. Ryan even told the teacher about that house on Bute. I have to say I admired his act and wondered how he was able to sound so cheerful about Scotland.

Thankfully, Ryan could talk for both of us. I had no wish to say anything. As far as I was concerned, the words floating around my head were better staying there. The whole time I was at my desk trying to listen to the teacher, images of Clive and what he had done to us kept flashing into my mind. The mocking smile when he looked in my direction that made my skin crawl. There was another expression I had seen his face, one that made me want to curl up and go to sleep and never wake up again – it told me that he had no intention of ever taking no for an answer.

My teacher, ignoring the fact that I must have looked as though I was daydreaming, smiled over at me.

'What about you, Phil? You're being very quiet, did you have a good time too?'

And glancing over at Ryan, I managed to tell my first lie.

'Yes,' I told her.

Luckily, before I was asked any more questions, she reminded me that I was going for my hydrotherapy the following day. It was something the school had recommended almost as soon as I had arrived, as they had my speech therapy. It was this teacher who nearly two years earlier had explained to Mum how it would help me and what I would be doing there. Basically, it was going to be some kind of swimming that would help strengthen both my leg and arm.

I managed a smile then – just being in water made me feel peaceful and calm. Seeing the look on my face, she said, 'I expect you missed going when you were away.' In truth, I had given it little thought – there was too much else on my mind. But I said yes anyhow.

For the rest of the lesson I tried to concentrate on getting simple sums right, but the numbers swam in front of my eyes. When the bell rang, I breathed a sigh of relief. All the class rushed out, except Ryan.

'Do you want me to stay with you, Phil?'

I shook my head.

It was on those breaks that, once I had eaten my lunch, I worked on my motor skills during the time my classmates were racing around outside. Something that took both patience and concentration. I was thankful that I could spend the time with those exercises that helped encourage the muscles in my left arm to work. There was no background noise, just a quietness that helped me concentrate on fitting those different shaped wooden blocks into their right holes. In my first year at school, I had been given huge balls of playdough to grip and turn into a ball, but I preferred those wooden blocks – they were less messy.

I know that some of the other children made jokes about it, not that I took much notice. There were other problems at school that I refused to talk about. Like the children who, when they thought there were no teachers listening, called me 'Spaz'. I knew they sneered at how my leg still dragged behind me, even after all my exercises, and that I still had difficulty with coherent speech, but on top of that, did I have to have red hair as well?

Talk about triple whammy!

'Carrot top,' my classmates called me teasingly, though that was nothing as bad as the taunts a few of the older boys threw in my direction.

Ryan would always take my side when he heard them. Told them to leave me alone. And if Leighton was around, he simply threatened to punch them if they didn't shut up. Being such a good football player made him well respected in the school and no one wanted to get into a fight with him. He'd always been protective of both Ryan and me, even if he was only four years older. Being called a Spaz was hurtful alright, but thanks to my brothers, I was able to ignore the culprits who threw those insults at me.

Ryan would tense up and scowl angrily, much to Leighton's amusement.

'You'll have to wait till you're a bit bigger,' he told him.

I was really sad when our elder brother moved on to the senior school. Luckily, it was not far away and he still came to meet Ryan and me so that we could walk home with him.

I never told him about the worst comment I heard, coming from the blonde-haired mother of the boy who called me 'Spaz' at every opportunity – 'I don't understand why this child is in our school. Should be in a special one for retards, don't you agree?' I didn't hear the other mother's answer, but I saw her nod in agreement.

'Everything alright, Phil?' asked Leighton when he rushed over to where I stood, my ears still ringing with that woman's voice.

'Yes,' I said.

20

Phil

It was about a week later when my mother announced that Uncle Clive and Auntie Maureen would be paying us another visit.

I felt my heart race at those words.

'Now aren't you pleased we'll be seeing them again so soon?'

Ryan managed to croak out yes, I just nodded my head.

'Can we take our bikes out, Mum?' Ryan asked her, clearly wanting to get away from any more talk about Clive.

'Yes, just be careful,' she replied.

I followed my brother out and I could see his face was flushed.

'Why is he coming so soon?' he asked.

A question we both knew the answer to. All I felt then was a growing sense of despair as I mounted my bike and pedalled out into the road as fast as I could. I wanted to get away from the house, get away from the sound of Clive's name, get away from everyone. I heard Ryan's voice calling out to me to wait, then he shouted for me to slow down and that made me pedal even more furiously – I didn't even want to hear his voice.

It was my leg that let me down. It just didn't have the strength to stop when I reached the end of the pavement. Instead, the bike swerved as it hit the road and I felt myself being tossed over the handlebars and my face connecting with the gritty tarmac of the road. All the air went out of me, I could hardly make a sound. And I just lay there, my face and body hurting so much but I was unable even to cry.

Then I heard the sound of running feet as one of our neighbours came rushing out of her house. Her voice was calm and reassuring as she told me to keep still for a moment.

'Just want to make sure nothing's broken,' she explained as her hands went gently over my body before she helped me sit up. But I couldn't see her face until I was sitting on the edge of the pavement and I could hear my twin's worried voice above me.

'He's alright, isn't he? He's going to be OK?'

'Yes, Ryan. Now if you want to help, ride back to your house. Carefully, mind. Tell your mum Phil's had a bit of an accident and I'm bringing him back, alright? His face will need a bit of attention, but faces heal quickly.'

She smiled at me. 'You're going to have rather a big bruise, Phil. Now let's get you standing.' And her arms went under mine as she helped me up.

Once I was on my feet, I could feel how much my face was smarting and I felt blood trickling down it. I almost welcomed that pain – it took my mind off everything else.

'No more cycling for you today,' our neighbour said. 'I'll wheel it back and you just grab my other arm.' And slowly, one step at a time, we made our way back to our house.

After Mum had thanked the neighbour profusely and I was seated in the kitchen, she took my face in her hand. 'Better get it cleaned up. You've taken a layer of skin off that side,' she said as she bathed it in a mix of warm water and Dettol, which really stung. When she was satisfied that she had removed all the dirt, she gently patted some antiseptic cream on my grazes, which made my face burn again. 'Best you rest now,' she told me. 'At least you're brave,' she added gently. 'No tears.'

There were, she just couldn't see them: they were trapped inside me.

21

Ryan

The ringing of the doorbell was a sound I had grown to hate. Except for Clive and Maureen, most of our visitors came straight in through the back door and into the kitchen.

All night, I had tossed and turned. I had dreamt of something that had imprisoned me. I couldn't move and all around me was darkness. My hands grasped the sheets that were twisted around my body. I tried to smooth them a little and then I felt my stomach surge as I remembered that Clive was coming. I could hear Phil muttering in his sleep and wondered if he too was a captive in his dream or whether it was because his face was hurting.

From the moment I got out of bed my nerves had been jangling at the thought of seeing Clive again. And when the bell rang, I knew he was just outside our front door, waiting to be let in. I could hear them chattering away as soon as Mum opened the door to them.

And then they were in the room.

'So, how are my little men?' were the first words that he

spoke as he entered the room before doing his usual hair ruffling. Both Phil and I had to force ourselves not to duck out of his reach. I had noticed the word 'my' even if no one else had – maybe he felt he owned us now.

'And goodness, what's this one been up to?' he asked, pointing at Phil. 'Been in a fight, have you? Well, what's the other one look like then?' he said with a laugh.

'He fell off his bike, he was going too fast,' Mum explained. 'They've been looking forward to seeing you, haven't you, boys?' she told him brightly, glancing in our direction.

I wonder even then if she guessed that for some reason we weren't.

'Yes,' I managed to say, feeling a tide of red creeping up my neck.

His hands gave each of our shoulders a squeeze, 'And it's good to see both of you too.'

What Mum and Dad would have seen was a benevolent uncle, what I saw was a certain level of complacency in his face. We obviously hadn't talked. But then, he had been pretty sure we wouldn't.

Mum disappeared into the kitchen, with Maureen following her, saying, 'I'll give you a hand.'

'Got some good photos of our trip,' said Clive, placing them on the table. 'Look, boys, there's a couple of you at the farm.' And he passed them over to us. In them, we actually appeared happy. But then we had enjoyed seeing the animals up close.

When Mum came back in, carrying a tray, she placed it down and picked a couple of photos up and smiled. For most of that afternoon remarks like, 'Oh, I remember that and what a lovely day it was,' rang in my ears.

I just wished we could make an excuse and disappear.

Later, we all ate together. The spare room was made up and I just prayed he would stay in it.

He didn't.

In he came, a finger to his lips, telling us to be quiet as he woke each of us up. I had my sheet pulled up to my chin as I waited to see what he was going to do this time.

'Is your face still sore then, Phil?' he asked.

'Yes,' I heard my brother say.

Not that Clive needed to ask that. Phil's bruise, which covered most of one side of his face, had turned a dull yellow and his eye still hadn't fully opened with all the swelling.

'Well, we'd better wait for it to heal, hadn't we?' he said gently as he tucked Phil's bedding in.

At this, I gulped. Was that really it? Had he only come into our room to say goodnight?

A question that was answered the moment he straightened up. The expression on his face when he glanced in my direction told me it wasn't.

I must have looked like a rabbit caught in the glare of headlights. One that was too scared to move when he sat on the edge of my bed and smiled. Still I said nothing, not even when he took hold of one corner of the sheet and pulled it down to my chest.

'Lie down now, Ryan.'

I could feel my teeth rattling with fear and I felt I had no other choice but to obey him. I knew Phil was not going to sleep but was lying stiffly in his bed, only too aware of what was happening. He would have seen that hand darting under the bedclothes and heard him whispering in my ear of what he wanted to do. Like me, he would have heard the sound of Clive's breathing as it grew heavier while he worked on my body. And I'm sure he must have noticed what I saw next: Clive's other hand stroking the front of his trousers.

But I didn't hear a sound coming from Phil – I guess fear was making him hold his breath. He no doubt did not believe that Clive was going to keep his word and leave him alone.

For once he did, though.

He straightened up and patted me on my shoulder.

'Sleep tight, Ryan.'

And then with that mocking smile on his face, he left our room.

I heard my brother climbing out of his bed as soon as he was sure that Clive had gone.

'Are you alright?' he whispered.

I couldn't bring myself to speak, not even when I felt his small hand take hold of mine. And I knew he wanted to comfort me as he sat on the floor, his head leaning against my bed. I felt a sob coming up from my chest.

'Go back to bed,' were the only words I could manage then.

That was the first time since I was a baby that I wet my bed.

*　*　*

When I realised in the morning that I was lying in a wet patch, I felt even more shame – if that were possible. Phil helped me wash and turn my mattress before we managed to make up the bed again.

'Don't want Mum to see it,' I told him just before the tears I could not stop began spilling out of my eyes. 'I mean, what would she think? She'd be angry. It's not as though we're little boys now.'

But we were, weren't we?

22

Ryan

To mine and Phil's relief, Warren had offered to babysit so that Clive could take our parents out for dinner.

'You two OK?' he asked us later that evening when he had watched us pushing our food around our plates. 'You both seem a little down.'

And all I can ask myself now is why did we not tell him then what our problem was? He was our big brother, wasn't he? The one who had always looked out for us.

Looking back, I suppose it was that dirty secret as we both saw it, one locked away so tightly, we were incapable of unlocking it.

Clive did not come near either of us that night. Just wished us 'Goodnight and see you in the morning' before Mum whisked us both up the stairs to bed.

After breakfast, which we all sat down to eat at the table, he and Maureen left.

'Long drive, need to complete some paperwork,' was his excuse.

Phil and I had to put up with hugs and the kisses on top of our heads before picking up their small suitcase to carry it out to the car. Then Clive uttered the words that made me quake: 'Be good to have you over when the boys have their next break from school. Only a few weeks away now, isn't it? God, teachers have it easy, alright! Not like hardworking guys like you, John. Thought we could hire a boat and go out on the river.'

The next words I heard came from Mum: 'Oh, that would be so lovely, Clive.'

More laughter and then I heard a welcome sound – the click of the front door closing behind them.

23

Ryan

I could not rid my mind of that invitation hanging over our heads. Inside, I felt such shame. Shame I could not see a way out of what we were enduring and shame that I was unable to protect Phil.

At school, my mind would drift off as images of Clive came into my head. Often, I would not even hear the teacher's question until it was repeated, along with stern remarks about daydreaming. I also felt my temper rise at the least little thing, something else I knew I had to try and control.

Even though Clive had not made any arrangements to visit again, I knew he was just waiting for us to walk back into his lair. As the days grew warmer, Mum asked me to encourage Phil to ride his bike, because over the weeks since his accident, he still appeared reluctant to do so.

'Come on, Phil,' I said more than once. 'It's sunny outside, let's get our bikes out.'

I hated seeing the doleful expression on his face when he just shook his head. Phil, who until then always had a cheerful disposition and picked himself up nearly every time something had upset him, appeared incapable of it now.

Mum still seemed to think that it was only his fall that had affected him and finally put her foot down.

'Phil, stop this nonsense right now! You know the bike helps strengthen your leg and makes you walk better, doesn't it?' Not that she waited for a reply before she said very firmly, 'You go with Ryan now, just don't go too fast and you'll be fine.'

What Mum didn't say was that she had noticed his leg dragging more again and his left arm was also weaker. I had also noticed him stumbling more. The difference was I understood what his problem was: the same one that was mine. His mind was just as full of the images of Clive coming into our room. I heard him crying out in the night and I knew he was being tormented in his sleep as well as his waking hours.

I had dreams too; I dreamt that a dark figure was crouching over me. In my dreams, I could even feel his hands weighing heavily on my stomach. My eyes would fly open as I sat up and then I felt the relief when I realised it was only a dream and that there was no one in our room except for Phil's small body huddled up in his bed.

Mum did show some concern and she asked me if anything had upset him at school.

The truthful answer to that was, 'No, I don't think so.'

I waited to see if she would ask more questions and try to get to the root of his behaviour, but she left it at that. She turned to me instead for her next observation: 'And you,

Ryan, you can't fool me. I know you've had a couple of little accidents. Had too much cocoa to drink before you went to bed, perhaps?'

I waited again for some more searching questions, but instead she provided her own answer after I had managed to say, 'Sorry, Mum.'

'These things happen,' was all she said. And although they happened several more times over the weeks leading up to our summer holidays, all she did was put a plastic covering over the mattress. The only question she asked me then was did I have bad dreams and I wondered if she had heard me calling out in my sleep. When I replied somewhat vaguely, her only comment was to say maybe I should stop looking at Leighton's comics if they were disturbing me.

Of course, I've wondered over the years why did she not put two and two together, or talk to the doctor. I like to believe now that it was just naivety. Abuse was not really a talked-about subject then whereas now nightmares and bedwetting would have rung more than one alarm.

24

Ryan

Since our holiday and Clive's visits there was no getting away from the fact that there were some changes in Phil, and not for the better. Despite everything that went against him and his constant struggle to overcome his difficulties, he had always been a pretty happy-go-lucky boy. One who chattered away, not bothered that it was only me who could completely understand him. And that infectious laugh of his made us all smile. But within a couple of months he was becoming just the opposite. His chatter was drying up more and more each day and we seldom heard him laugh.

I knew my brother's deterioration both in speech and movements was noticed, not just by our brothers, but our teachers as well. Not that they were aware of his restless sleep, the bad dreams he had and the whimpers I heard coming from him in the night. I never told anyone about the times I went over to his bed to waken him from his nightmare.

'It's just a nasty dream,' I would say when he looked up at me with frightened eyes.

On those nights, I would tell him that everything was alright – that there was only us in the room. I might have tried to shrug off the thoughts of Clive molesting us, but I did not succeed for long. When I met up with my friends, I was able to push it to the back of my mind though.

Phil was unable to do that.

I noticed that his leg had started dragging more and his speech was almost as bad as when he first started speech therapy. If Mum noticed too, she said little. Warren was the first person to mention it to me. When he came round to see us, he caught my eye and jerked his head towards the garden, which was his way of saying he wanted to talk to me out of earshot. He asked if I knew what was bothering Phil for he was convinced there was something upsetting him.

'Has there been more bullying at school?' he asked.

'No, I haven't seen any. They've got used to him now.'

'Anything else you can think of?'

I swallowed before saying, 'I think his leg still bothers him.'

'Well, it's a nice day, so come on, I'll take you both to the park. That will cheer him up.'

Patting my shoulder, he went into the house to tell Phil we were going out.

25

Phil

Warren was right: I loved going to the park, being put on the swings and having him push me until I felt I was flying right up to the sky. Or that's what I was able to imagine when I leant back and gazed up at it.

I knew everyone was concerned about me, but there was nothing I could do about it. The thought of spending a week in Clive's house was tormenting me almost every hour of the day. All I could think of was him. He would wait until Mum and Dad and, I suppose, Maureen were all tucked in bed and then come into our room to do things I couldn't even put a name to. It wasn't just his face I could see in my mind, but those long-fingered hands of his, so smooth, with such neatly trimmed wide nails, that I hated the thought of him touching my body. They were so different from Dad's, which at weekends showed grime-rimmed nails after a day working on the engine of the van. And unlike Clive's, they bore the roughness of hard manual work.

I understood why Ryan wanted to talk to me about what

was happening between Clive and us. After all, it was only the two of us who knew the truth about him. But I couldn't. If I did, I was frightened I would see him even more clearly, hear the sounds he made louder and smell his musty scent all over again. More than that, even letting him into my mind made me feel dirty and ashamed. I just knew that if I uttered a word about his visits to our room, I would feel even worse. And my body would ache even more. There were times when I wanted to explain those thoughts to Ryan. In my mind, I said to him, 'I would feel even more miserable if I talked to you about it, wouldn't you as well? Just thinking about it hurts me inside, it really hurts. Don't you feel the same?'

Even that I could not manage to articulate.

But most of those anxieties slid away a little when I heard the word 'park'. It was enough to make me smile up at my big brother. He would take me to the swings and while on them for just for a short while, I managed to feel like a normal little boy. Back on the ground though, I was aware of that dragging leg that people saw. I knew some pitied me and others thought my mind was as weak as my leg was. A fact that since I had begun school, I had managed to cope with.

Apart from the park, the only other place where I could forget Clive was when I went for my hydrotherapy. Water, I had found, since the first time I was immersed in it, had a really peaceful and calming effect. Ever since I had been going for that type of exercise, together with riding my bike, I had felt the muscles in my leg grow stronger. I can still remember the first time Mum left my buggy at home and I managed to walk the whole way to school. I felt such a glow of happiness then. My teacher looked almost as pleased as I was when he came to the gates and saw me standing there.

And on the way home I still felt the same, even though my leg was dragging and I was a bit lopsided with the exertion of the day. I felt so proud that I had managed to walk unaided. But after my accident, I no longer felt safe on my bike. I was scared my leg would let me down again. Even worse were the other fears that refused to leave me alone. The ones that brought me out in a cold sweat. I had begun to be concerned about what my classmates thought of me: could they see I was hiding a dirty secret? That was the worrying thought that nibbled away at the small amount of confidence I had built up once I managed to walk.

When I was asked a question that knot of fear grew heavier. What if my words let me down and I just uttered some embarrassing garbled rubbish? Even when I knew the answer to a question the teacher was asking in class, my good arm froze even more than my bad one. I was unable to lift it, unable to let the class hear my voice.

Already I looked weird enough to them, didn't I? So, sounding it as well would only make things worse.

I felt Ryan glancing at me in the classroom. I knew without him saying anything that he was worried about me. I wondered then if he felt as I did, that something had altered in my body. My leg felt heavier, my arm limper and now my mouth was beginning to find it harder to shape words that people could understand. The woman who supervised my hydrotherapy asked if I had missed having my treatment over the holiday. Maybe she too had seen that my limbs were weaker and put it down to me having missed a few weeks with her. Though she must have mentioned something to Mum, because I overheard her telling Dad that she thought I was getting worse, not better.

Today, I understand that the problems I had then were caused by a mixture of anxiety and depression. Both Ryan and I can talk about it now. We've googled different sites which explain just how abuse damages children, sometimes for life. Something that my brother and I decided several years ago was that we were not going to let this happen to us; he insisted we should put it behind us and move forward. But at least the articles we read explained all those aches I had as a child.

It was most probably my belief that my leg was going to let me down that caused my second accident.

26

Ryan

Mum had an appointment at the hospital. All I knew was that it was something to do with her leg. We could all tell, by the way she winced when she had to carry her groceries in and the deepening lines on her face, that it ached continuously.

She told Phil and I that as she didn't know how long she was going to be at the hospital, she had arranged for her friend to look after us.

'Marianne will collect you from school if I'm not back,' she told us both. 'Leighton can go to Warren's and do his homework there.'

Marianne was the one who always offered us cake when we went round her house with Mum so I smiled at the thought of going to hers and Mum gave a little laugh when she saw the gap where my baby teeth had fallen out. Not that having a gap in my front teeth bothered me – in fact, I was really pleased about it. Those baby teeth were doing exactly what I wanted them to do: dropping from my mouth to land on my pillow while I slept. Mind you, at least one had been helped by me twisting away at it. I was all ready for my grown-up ones to replace them. At night, I would push my tongue up to the small part of my exposed gum to try and feel for the hardness of a new tooth growing. That gap in my mouth would not be there for long, I told myself every morning when I looked in the mirror.

Of course, I was not the only boy in the classroom with a gappy smile. Most of my classmates had them and we kept comparing how many teeth each of us had lost. Except for Phil. His baby teeth appeared to be reluctant to leave his mouth, something I enjoyed teasing him about.

'You know why that is, don't you? It's because I'm older than you,' I kept saying, which raised a smile. 'Try wiggling them, they might come out then.'

And obediently, Phil would stick a finger in his mouth and try to wobble the front ones. Then he would sigh loudly when they refused to move.

'Not ready to leave your mouth then,' I would say each time.

Not that either of us knew then, my twin being a little late with getting his big boy teeth was going to turn out lucky for him.

*   *   *

As expected, Mum's friend was standing at the school gates waiting for us. I had always liked Marianne, who, with her short grey hair and kindly eyes set in a pale crinkly face, always gave Phil and me a warm welcome. I greeted her, but

Phil seemed as if he was in a world of his own. He managed to mumble hello and that was about all he said when we walked with her to the terraced house where she lived.

I was beginning to get used to his bouts of silence, although I kept wishing he would confide in me a little. He always had before Scotland, but since that holiday, he had kept most of his thoughts locked up.

I thought Marianne's house, with its comfortable brightly coloured chairs and a conservatory where we could look out at all her terracotta pots full of flowers crammed on her patio, was much prettier than ours. Its walls were covered by various paintings and a large bookcase, where hardly another volume could be squeezed into it, helped make the living room feel cosy.

'Have you two any homework to do?' she asked.

'Just a few sums,' I told her.

Homework was something that had only begun that term. Getting us gradually prepared for when we would, like Leighton, have enough to keep us busy all evening.

'How long will that take?'

I grinned up at her. 'Only a few minutes. We only have ten to do and they're easy ones.'

'Well, in that case, why don't you get them out of the way while I get you something to eat?'

Out came our notebooks and with his brow creased, I noticed Phil staring at the questions but hardly writing anything down.

'Copy mine,' I suggested for I had nearly finished and his page looked as though he had barely begun.

I received a dirty look in response.

'Teacher would know, wouldn't he?'

Putting his head back down, he scribbled away for a few minutes, then closed his notebook and stood up. I could see he was troubled and then I noticed him staggering a little.

'Want to look at the garden,' he said as he walked towards the conservatory.

I was still trying to find the answers to the last couple of sums when I heard a loud crash, followed by a scream. Marianne came rushing out of the kitchen as I too shot to where the noise had come from. I could see straight away what had happened: Phil had tripped on the small step between the living room and the conservatory. Marianne's sewing machine, which had been on a small table, was now on the floor with my brother lying across it.

'Just stand away, Ryan,' she told me and I could hear the nervousness in her voice.

She managed to lift Phil up and I could see his eyes were nearly closed and there was blood coming from his mouth. She carried him carefully over to the settee, telling me to fetch a first aid kit, which was in a kitchen cupboard. I could hear her voice murmuring to him as I bent down to open the cupboard. She kept saying his name, 'Phil, Phil, come on, Phil, please open your eyes.' He whimpered then, a sound that told me he was hurting. I was scared of what I was going to see when I returned to where they were. My hands were shaking when I opened the cupboard and took out the first aid box. I carried it to the settee and I saw his head was on her lap.

'Phil,' I whispered as I felt the tears spilling from my eyes. He looked so terrible, his face was ashen and his mouth such a bloody mess.

'It's not as bad as it looks, Ryan,' she told me. 'It's his gum that's cut. That's where the blood's coming from. But it looks as though he might have smashed his front teeth on the tiles. Get me a cup of warm water from the kettle. It boiled a while ago so it's sterilised but not too hot.'

When I placed the cup in front of her, she looked at me earnestly. 'It's that left leg of his, isn't it? Your mum told me it's been letting him down.'

'Yes, it keeps giving way,' was all I could manage to say as I watched her wash the blood away from my brother's mouth as gently as she could. I could see him wincing, which meant that although his eyes were shut, at least he was not unconscious.

She kept talking softly to him but there was no response. Instead, he just lay there and even when he finally opened his eyes when she coaxed him, there was a completely blank expression on his face. It was that blankness that worried me more than the blood. And what was making me even more upset was that I could feel Marianne's worry. There was just no reaction from him at all when she said his name again.

This was much worse than the day he had fallen off his bike – he had managed to pull himself together then.

How much does it hurt him? Will he be alright? Is anything broken? Those were the questions spinning around in my head. But before I was able to fire them at Marianne, she told me again that I mustn't worry, that he was conscious. I noticed as she spoke that her fingers were pressed lightly on Phil's wrist while she kept glancing down at her watch. That told me she was taking his pulse, something I had watched Mum do a few times when one of us was sick. Just as more tears began to spill down my cheeks, the doorbell rang.

'Oh God, that will be your mother! Can you let her in, Ryan?'

I wiped my eyes hastily with my sleeve and bolted to the door. 'Mum will know what to do,' was the sentence running through my head as I tried to tell her that Phil had had a bad fall.

'Alright, Ryan, now calm down. I'll see for myself.'

And without another comment, she was in the lounge.

'Accidents happen all the time with boys,' she told Marianne, who looked as though she was about to burst into tears any moment.

'Mmm ... Now come on, Phil, I know you're in there so look at me.'

Nothing like Mum's no-nonsense voice to stop panic. On hearing it, my brother finally opened his eyes. 'Good, I thought you were awake. Now I know everything hurts a bit, we'll get that fixed. Your mouth's still bleeding a little now, but not enough to worry about.' And bending down, she peered closer. 'Thought as much, it's just your lip and gum that's been cut. You're going to be fine. Still, I think I'd better get the dentist to have a look at you. Looks as though you're going to lose those front teeth you've been trying to wobble out for ages so I don't think you're going to be sorry about that, but I just want to make sure. OK?'

He managed to mumble 'Yes', which was rewarded by smiles from all of us leaning over him.

I felt so relieved that our mother was there and taking over. There was nothing so reassuring as her practical comments that day.

Mum borrowed Marianne's phone and made her call to the dentist. I could hear her giving details to one of the dental nurses and then thanking her, before saying that she and Phil would be there in about twenty minutes.

'Right, Marianne, he'll see us as soon as we get there. Do you have a mini cab number? There's no way this child can walk there!'

She must have been more worried than she was showing to spend money on a taxi. That was not something I'd ever known her do.

'Yes, I'll ring for you. And shall I let John know where you are so he can pick you up?'

'Thanks, that would help.'

Marianne told Mum that the least she could do was look after me and they could collect me on the way back.

'Well, if you don't mind putting up with him,' said Mum.

'I'll get him a snack. I didn't have time, what with Phil falling down that step.'

My mother turned to me then.

'Have you finished your homework, Ryan?'

'Eh no, but nearly.'

'Well, you'd better get it done then before I get back.'

'Mum!' was the only part of my protest I was able to get out. Didn't she know I was hardly in the right mood to open an exercise book again?

'Wasn't you that was hurt, was it? No excuses!' was her firm response before turning her attention back to Phil. 'Now, we'd better get you up and on your feet, hadn't we?' she told him calmly before putting her arm around his small body as she gently helped him sit up. 'Well, that's step number one, next one is to get you standing, isn't it? Just slide your legs down onto the floor ...'

Keeping his gaze on her, Phil moved as she had told him to do.

'Good boy! Now the taxi's here and you're going to have to take a few steps.'

Taking his hands, she pulled him up until he was standing. Both Mum and Marianne helped my brother out to the taxi and within seconds, he and Mum were gone. I felt more tears welling up then. Somehow I managed to get the question out that I had wanted to ask before Mum came: 'Is he going to be alright?'

'Yes, he is, Ryan,' Marianne told me. 'He's just a little shaken. And as your mother said, it was only his lip and gum that was cut. That's what caused all the bleeding. The dentist will fix that and he'll be right as rain in the morning, you'll see.'

'Good,' was the only word I could manage. I didn't think for one moment that there was much chance of Phil being alright as he hadn't been his normal cheerful self for weeks.

'Now eat the sandwich I've made for you and here's some

lemonade as well. And when you finish those sums, there's homemade chocolate cake waiting to be eaten.'

I tried to smile for her chocolate cake was really good, but all I could think was how I wished Mum had taken me with them. If I'd noticed he had a problem with his leg, Phil must have known too so why wasn't he more careful on the step? The answer to that question came straight into my head: because his mind had drifted into its dark place and he hadn't seen it.

I just wanted my cheerful brother back, but I had no idea how I was going to make that happen.

*   *   *

It seemed ages before Mum returned, this time with Dad, who she had left in the car with Phil. When I climbed into the back with my brother, I saw he was almost asleep. He hardly stirred when we reached home. Dad just leant into the car, picked him up and carried him in.

'I'll take him upstairs, think that's the best place for him. I'll stay with him until you bring up some soup, Audrey.'

'Yes, that's about all he'll be able to manage today. Ryan, stay here,' Mum said when she saw me move to follow them. 'He needs to rest. It's better if you don't try and talk to him tonight. He's had a couple of injections, that's why he's sleepy. So, tiptoe when you go up to bed, won't you?'

'Alright, Mum.'

'Still, at least it was his baby teeth he knocked out,' she told me with a wry smile. 'The dentist said the ones that are growing up to replace them aren't damaged so he won't be having that gap forever now, will he?

'His mouth's going to hurt for a while and he'll probably have a headache for a bit. He'll only be able to eat soft food so I'm going to keep him off school for the rest of this week.'

* * *

During the time Phil stayed at home, the fact that he hardly talked didn't appear to worry our parents – it was put down to his mouth hurting.

Was I really the only one who knew there was more to his silence than that?

27

Ryan

Summer came early that year. With it came the feeling that our holidays were just around the corner. On every break I could hear my classmates' excited chatter as they tried to outdo each other in describing their holiday plans.

'We're going camping in Norfolk, our tent's really huge and Dad's going to set it up right by the beach. It's really great there,' one of my friends boasted.

Though I thought he looked a bit peeved when his friend Matt, whose mother drove him to school each morning in her sleek red sports car, told everyone within earshot that he was going on a plane. His parents were taking him and his sister to Spain for three whole weeks! As many details as he could manage without drawing breath were blurted out – about their apartment (gigantic) and the huge swimming pool there.

'Mum says it never rains there so I won't have to take my mac,' he added gleefully before thankfully running out of steam.

Then there were some of my classmates who, shuffling their feet a bit, had to admit that they didn't have much planned. They would be staying at home, maybe going on visits to some of their relatives.

'What are you and Phil doing on the holidays then?' one boy asked.

A question that made my heart sink. It reminded me of just what was in store: a whole week staying at Clive's house. Not that this was going to stop me bluffing a bit. After all, I still wanted my classmates to think we were doing something interesting. I described my uncle's house, the restaurants he took us to and managed to mention the river trip that Mum had told us about. No one appeared impressed. Camping by the sea and a holiday in Spain had trumped a visit to an uncle, no matter how big his house was. To my classmates, Cambridge was just another town and its river was not for swimming, was it?

If I had made my friends think I was looking forward to our holiday, I must have been pretty good then at bluffing.

I didn't have to look over at Phil to sense that these questions were having the same effect on him as they had on me. The only bit of good news was when Mum told us that Clive was going to be away for most of that summer. Which meant that he wouldn't be able to make it to our birthday party in August.

'He's been invited to stay at a friend's villa in Marbella in Spain,' she told us with a touch of envy in her voice. 'He certainly has a lot of good friends, doesn't he? But you know Clive, he's always so thoughtful. Even though your birthdays are quite a few weeks away, he's arranged some really nice things for us while we are there. I'm looking forward to the river trip, it's not an ordinary one. Trust Clive to arrange something special for all of us.'

And no doubt he's arranged something especially for Phil and me, I thought despairingly.

* * *

I can hardly remember the last day in the classroom; too many thoughts about going to Cambridge were in my head. I know that goodbyes were said as the class rushed out, squealing with excitement.

An emotion neither Phil nor I felt.

Of course, the teacher had asked us a few questions. Told us we were lucky to be spending time in such a beautiful city – 'All those marvellous ancient buildings you'll be able to see on your river trip. I expect you'll have plenty to tell me after the holidays.'

Well, no doubt we would, but nothing suitable for his ears. Though somehow I made myself look interested when the teacher talked about it. I could hardly tell him that unless a wizard lived there, old buildings didn't interest me much.

I had seen enough of them in Scotland.

* * *

Phil and I were aware of how much our parents were looking forward to spending a whole week at Clive's. By the time we had got in from school, Mum had done nearly all of the packing and our bikes were already in the van.

'Warren's coming round for supper,' she told us. 'He's going to take Leighton back with him. Don't know why he would rather stay here and practise football than come with us, but that's boys for you, I suppose.'

How I wished I was old enough to be in a team like Leighton then I could have used the same excuse. A thought that made me feel guilty: Phil was never going to be able to play football. I would be a pretty bad twin if I let him go alone to be at Clive's mercy, wouldn't I? I just hoped that he would manage to get through this holiday. I had heard Mum talking to Dad about him and she mentioned that she was still a bit concerned – 'His coordination's still not good. And he's not really got over that last accident. I just hope this holiday will cheer him up.'

'Yes, he does seem a bit down, wonder if he's got problems at school? Have you asked him?' Dad asked thoughtfully.

'Yes, he says not. Though Leighton told me there's still a little name-calling, but nothing too bad.'

Well, I did say I was good at eavesdropping. I don't think my parents ever worked out that the only two places to have a private conversation were either in their bedroom or at the bottom of the garden.

Mum waited until supper was over to send Phil and I up to our room to sort out what we wanted to take with us – 'Books, games, things like that,' she told us a little impatiently when we asked her what she meant. 'You too, Leighton. Sort out what you need to take to Warren's. So, off you all go!'

That told us we were not wanted downstairs for a bit. They clearly had something they wanted to talk about out of our earshot, though I guessed it was about Phil. I had overheard Warren telling Mum that he too was concerned.

'He's just not been his usual happy-go-lucky self,' he said more than once.

'Well, he has had two nasty accidents,' Mum pointed out.

'I know, Mum, but I don't think he was his normal self before either of them.'

Our mother had not appeared worried until that fall at Marianne's. I heard the kitchen door close and tried to stop thinking about what they were talking about downstairs, busying myself putting the things I wanted to take with me in my satchel. I remembered then that my Lego, that I really wanted with me, was downstairs in the sitting room and I was pretty sure that everyone was still in the kitchen. So, thinking I could just dart in and grab it without being seen, I crept as silently as I could down the stairs.

It was when I reached the hall that I heard Warren's voice:

'You know, Mum, if he doesn't seem better after the holiday, maybe he needs to see someone.'

'Like who?'

'Well, the doctor for a start, he might recommend a therapist. Maybe Phil's finding it difficult to cope with his disabilities now he's getting a little older. I know you mentioned that Leighton said there was still a bit of name-calling, but I don't believe that's the real reason for the change in him.'

'All I can think is that it might be. Remember, I went through this too when I was his age, Warren?'

'Oh, come on, Mum! He's put up with that ever since back when he had to be wheeled around in his buggy. And even if it bothered him, he seldom let it get him down. He's managed to take it in his stride. There's got to be another reason and if he's no better after the holiday, it needs looking into. Maybe he might open up to someone who's not a teacher or a member of the family. And if you can't get the right person on the NHS to have a talk with him, then I don't mind paying for it. In fact, I already have the name of someone who specialises in children's problems.'

I might not have understood everything I heard, but I gathered from what had been said that Warren wanted Phil to talk to someone. Not that I was sure exactly what that meant but I worked out from their conversation that it was an adult a child could tell anything to.

Could someone like that look into our heads and see our dirty secrets? And what would they think of us, if they could? Wouldn't they just say we were nasty little boys?

I decided that it was not worth going into the sitting room to collect my Lego after all. Instead, I crept up the stairs. I didn't tell Phil what I had heard until much later. It was something I pushed to the back of my mind until we were back in Cambridge.

* * *

It was the usual journey there, van packed, bikes and a couple of suitcases in the back, flask of tea for Mum and

Dad, a couple of soft drinks for Phil and me. As soon as we were in and safety belts clicked shut, we were off.

As we were expected at Clive's for lunch, Mum had pointed out that for once she didn't need to pack food for us all, though as we were on holiday, she did allow us to have a few sweets to suck. No doubt to keep us quiet while we looked out of the windows, counting how many blue cars we saw.

Almost as soon as we pulled up in front of Clive's house he shot out of the door to greet us. Both Phil and I had our hair ruffled as he said with his wide, 'caring uncle' smile, 'Hi, little men, great to see you both,' and of course he also greeted my parents, giving them his 'You are my best friends' smile.

Mum and Dad took their bags up to their room and after being told we were in the same room as before, I carried ours. Auntie Maureen was, as usual, in the kitchen organising lunch, which we ate outside on the patio. *More green stuff*, I thought. I hated salad, but sensing her watching us, I managed to eat some of it.

The thought that kept running through my mind was just how far our bedroom was from the one our parents were in. And there was another spare room near theirs, but no one seemed to wonder why we hadn't been given that one. It was not hard to guess why Clive had allocated rooms this way.

Over lunch, he talked about the boat trip he had arranged before going into detail about his friends in Marbella, business ones he managed to slip in, and the lovely place they had there.

'We're certainly lucky to be spending the summer there,' he told us.

I closed my ears to his voice as much as I could. They only pricked up again when he confirmed that he and Maureen would not be back until the end of September or even the beginning of October. How many weeks would that be? Certainly, October seemed a long way off. I wished that he would like it so much over there that he would decide to move to Spain for good and be near to where his friends lived.

'Oh, lucky you!' sighed Mum without a hint of resentment.

Lucky for all of us, I thought.

'Now, are you two going out on your bikes?' she asked, only to receive a shake of the head from Phil, who, gazing at his shoes, muttered that his leg was hurting. She decided to ignore that plea and didn't complain when instead of going outside, we asked if we could get one of our board games out.

I've forgotten most of that evening and what the title of the film was that they all wanted to watch on TV. Maureen had put out bowls of popcorn and everyone had a drink. The curtains were closed and Clive turned the big lights off, saying it 'would be like sitting in the cinema'. But I can remember him pulling me down onto his knee. I could feel his hands under my jumper, touching my back and stroking the top of my underpants. Worse still was finding that the part of him I could hardly bear to think about starting to feel hard underneath me. I just wanted to wriggle away, to say I wanted to go to bed or that I was tired, anything not to have to stay where I was.

It was Dad who looked at his watch and said us boys should have been in bed an hour ago:

'We all have to get up early tomorrow, so off you go now.'

'And don't forget to brush your teeth,' Mum chipped in as we made our way to the door.

Part of me was relieved to get away from Clive's hand, the other part was fearful that he would come into our room later – a fear reflected in my brother's eyes.

That night, I was far too tense to fall asleep. My ears were on full alert as I listened for the sound of Clive's footsteps padding down the corridor. Every little noise that a house makes when settling down for the night caused me to stare at the door, praying that I would not see it opening.

If he came, would it be to play that Up and Down Game?

By then, I knew that it really wasn't a game, just an excuse to put his hands on the parts of our bodies we hated being touched.

If he came later in the night, would there be enough time for him to play that game with both of us? Or would it be quick, with him out of our room in just a few minutes?

In the end, sleep finally took over. It was not until I heard the sound of Mum drawing back the curtains and saying that it was time to get up that either of us woke. *So, he hadn't come*, I realised. I think now that was part of the game he played with us. He seemed to intentionally let us be frightened, not knowing whether he was going to come into our room or not. This would keep our nerves on edge and make us more vulnerable. And frightened small children are easier to control. In Clive's case, I'm pretty sure he found it even more enjoyable to see fear in our eyes.

Later that morning, pointing out buildings of interest on the way to my parents, Clive drove us all into Cambridge. Did we enjoy the river trip? To be truthful, while I liked looking over at the small boats rowed by happy-looking, young university students, I could have done without hearing his voice going on and on, showing off his knowledge. He was in his element, acting the part of tour guide as he pointed out still more buildings of historical interest to us all – not that Maureen appeared very interested.

The special side of the trip that Mum had mentioned was the afternoon tea served on pretty plates that she remarked on. There was certainly tons of food – tiny sandwich triangles, big fluffy scones with jam and whipped cream, followed by an assortment of cakes.

Phil and I could hardly resist trying one of each cake. Not that tucking into scones and cakes was enough to completely stop me thinking of what our uncle might have in store for us that night.

When we returned to the house, he told us all that he was celebrating a big deal he had just made and giving us first a couple of fizzy drinks, he then opened a bottle of champagne.

'I should put some wine aside so it will be there for your eighteenth birthdays,' he told us.

Not that we understood why he would want to do that then. Words like 'laying down' and 'vintage' floated in the air, not that I think my parents understood a word of what he was talking about either. Mum hardly ever drank and

Dad's taste was more for a pint of beer than wine. But then Clive loved showing off his knowledge, especially to people he knew could never tell if he made a mistake.

Funny I had worked that out, even then, but they hadn't. Maybe because I had heard boasting at school, followed by the name 'show-off' being shouted at them.

Another bottle was opened, more glasses filled, and then I noticed that Mum's face was growing rather pink, her laughter a little shriller when Clive topped up her glass again.

'Oh, I really shouldn't,' she said before taking another sip.

'I think I'll order a takeaway tonight, Maureen,' said Clive. 'Don't think anyone feels like cooking, do they?'

'Well, *I* don't,' she replied firmly before he crossed over to where the phone was. She picked up a handful of menus tucked behind it and handed them to him.

'Now, Chinese, Indian or Thai?'

'Never tried Thai,' was Dad's answer.

'You'll love it! Just leave it to me to order then, John. Think I can guess what you'd like. Do you both like prawns?'

'Yes,' came the reply in unison.

'And which do you prefer, hot or mild?'

'Eh? Mild.'

He then asked Phil and I what we would like as he ran a few dishes past us. Chicken with peanut sauce sounded good, as did a couple of others whose names I could not pronounce. What on earth was pak choy, I wondered when I heard Maureen saying we should have some of that.

Clive got busy on the phone and it was clear that this

was another place where he was known. Some laughter and conversation before he turned around and beamed at us.

'Be here in about half an hour, it's not far from here.'

He put some nuts and crisps out in small bowls.

'That'll help soak up the bubbles,' he told the adults as he topped up everyone's glasses. 'And now for some music ...' Going to his sleek black music system, he carefully placed a record on it. 'Can't beat the old vinyl, John, now can you? I haven't time for all those cassettes coming out and no doubt there'll be more new gadgets around next year. Mind you, I enjoy the eight-track in the car ...'

There he was, boasting again. We had a radio in the van and that was what Dad played.

More chatter went over our heads, and a lot more laughter, not that Phil and I could see what was so funny. I was grateful when the doorbell rang and an assortment of boxes was placed on the table.

'Tuck in, everyone!'

Phil and I didn't need much encouragement.

I heard the pop of another cork coming out of a bottle. This time it was wine that he poured into everyone's glass except ours.

'I always think a Riesling goes well with Thai,' he explained to Dad.

The food was like nothing we had ever eaten before. Some dishes were sweet but hot and we loved all the different flavours, especially the peanut sauce. By the end of the meal I could see that Mum's eyes were a bit glazed. Phil and I escaped as soon as we could – the Snakes and Ladders board was in our room and I wanted to get away from the adults and play on it.

Another thing I had learnt in Scotland is that children don't like to see their parents getting tipsy – flushed faces and loud laughter unnerves them. Standing outside the dining-room door for a few seconds, we listened to their slurred voices and grinned at each other, shrugging our shoulders.

No one would be coming into our room that evening.

We were wrong on two counts. First, it was Mum, looking a little sheepish, who told us to make sure that teeth were brushed and that we were not to stay up too late. I noticed that she stumbled slightly when she left the room, saying, 'I'm off to bed now,' before closing the door, leaving us trying not to laugh.

Not expecting another visit, for surely even Clive would be making his way to bed, we carried on playing our game until our heads were drooping. Remembering what Mum had said about brushing our teeth, we did as we were told as fast as we could, then climbed into bed and fell fast asleep.

Too young to understand the effect of alcohol on others, we had completely underestimated Clive's capacity for it. Looking back, I expect his intention that night was to get them all pretty legless while he consumed a lot less. After all, he was the one who had busied himself topping up glasses. I think now he knew exactly what he was doing when faced with two moderate drinkers. Everyone's heads were going to hit their pillows until morning, leaving him with the freedom to wander unnoticed down to our room, where he could stay as long as he wanted. Though I still don't know if that applied to his wife or whether she knew what he was doing.

It was a hand on my shoulder that woke me. Opening my eyes, I looked up into a face which was the last one I wanted to see.

'Everyone's fast asleep,' he told me as if I would be pleased to hear that piece of information. 'God, Maureen was snoring her head off when I left her! Didn't listen at your parents' door, but I don't think anyone will be waking till well after the birds start cheeping. Gives me plenty of time to spend with my favourite nephews, doesn't it?'

His voice was sending coils of fear into my stomach, as did his appearance. He looked so different from the well-dressed, suave man I was used to seeing. Gone were the smart chinos and the soft blue sweater, in its place a dark blue dressing gown. I could see his pale hairy legs poking out from the bottom of it and realised that he was not even wearing pyjamas. The act he put on in front of my parents of being the benevolent uncle had totally disappeared as well.

It was the real Clive who was sitting on my bed, the one I had grown to feel total repugnance towards. Only then I felt more than that, I felt frightened. There was something scary about this version. I wanted to tell him to go, to threaten that I would tell my parents if he didn't. But the words stuck in my throat and instead, I felt myself cowardly pulling my sheets up to my chin and looking at him pleadingly.

I hated myself for that. Even more so when I caught a glimpse of amusement in his expression. Clive had read my thoughts as easily as he read his newspaper. He was completely aware that with hardly saying a word, he had managed to instil enough fear in me to stop me saying anything.

'So, you're awake, are you? Were you waiting for me?'

I wanted to say that he had woken me, scream out that I didn't want to be touched, but those words also refused to leave my mouth. Then I thought of Phil – how much harm was being done to him? From somewhere deep inside me, I managed to find the courage to speak.

'Leave Phil alone, please, Uncle Clive,' I begged him. 'He's not been well for weeks and Mum's really worried about him.'

I looked straight into his eyes then as I managed to bring up a sentence which made him pause.

'I heard her saying that if this holiday doesn't make him better, she'll have to take him to the doctor.'

Whether he believed me or not, that last bit seemed to work.

'Alright then, Ryan, more time for you then,' he told me gloatingly.

Was Phil even awake? I really hoped that he was not. Just seeing Clive in the room would make him worse.

* * *

That night, which is still etched in my mind, there was very little chat, just commands. And the unspoken threat this time was if I didn't obey him, he would turn his attention to my brother.

'Out you get, Ryan! You know what to do, don't you?

That's why I've put the rug in here. I like to make you comfy. Shows just how thoughtful I am, doesn't it?'

By then, I was too afraid of him to protest any further. I guess he wanted the picture of him kneeling over my prone body, his face flushed, hands moving on those little parts of me. Those hands, as though with a life of their own, could not resist starting the pulling and rubbing.

Just when I thought he had nearly finished with me, he did something he had not tried to do before. Gripping my hand hard, he pulled it under his dressing gown.

'My turn now, Ryan. See no reason why you should have all the fun.'

Without uttering another word, he put my hand over something hot and hard. He coiled my fingers around it and his hand remained tightly covering mine as he made mine move up and down.

'Yours will be as big as this one in a few years,' he whispered in my ear and I could feel his hot breath on my cheek. 'Think what fun we'll have.'

Did he want my nightmares to be full of the sound of his breathing as it grew faster and came in gasps? Then it turned into a loud groan and I could feel his weight as he nearly collapsed on top of my body while that horrible sticky liquid spurted from him onto my hand and tummy. Did he want the smell of his aftershave mixed with something more unpleasant and musty to remain in my nostrils? Did he know that everything about that night remained forever lodged in my mind?

Did he know what hate was? I did, because I felt it then.

28

Ryan

The night after Clive had come into our room, he and my father made their usual excursion to the pub. I guess now that Dad had wanted someone to confide in about some of Mum's concerns about Phil. A therapist was out of his league, he would have had little understanding of what it was that they did, whereas Clive, being a worldly man, would have known. Not that I worked all that out then, but I have now. It explains Clive's actions the following day. I expect Dad had also told him that Warren had been worried enough to tell Mum that he could pay for someone privately if the NHS could not help quickly enough. Not only that, he had done a bit of research and he had told our parents that he had the name of someone who was highly recommended.

And what was the last thing Clive would have wanted?

A disturbed child talking to a therapist.

Not that I understood then the trouble that he would be in if Phil talked. The police would have been knocking on his door within minutes.

Now I like to think that Clive must have had a sleepless night worrying about what he could do to stop Phil's problems being taken any further by the family. He didn't have much time to come up with a plan to turn my brother back into the cheerful little boy he had been not that long ago. I expect he spent the best part of the night turning it over in his mind.

Over the last few years I have taken various courses. From what I have learnt, it seems that there are two main things a child psychologist looks for in a child who is showing signs of anxiety: bullying or abuse. If the child is being extremely secretive and uncomfortable, then abuse is more likely to be suspected. I have no doubt that Clive would have been only too aware of this.

Another thing he would have known is that a child of Phil's age would be believed. An older one might have made it up as an act of revenge, though that is pretty unusual, but not a 7-year-old. And Phil would have ticked both those boxes: high levels of anxiety and secretiveness. For hadn't Clive used those subtle threats to make us obey him?

So, what did Clive do? He took us out to a cafe. Of course, he had a plan, one that seemed pretty innocuous when he invited us to go with him to the place that did the best ice cream. What he had worked out to hopefully save a spell in prison and the loss of his reputation was something he needed to get us alone for. He might have had Dad thinking he was wonderful, but I had my doubts whether Warren felt the same. And it was he who was pushing our parents to take Phil to a professional to seek help. And if the truth came out, he must have known how many people would turn against him.

'Right, boys,' he had said early that afternoon. 'The sun's shining and what do we want on hot days? Three guesses!'

No answer from us, just a couple of sideways glances at each other.

'Why, ice cream of course. So, come on, you two, I'm taking you to that place you like so much.'

If Mum had been paying attention, she might have noticed that the invitation had not filled us with joy. But she wasn't anywhere near us. Instead there was only Dad, looking as though a weight had just been lifted from his shoulders. I'm sure he had asked Clive if he could try and sort everything out. After all, over the last couple of years hadn't he formed a close bond with us boys? And often children find it easier to confide in a close family friend than their own parents. And Clive would have told him that he would try his best. I wonder when he took us out that day if he was pretty confident that by hook or crook, or in any case by bribes and threats, he was going to silence us. Believing that we had little choice, the two of us meekly followed him out to the car, wondering just what he had in store for us next. Instinct told me that his interest in taking us out was not just about buying us ice cream. He had something up his sleeve, not that I could guess what it was.

His mask was back in place, that of the 'benevolent uncle', whose face creased into warm smiles when he looked at us. Our parents might have been fooled and were happy that he enjoyed spending time with their sons and giving them little treats, but it didn't work on us, no matter how many smiles came in our direction – we were past being fooled.

True to his word, he didn't stop at his shop, which I was praying he wouldn't, but drove straight to the cafe. As he pulled up, he said, 'Recognise it, boys?' We did of course, it was where he had taken us when I still believed he cared for us. If anything, being reminded of those times when I had felt happy being there with him made me feel sad.

'In we go then,' he announced cheerfully as he opened the car door to let us out. He put his hand out to help Phil, who more or less ignored it. 'I'm alright,' he said gruffly as he walked slowly beside me. I felt proud of him for that, but I tried not to smile when I noticed Clive looking somewhat taken aback at my brother having the courage to snub him.

I think both of us thought he was up to something, we just hadn't worked out what it was. Neither of us had any idea that his aim was to ensure that we did not talk.

He waited until the ice cream was in front of us and a couple of spoonfuls had already slipped down our throats before he began to show his hand. It was Phil he turned his attention to first.

'Your dad told me last night that both he and your mum are worried about you, Phil,' he said, trying to appear genuinely concerned. 'That last accident of yours really upset her and maybe you don't know this, but being worried is really not good for her. We don't want her getting ill, now do we? That's what your dad is scared of. He thinks she just might and he's pretty concerned about that.'

Hearing the words that Mum might be getting ill made

me feel a little sick and my hand holding the spoon piled with ice cream remained suspended in mid-air. I could hardly think how bad it would be if she was no longer in charge of our household.

Clive saw the flutter of worry on both our faces. He must have been pleased that he was getting through to us. He leant forward then, no doubt because he didn't want anyone else to hear his next words. What came then was a strong hint that he would leave us alone if Phil stopped upsetting Mum. Well, let's say it was a hint followed by a thinly disguised threat. Even then, I didn't believe that he meant he would stop what he was doing to us forever. Not that I told my brother that – I so wanted him to be happy again that I thought it was best to keep these suspicions to myself.

I listened intently to Clive as he made his first move.

'You've nothing to worry about here, Phil, nor you, Ryan. We're just going to have a nice holiday. Maybe I forgot just how young you were when we played some of our games.'

A statement we could hardly comment on.

He quickly followed up that semi-promise with one of his subtle threats.

'So, the job for both of you now is to make sure your mother has nothing more to worry about, isn't it?'

We both managed to say yes to that.

Not that he had finished. His next threat was a masterpiece:

'If she got ill, who would look after you? I expect your dad would ask her sister if you could stay with us. And I think you'd be better off in your own home, don't you?'

The answer to that was a very definite yes. The thought of

staying with him without our parents was just too horrible to contemplate, though neither of us said that. We just nodded our heads, but both of us knew exactly what he meant. He would leave us alone if Phil made efforts to appear more cheerful, then Mum's worries would disappear and we would all be happy again. We were naive enough then to believe all of that fabrication.

'Now finish your ice cream before it melts,' he told us, and lifting up our spoons, we quietly did as he asked. Not that us spooning up half-melted ice cream into our mouths stopped him from talking.

'We've got another treat planned for both you and your parents. Another visit to my favourite restaurant. You enjoyed it that night we went last time, didn't you?'

The truth was that we did, so heads were nodded dutifully again.

'And now I'm going to ask you to do one simple thing when we get back. It's not for me, it's for your mother. I want to see you both out on your bikes. Just for a short time, because that will really make her happy. You know your leg has improved since you started riding, don't you, Phil? That's another thing that pleases her. Your dad told me she gets upset when you keep saying you don't want to. So, will you do that for her, if not me?'

'Alright,' muttered Phil, not that he looked as though he thought it was.

But Clive was a businessman who was successful in obtaining large orders from building firms all over the country. His motto must have been 'give the punters what they want'. That was after he had convinced them of exactly what that would be, so the two of us were pretty easy targets for his next negotiating stage: sealing the agreement. He knew when it was the right time to change a subject, which he casually did in a few seconds.

'Oh, by the way, boys, I'm really sorry I'll be away for your birthdays. I would have liked to take you all with us, but perhaps another time. But now, presents! I think you two had better help me out there. Things have changed since I was your age so it would be better if you told me what you want, so that I can make sure it's there on your birthday. Now, Ryan, you go first.'

'A satchel,' I blurted out. 'One like Leighton has.'

'Well, that sounds very reasonable. Anything you need to go in it that would help with your homework?'

'Umm, some new exercise books and a better pen?'

'And how about a dictionary? Nothing like a nice new one to make you want to use it.'

'Well, yes, thank you,' I said quickly. A new pen and satchel for school was what I had wanted for ages.

'Anything to help you with school, Ryan. Education is very important.'

'Now, Phil, what do you have in mind?' he asked, looking over at him.

I noticed Phil chewing his lip. Had he recognised what Clive was doing? From what I can remember, it was only much later that we realised that Clive had both threatened and bribed us. Or deep down, did we already know? Even so, neither of us wanted to sound too greedy.

'What I would really like,' Phil said slowly, so that Clive could understand each word, 'is a Walkman.'

Well, that surprised even me.

'You like music then?'

'Yes, my brothers have loads and I listen to it when I'm with them.'

'Well, you know what then, as I'm sure you'll share it, when you get it that is, why don't we go into the music shop and choose a few cassettes? Would you like that?'

Of course we would, a Walkman would be really cool.

'And is there anything else you can think of?'

If I was surprised by Phil's first request, I was just about speechless when he made his second.

'And to help get my leg better, I would like more water therapy. I can't have more than one session a week for free.'

For the first time that day his innocent blue eyes looked straight into Clive's.

'That would make it easier to ride my bike and make Mum happy, wouldn't it?'

'Well, yes, you're right, it would. So how many times a week would you like to go?'

'Three times a week.'

If anything, I thought Clive looked genuinely bemused by Phil's firm and precocious request.

'I'll arrange that with your mum,' was all he said, before calling the waitress over and settling the bill.

* * *

Back at the house, we asked Mum if it was alright to take our bikes out. If she was surprised at that request, she made a good effort to hide it.

'Of course you can. Just don't ride too fast, Phil,' was all she said.

The following morning, when our sleep had been undisturbed, we sauntered down to the kitchen, demolished a large breakfast, then asked if we could take our bikes out again.

This time our mother was unable to hide how pleased she was and practically beamed.

'Of course it's OK, Ryan. Fresh air will do you both good.'

I could see the pleasure in her face as we trotted out.

Phil was still a bit nervous, but after we had been out a few times, he became pretty relaxed. I made him laugh when I teased him about the Sony Walkman he was about to receive. In fact, for the first time in weeks, a wide smile sat on his face when he thought about it. But the downside of him looking as though his old self was finally putting in an appearance was that Clive, of course, received all the credit – Mum and Dad must have thought he was a miracle worker. They had no idea that it was a mixture of promises, threats and a good dose of bribery that amalgamated to cheer the pair of us up.

I'm not saying that after our talk with Clive, Phil went straight back to his old self. I don't think he ever really did. He was far warier of people, especially men, for a very long time. But then so was I. In addition, the pair of us were even happier to know that once we left Clive's house, we would not have to see him for months.

On the morning of Phil's and my birthday, we received several brightly coloured parcels. New jumpers from Mum and Dad, trousers and a couple of shirts, as well as some toy cars and more Lego from our brothers. When we had expressed our delight in everything that the family had given us, Mum placed two more parcels on the table.

'You know Maureen and Clive are really sorry they can't be here, don't you?'

'Yes,' both of us managed to say in unison as we tried to stop smiling with the sheer relief on hearing those words.

Right up until the day of our birthday we had both been dreading hearing the news that Clive and Maureen had decided to return. That they were back from their holiday and were going to be staying with us after all. Even though postcards were arriving with pictures of sun and sea and yellow sanded beaches, they were just a reminder that their absence was only temporary.

'Missing them, are you?' Mum asked, thinking we had been hoping for a surprise visit for our birthdays. 'They'll be back in October and we'll be seeing them then. And October's not that far away. I'm sure you wish they were here.'

Now that was a bit of a difficult one. What could we say? Somehow we forced ourselves to smile and managed a mumbled yes.

'Now, boys, nothing was going to stop them from making sure you got your birthday presents on the day. These two are from Maureen and Clive. That one's yours, Ryan, and this one's for you, Phil,' she explained as she passed them over.

I really doubted if Maureen had much to say in choosing

them, I thought as my fingers busied themselves untying the string. She was most probably annoyed that her husband had spent so much money on us. I wondered how he had managed to explain that one away.

Not that I was in the least bit bothered.

The next effort we had to make was to appear totally surprised when we saw the contents of our parcels. At least when I saw mine, squealing with excitement was not a problem. The satchel I had asked for was even smarter than Leighton's. Not only that, when I rummaged inside I found several brightly coloured notebooks and a sleek silver pen.

It was not difficult to look pleased with all of that, was it?

Not for Phil either. When he unwrapped his Sony Walkman, he also found a gift token inside for him to buy some music and he gave a spontaneous gasp of pleasure.

'Goodness me!' exclaimed our mother. 'Your uncle's certainly been very generous to you both, hasn't he? I have the address of where he's holidaying, so you'll have to write to him to say thank you. Tell him it's your new pen you're using, Ryan. That will please him.'

'We will,' we replied. Not that we had any choice – Phil and I knew Mum well enough to know that she would be standing over us until the letter was written to her satisfaction.

'And look, Ryan,' said Phil, showing the gap where his front teeth were still missing as he grinned widely at me. He was holding up a pair of headphones. 'There's two lots of these, means we can listen to the music together. Now, that's cool, isn't it?' And I had a picture in my head of us walking to school joined by those headphones and burst out laughing.

'We'll look as though we're tied together, like Siamese twins,' I said and the pair of us doubled up and broke into a spasm of giggles.

'We're going to look really smart when we go back to school,' said Phil once he got his breath back.

'We will!' I replied.

How our classmates would envy us.

Mum butted in then. 'Right, you two, time to put your presents away! They can go in your room and when you come back down, you can clear the table. You haven't forgotten we have a party to get ready for, have you?' Her voice might have sounded stern but I could see that the sound of Phil's laughter had really put a smile on her face and she looked relieved.

The fact that our birthday arrived in the middle of the school holidays when quite a few of our friends were away did not deter the family from organising a celebration. As far as they were concerned, although it fell on Phil's and my birthday, it was not just for us but for everyone. With our brothers, their wives or girlfriends and a few more relatives, we were a pretty big family. There was no way they could all fit in our house comfortably, even if half the guests were happy to sit outside, so Mum, as she always did for large family gatherings, had hired the village hall. Phil and I had invited friends who had not gone away, Dad invited his brother, who was bringing his wife, while Mum's younger sister was coming with her husband and two sons. Then there were people my parents knew locally and of course, our neighbours. All told, this meant a real mix of age groups.

It was the custom in our area that when parties were thrown, everyone would pitch in. Some delivered their dishes of food to the hall, while others brought them to the house. As Mum was busy cooking, Dad had taken Leighton with him to help at the hall. It was my job to rush to the front door every time the doorbell rang and let in whoever was bearing a dish. With all that hustle and bustle, thoughts of Clive faded from my mind – I was too busy having a good time.

I tried hard to push back the memory of the nightmare I had had the night before. It was when I woke in the small hours that I was convinced that Clive would never leave us alone, for in my dream he was sitting on the edge of my bed and it was only his face that I could see. Even though I tried not to, I still couldn't stop myself from hoping that he would go back to being the 'nice uncle', the one I had liked so much initially. The one who made me feel special, the one I believed had enjoyed the time he spent with me as much as I did. That was the person I missed.

As an adult, I now understand that this was all part of his grooming tactics. And as for that chat in the ice-cream shop with Phil and me, when he pretended to show a little concern, was I so naive that I had not seen through it and recognised blackmail when I heard it? Of course I should have faced up to the fact that his one and only concern was to ensure that Phil did not meet up with a therapist. But then Clive was, as I have learnt over the years, an exceptionally devious man.

I forced myself to push aside all those bad thoughts. This was our special day, wasn't it? And I was young enough to be made a big fuss of. I had been given loads of presents already and I knew when the guests arrived, more would be coming. And what child doesn't love presents? So I made myself think ahead to the good time we were going to have.

'Now don't forget we've got my sister, Auntie Elaine, coming with her boys. That will be fun, won't it?' said Mum, interrupting my thoughts.

As I could hardly remember them, I thought I would rather spend time with my friends, but I agreed anyhow. I could sense Phil wasn't happy. Maybe he had forgotten that we had met them before and they all seemed very nice. The boys had been friendly enough and their father had chatted away to us. Later, I came to understand that it was the word 'Uncle' that had scared him. It was around then that he seemed to have begun to think that the word meant only one thing. The only exception seemed to be our dad's brother, whom we had known all of our lives. Tiny seeds of suspicion of all men we didn't know had been sown and were already beginning to grow. With me, it took a little longer than Phil, but that didn't mean I wasn't beginning to feel it. Already we didn't like our hair being touched or ruffled and we shied away when one of Dad's friends stretched his arms out to give us a hug.

Everyone put it down to us thinking we were too big to be treated like babies. Well, that was the excuse that was made and joked about by the adults, but really, neither of us liked being touched by any male who was not part of our immediate family.

I noticed the worried look that came over Phil's face when Mum told us that her sister and her family were going to stay. Within seconds, it was replaced by relief when she added that they had booked into a local hotel. Not that I said anything to him, I was too busy thinking about the party. My brothers had let slip that they had hired a magician as part of our present and I could hardly wait to see my friends' faces when they saw that.

Ian and Allen came over to give Mum a helping hand and all of us carried the remaining dishes from our house over to the hall. The table was practically groaning with all the food that was already on it and it took a bit of manoeuvring by Mum to get the rest on.

'I hardly needed to cook, did I? Looks like the whole village spent hours doing it! Anyway, that's everything done on my side, I'm leaving everything else that needs doing to the men. Time to go and get ourselves ready now,' she told us. 'Though first, I'm going to sit down with a cup of tea.'

Phil and I got ourselves washed, making sure that the backs of our necks and our fingernails had been scrubbed clean. We knew that before we left the house Mum would be inspecting both. She had put out clean clothes for us on our beds, which we pulled on and then took ourselves back downstairs. After she had given us the once-over and tidied our hair to her satisfaction, we all walked over to the hall, where we could already hear music playing.

'Old folks' music,' Leighton whispered, making us both giggle.

The magician in his top hat and tails was already there. Most of his tricks were going to be done outside, he told us.

'You all like magic, don't you?'

'Yes,' each of us replied enthusiastically. Then I tried to tell him all about the place where Merlin had once lived. I must say he did his best to look impressed, but I don't think he had a clue what I was talking about.

'Well, you and your friends will be getting a few surprises in a while,' he told us before sauntering off to chat to my older brothers, who he knew well.

I noticed that a small stage had been erected outside. The three of us called to our friends who had arrived and there was a scramble to make sure we were sitting the closest to it. Once the magician saw all the children were seated, he greeted his audience and called a couple of people up to help him with a few of his tricks. A white rabbit was found under a hat and silk scarves appeared out of thin air, or so it seemed. I thought it great fun and when he was walking around, he found a couple of chocolate coins behind my ears and some jelly babies behind Phil's. Then it was time to eat. It's a wonder none of us were sick because we stuffed so much into our mouths, washing it down with juice and fizzy drinks.

Just when I thought I couldn't swallow another morsel, Mum came out carrying our birthday cake. As we were boys, she had managed to ice it in blue and white. We were told to blow out our seven candles together and make a wish. Phil and I breathed in as deeply as we could and then let out the biggest puffs we could.

'Make a wish now!' our brothers yelled the moment the candles' flames were extinguished.

I wondered if Phil would wish the same as me – that Clive would never return from his holiday. I stopped myself from wishing he would drop dead, because I knew that would be a wicked thing to do, wouldn't it?

*   *   *

It was sometime later that day that Mum's sister Elaine and her husband Martin invited us to visit them on the Isle of Dogs in London – 'You haven't seen our new house yet and we have plenty of rooms,' Martin assured our parents.

'And it would be great to be able to spend some time with you again, Audrey,' Elaine said with a smile, which made Mum look really happy. 'I'm sure a few days' break would do you all good and there's so much to do in Docklands and in London.'

'It would! The boys have never been to London.'

'And do your boys like Chinese food? I know ours do. There's a great Chinese restaurant near us, it's on a boat! Really lovely at night, all lit up with Chinese lanterns and the food's wonderful. The chefs there take a real pride in it. We'll have to go there for a night out. The kids can always sleep in late the next morning, can't they?'

I must say it sounded good to me.

'And I have a really famous neighbour,' Martin chipped in. 'Gary Mason – remember him, John?'

'I do, he was a really famous boxer in his time. He's still alive then?'

'Indeed he is.'

*   *   *

'I wish I could come with Audrey, but I have to be at work early on Monday, plus Leighton's playing football on Saturday and I promised him I would go. Can't let him down.'

It was Warren who noticed Phil's face drop when he heard that Dad wasn't coming. Believing it was because Phil thought we could not go without Dad, he quickly chimed in, 'Not a problem, Dad. Vicky and I will take them.'

What Warren didn't understand was the reason Phil beamed at him when he made that offer. It was because he thought Warren would be staying with us as well. For out of everyone, Warren was the person who made Phil feel the safest.

'It's a shame Leighton and your dad can't go with us,' Mum said to me later. 'But you know Leighton and his football, and your dad's not much better.'

I was sorry too that Leighton wasn't coming. He was always such fun to be with and not only that, he was the one who always managed to make Phil laugh. Still, he would never let his team down by not playing a match, even if it was a friendly against the top team in the league. It must have been because the holidays were nearly over that the boys wanted to make sure that they were still up to scratch before the new league started when the schools went back. And Dad wouldn't want to not be there to cheer him on.

As if reading my mind, Mum said, 'Don't think your dad's ever missed a match when Leighton's playing. And isn't it good of Warren to offer to take us all the way there? I know he had his own plans for the weekend. He told me he didn't want me struggling with you two and our luggage on trains and buses, especially if that leg of Phil's gives way again.'

I was aware that Warren was also concerned about Mum's health. I knew from snippets I had overheard that her doctor had made her more than one appointment with the hospital. Phil and I were a bit worried about her as well, although for slightly different reasons. Warren had spoken to Leighton, Phil and me about it when Mum was out of earshot. He told us that we must all help her as much as possible. Making our own beds was something even Phil and I could manage. It was also up to us to make sure all our toys were put away and our clothes hung up.

'Don't want to see her picking up after you when I come round.'

Warren was pretty firm that time, which for him was quite unusual.

As he had told us not to mention that conversation, Mum must have wondered what had come over the three of us when we all started being so helpful! She certainly looked rather surprised when I picked up a tea towel and offered to help with the drying up.

The day before we were leaving for our visit to the Isle of Dogs, she made sure we packed as little as possible. 'Everything we were taking has to go in the boot,' she told us. 'There won't be room for anything but ourselves once we cram into the back seat.'

When Warren turned up the next morning, his girlfriend Vicky insisted on sitting in the back with us – not that Mum protested too much. Vicky laughed when we asked if the Isle of Dogs was called that because there were a lot of different breeds there.

'There have been many stories about how that particular name came about,' she told us. 'So shall I tell you the one I like the most?'

As both Phil and I liked stories, her question received an instant yes.

'A long time ago, when thick forests covered much of our land and animals roamed free, a royal princess discovered a strip of land that had no name ...'

'What animals?'

'Bears and huge pigs with fearful tusks. Now, the princess was a great hunter, so she asked her father if she could have a lodge, along with stables for her horses and kennels for her hunting dogs, built there. A request that he, being proud of her accomplishments, granted. For she was bolder and more skilled with her bow and arrows than either of her brothers. The princess was happy that soon she could hunt in a place which was almost unknown. On that piece of land that she now saw as hers, she only needed the minimum of servants. All her finery, her furs, velvet cloaks and jewellery could be left in the palace. She would be able to live as she wanted; no more courtiers who bowed and scraped whenever she moved.

'As soon as the wooden lodge with its stables and kennels was completed, she had her hunting dogs brought there. They would be her guards for no trespasser would dare come near her when they heard the sounds of their barking.

'When the moon shone down, it lit the way for the forest's

nocturnal animals to forage for food. As they pushed through the overgrowth, they quickly disturbed the sharp-eared canine guards. The sound of their blood-curdling baying was carried by the wind right down the Thames and right out to sea and into the fishermen's ears. Like the animals, they used the moon's silvery light to guide them, cast their nets where they believed their catch would be the most successful, then waited silently for the fish to swim into them. But those blood-curdling sounds brought to them by the wind filled the men with panic. It was the ghosts of long-dead seamen who, unable to rest in the sea's depths, were cursing the ones above them is what they told each other.

'They were doomed, the fishermen believed.'

'What happened then?'

'They went to the palace, for the people who dwelt within those walls were known to be the wisest in the land. And surely, they would know how to persuade those spirits to leave. The men of the palace doubled up with merriment when they listened to the fishermen's woes. They could not tell them it was only the sounds of the princess's hounds that had been heard, for they were bound to secrecy. But then, not wanting the fishermen to desert their lives on the water, they thought of how they could remove their fears.

'It's only the souls of ancient dogs that you hear, they told them. The king and all the kings before him have used that piece of land as a burial ground for their hunting dogs. It's their souls calling out to their masters that you can hear at night. A story that spread to every corner of the land. And that is why today, it is still called the Isle of Dogs.'

I don't know if we really believed all of that story, but we certainly loved her storytelling – she was just brilliant at it.

'Tell us more,' we kept saying and Vicky managed to keep us amused for the rest of the journey by inventing a few more stories about the golden-haired princess and her baying dogs. We finally stopped pestering her as we reached the outskirts of London and were absorbed by the sheer size of it. Warren drew our attention to a massive skyscraper being built in the distance. It was silver and had a glimmering blue-pointed top.

'That's Canary Wharf, it's going to be a new financial centre. It's even getting its own station once the new Docklands Light Railway is built.'

Once we arrived on the Isle of Dogs it was hard to imagine that many years ago, a princess had ridden her horse over that part of London. All we could see were huge concrete and glass buildings that towered over the whole of the area; a few were finished with trees and gardens surrounding them, others had 'For Sale' or 'To Let' signs up and there were still more under construction.

'Interesting, they seemed to have started with the residential. All these flats and houses are new. Almost there,' said Warren as he took a turning and pulled up in front of a barrier with a uniformed security person. The barrier was lifted when Warren gave his name and he drove us slowly into the residential estate until we came to Martin and Elaine's house, a large redbrick modern, double-storey house with a small front pebbled garden with pots of brightly coloured flowers in the porch. The houses were built around the edge of the water and we would soon discover that the Isle of Dogs is full of waterways.

'Is this it?' gasped Mum in amazement.

'Yes, Mum, we've arrived. Lovely house, isn't it? Imagine living right on the edge of the water!'

As Warren opened the boot and lifted out our belongings, Martin and Elaine came out to greet us. Hugs were given to Mum before Martin bent down slightly so he was on the same level as us.

'You boys are growing up alright,' he said. 'Quite the little men now, aren't you?'

At least he didn't ruffle our hair. That would have made things even worse. But he wasn't to know just who and what his greeting reminded us of. I saw Phil stiffen as red blotches appeared on his cheeks. Luckily, I think Martin thought Phil was the shy one out of us two and was merely blushing.

Their two sons greeted us the moment we entered the house.

'Come on, let's go into the garden,' the younger one, Tim, said, almost as soon as we walked through the door.

'I'll show you our goldfish,' the elder one, Robbie, added, while Tim muttered about taking us to where his rabbits were.

'Where do they live?' asked Phil.

'In a hutch at the bottom of the garden,' was the answer.

I must say the thought of meeting some rabbits sounded a bit more interesting than looking at fish. Not that I said so because Mum had given us a lecture on getting on with our cousins and being polite.

Outside, we walked over to a small pool and that's when I saw several large golden fish swimming around lazily. They were, I thought, quite beautiful, though after a couple of minutes I couldn't stop myself from fidgeting. Looking at fish, even beautiful ones, was pretty boring. After that, it was down to see the rabbits. There were two pink-eyed, fluffy white ones in their run, munching away at some green stuff and more or less ignoring us when we approached.

'They like being stroked,' Tim told us, leaning over to run his hand over one rabbit's back. 'You can give them a stroke now.'

Both Phil and I leaned over as well and stroked the rabbits. Neither seemed at all perturbed at strangers touching them.

'They're not frightened by strangers,' Robbie explained when I mentioned that I was surprised at them being so docile, 'because no one has hurt them ever.'

Hearing those words made Phil smile at him. Being kind to animals was something he felt was very important. Because, he told me once, they only have us to look after them.

Outside in the garden I was pleased that my brother looked so relaxed as he chatted away happily to both the boys. Not that I thought they understood much of what he was saying, but they were kind and smiled away at him as though they had understood every word.

It was not until we were called to come in for lunch that everything changed within seconds. Warren and Vicky were standing, clearly in the middle of saying goodbye, when we walked in. I could hear Elaine saying that she wished they could have joined us but she understood they had to get going.

'Afraid so,' Warren said smiling. 'We're expected at Vicky's parents on the South coast sometime this afternoon.'

'Yes, you're cutting it a bit fine, but you can join us next time you come.'

Before Warren had a chance to reply, Phil moved from where we were and placed himself right in front of him and Vicky.

'Are you really leaving?'

I, who knew every expression in my twin's voice, heard his fear. Unfortunately, Warren didn't recognise this.

'Yes, mate, got to get off now, got a long drive in front of us.'

'I don't want you to go!' Phil shouted.

'We can't stay any longer, we're expected at Vicky's parents' house for dinner.'

Phil just stood there and then his mouth opened and the word 'Noooo!' turned into a high-pitched scream that rocketed around the room. Before Warren could stop him, he rushed into the downstairs lavatory, slamming the door behind him. We heard his gulping sobs and then the key turned.

For a moment there was complete silence in the room. No one else could understand what this outburst was for. It was so unlike him for Phil was the placid one, the good-natured twin, the one that everyone felt protective towards.

It was Warren who moved first. I heard him knocking on the toilet door.

'Come on, Phil, come out. Whatever's upset you, we can sort it out.'

More sobs came through the door. The tone had changed

and Phil sounded more and more distressed. Vicky looked almost as worried as Warren had. I think Mum was too shocked to do anything.

Elaine and Martin told the boys that they could go outside if they wanted. 'Warren will find out what the problem is,' she told them. 'I'm sure it's nothing to worry about.' A little bewildered, they both scarpered as fast as they could back into the garden.

I could hear Warren asking Phil again to come out and talk to him. He turned to me then as nothing he had said had stopped my brother's sobbing.

'Ryan, whatever's got into him? This is not like our Phil, is it?'

'Let me try,' I offered. Moving over to the door, I got down on my knees and tried to see under it. 'Phil, it's me. Just tell me what's wrong.' For the gargling sounds mixed with sobs were indistinguishable even to me.

Hearing my voice telling him to take a deep breath before he tried to explain what the problem was helped lessen the sobs. After what seemed like hours, but was in fact only a couple of minutes, a torrent of words came through the door. It was lucky that I was the only one who could understand them.

'What was he saying?' Warren asked and I quickly told him as much as I could, leaving out the last thing Phil had said to me: 'Is he going to come into our room too?'

Just hearing that one sentence would have told Warren a lot.

Of course, now I wished I had repeated it word by word.

If I had, Phil's and my next few years might have turned out very differently. Clive would never have been allowed near us nor any other children again. And knowing Warren, no doubt the police would have been hammering on our uncle's door well before we returned home. But back then, the fear of what Clive did to us being discovered was too deeply ingrained for me to talk. Instead, I pulled myself up, tugged Warren's sleeve so that he bent a little towards me and whispered in his ear my version of what Phil had told me.

'He thinks he's being left here. He's been worried since Mum has to go to the hospital about her leg that she won't be well enough to look after us.'

'Wherever did he get that idea from?'

'Don't know,' was my answer, as I could hardly tell him it was Clive who had put that idea in his head.

'Well, let's try and get him to come out. You'd better stay with me.'

'Phil,' I said through the door, 'Warren's with me. He's worried about you. Now listen to him, will you? He's not going to leave you here.'

I moved away to let Warren stand closer to the door.

'Phil, I promise you that Vicky and I are coming back to collect you on Monday morning, then we'll all be driving back home together. And you know I've never broken a promise to you, have I?'

The sobs reduced to small hiccupping sounds as Warren kept talking calmly to him.

'Now come on, Phil, open the door. It'll be me who'll get

into trouble if I have to break it down, won't it? No one's cross with you. You mustn't think they are. Everyone's just worried about you being so upset. I'm sorry, it was all my fault, I should have explained to you that Mum needed a little holiday and she wanted both of you here with her. And of course, we're all going back together.'

A few more seconds of silence, then we heard the key turn. Standing in the doorway was my brother. With his flushed face and tear-stained cheeks, he was such a sorry sight. Warren opened his arms, wrapped them around Phil and then, picking him up, held him tightly to his chest. Soft words were whispered, words that told him he was very much loved, before Warren carried him back into the sitting room.

'All a little misunderstanding,' he told everyone. 'I'm going to take him into the garden and we're going to have a little chat.'

I can't remember how long they were out there – I don't think it was very long. When they returned, Phil was holding on to Warren's hand. There was no sign of tears, though he was still flushed.

'I'm sorry,' he said.

'Oh, darling, you've nothing to be sorry about,' Elaine said warmly, giving him a sympathetic smile. 'We were just sorry you were so upset. Now we're all going to forget about it and have a lovely time over the next few days, alright?'

Phil managed to give her a grateful attempt at a smile, even if it was a little wobbly.

'Well,' said Martin, springing to his feet, 'what I think we need is a little ice cream. That'll make you feel even better. Luckily, we have some in the freezer. My boys would eat it for breakfast if they could!'

Within minutes small dishes filled with strawberry ice cream arrived.

Warren bent down to give both Phil and me hugs. 'Now, you two enjoy your visit and you can tell Vicky and me all about it when we drive back. It will be your turn to entertain us. See you in a few days. You have a nice time. You hear me?'

'Yes.'

And then the last goodbyes were said.

Over the next few days, Elaine and Martin were true to their word, making sure we all enjoyed ourselves. Phil's meltdown was not mentioned once. Nor did our cousins question us about it – they just carried on being friendly and got us to play some games with them.

I was the only one who knew what had caused it.

And I was the one who dared not say a word.

29

Phil

After my meltdown it was almost as though, without saying a word, Ryan and I had made a pact. We were not going to talk about Clive; not to each other and certainly not to anyone else. What happened between him and us was our secret. No one would like us if they knew about it, of that we were both utterly convinced.

I hated to think what my school friends would say if they found out. They thought I was odd anyway. Their parents were always friendly when we met; I think with my poor speech and dragging leg they just felt sorry for me. But if our friends found out what we were made to do with our uncle, their parents wouldn't want either of us in their homes. Why would they? Rumours would spread until our neighbours, and the parents of the boys we played with, wouldn't want them mixing with us, for weren't we dirty little boys who should be avoided?

Invitations to our family parties would be turned down, which would hardly have made us popular with our own family. We had come to understand that we had little choice but to keep quiet. It was Clive who was the dirty one; it was he who made us do those things. We knew that, but would everyone believe it? It took a couple more years before we learnt another name for him: 'Perv'.

There were a few occasions when I also worried about Ryan. I could tell his feelings for our uncle made him feel confused. He was the one who had initially felt close to him. I remembered the first time Clive had taken us to his 'favourite restaurant'. He had shown us his thoughtful side then, hadn't he? Even booked a table near the door so that I could walk in.

And that tinge of pride in his voice when he introduced us to his friends. But it was Ryan he felt that pride for, not me. I had seen the expression on his face when he saw me dragging my leg and the impatience in his voice when he had to ask Ryan what it was I had said. Ryan might have pictures of the good times with Clive dancing in his head, but they didn't dance in mine.

I also understood that he still missed the man he had once seen as the benevolent uncle. Most of the time I had known that this man had never existed. I think this was something that Ryan had not come to terms with yet. I didn't believe for one moment that Clive would keep his word about leaving us alone. He had never said it was going to be forever, had he? Then he couldn't be accused of breaking his promise. I know I didn't believe it was over and from the whimpering sounds Ryan made in his sleep, I guess he didn't either.

I kept telling myself that even if it began again, it couldn't get worse, could it? At least that's what I told myself during the daylight hours, but like Ryan, my dreams told me something else. There was one dream that visited me nearly every night – the one where I knew I was awake, but I couldn't move, not even an eyelid. I was trapped by an unseen force that bound me there.

What my brother and I were afraid of was hearing the word 'Scotland' coming up in conversation. The place was too full of bad memories for us to ever want to visit again. In fact, the adult me still feels an anxiety attack coming on whenever I hear people talking about Scotland and how beautiful it is there. I won't even stay in the room if there's a programme about it on TV – horrific memories will flood into my mind if I do.

Back then, I think we both knew deep down that Clive was just waiting for us to go back there. What could be easier for him to get us alone than staying in a holiday home far away from our brothers and friends? Under the guise of giving our parents time off, he could get us alone far too often. So, I was not really fooled by him not coming into our room the couple of times he had visited us, or we him – I knew that he was just biding his time.

30

Ryan

I was aware that since we had that talk in the ice-cream shop, we had seen less of Clive. He and Maureen were back from Spain, but the phone calls were fewer. Nor were there any last-minute ones announcing they were on the way over and could Mum and Dad join them for dinner at their hotel. Instead, there were just a couple of fleeting visits when they were on their way somewhere else for 'business meetings'. And there was only one invitation for us to go down and visit them.

The only comment I heard Mum make to Dad about them was how hard Clive worked. They clearly had not worked out that maybe Phil and I were the attraction, not them. When we were all together, had they not noticed those sideways glances he kept throwing in our direction? I recognised the expression in his eyes. Hadn't I seen it often enough when he slunk into our room? It told me a lot more than his words had. That he still wanted to get his hands on us and was just waiting for the right time. And instinct told me that what Clive wanted, he made sure he got.

There had been nights when I had wished that someone would walk into our room and discover him groping us. Then everything would be out of our hands, wouldn't it? Then again, I was also afraid of what might happen if they did.

Wouldn't Phil and I be blamed as much as him for going along with it?

*   *   *

It was a few days before Christmas when our hopes of not returning to Scotland were dashed. The invitation to join Clive and Maureen for the Easter break was written inside their card. A big fancy one with a picture of his house on it. I saw Mum's face break out into a smile as she opened it before she read it out happily over the breakfast table.

I might have known that he would leave that invite lingering in the air for as long as possible. He would have worked out that the longer Mum and Dad had to wait for it, the more excited they would be.

Crafty old Clive; my instinct about him had been right. Of course, he wanted us to go with them to Scotland again. I felt something like a solid brick settling into my stomach when Mum's voice broke into my thoughts:

'Won't that be lovely, going back there? I didn't think he would be so generous as to invite us for a second time. But he has, he says it's our Christmas present. He's just so kind. I bet you're excited about it, Ryan. Something to really look forward to.'

It was a good job that Phil wasn't in the room then. I don't think he could have forced the muscles in his face to form a smile and mutter, 'Sounds great, Mum,' as I did.

As soon as I could escape, I pulled Phil to one side and broke the news. His reaction was pretty stoic: 'I expected that,' was all he said.

We hoped that Leighton would come as well this time. At least there would be some protection and we could ask that a third bed be placed in our room, couldn't we? But no, when I asked him, he told me that he would rather stay with Warren, meet up with his mates and keep working at improving his football.

I don't remember much about that Christmas and what we did during the holiday – rode our bikes and went to the park, I guess. Certainly, any good memories of that time were blighted by Clive's invitation. But I do remember how fast the time flew between winter and the start of spring. It was as if the winter which dragged from dreary dull day to the next was suddenly on fast forward. Once daffodil shoots pushed through the soil and enormous chocolate eggs were on display in shop windows, there was no getting away from the fact that Easter was just around the corner. And there was nothing we could do to prevent the arrival of our impending holiday. Nor could we push it to the backs of our minds for just a few minutes for Mum and Dad hardly talked about anything else.

The week before school broke up, Dad made sure that the old van was serviced – 'We can't have it breaking down and ruining our holiday.' Mum had been sorting out our holiday clothes. In the year since our last trip we had grown so she spent a lot of time going through our things and discarding items that were now too small. Then came the dreaded day before we due to leave. Cases and satchels were packed and placed in the hall. As usual, we were leaving at the crack of dawn.

A year earlier, excitement had kept us awake the night before, but this time sleep evaded us for a very different reason. I know we must have drifted off eventually. It seemed as if we had only been asleep for minutes before Mum shook us awake and, thick-headed, we stumbled down the stairs.

This time we did not play games on the journey, no looking for cars of the same colour. Instead, Phil placed a Guns N' Roses CD in his Walkman, plugged in the two sets of headphones and leaning back, we let the music fill our heads. Spending time with our older brothers had certainly introduced us to a very different kind of music to the tunes we heard on children's TV. Our brothers' taste was for us, we had decided. It had not taken long for us to come to love the sound of Rock. Which was more than could be said of Dad's view – 'It's just a lot of shouting,' was his summing-up.

As before, we stopped for a picnic almost as soon as we had crossed the border into Scotland. To our parents, the miles of rugged scenery told them that their holiday had just begun.

Which was not exactly what Phil and I were thinking.

31

Ryan

The only difference to our journey that I can think of was that this time Clive was not waiting for us at the ferry – he had gone a few days earlier. 'Had some people to see,' he had told our parents and this time, Dad knew exactly where to go.

Mum insisted that Dad stop at one of the small towns on the way so that she could buy groceries: 'Don't want them paying for everything as usual, they even sent us the ferry tickets,' she told him before turning to us. 'And you two can stretch your legs for a bit.'

At least we could jump out and look in the shop windows. Not that we were particularly interested in what was behind the glass, our minds were too full of what it was going to be like when we were back in the house.

Of course, Clive came racing to the door as soon as he heard our van pulling up. Big hugs and pats on the head, our shoulders squeezed. The usual comments of 'Great to see you all', followed by, 'How was your trip, John?' And finally, 'Maureen's in the kitchen getting us all some late lunch' were all exchanged before he picked up a couple of our cases and ushered us in.

No, nothing had changed, although Maureen's greeting to Phil and I seemed even more forced than the last time we had seen her. Not that Mum seemed to notice; she was too busy passing over the shopping to her sister and telling her how wonderful it was to be back there.

'How you two have grown,' Clive kept saying. 'You're going to need bigger bikes soon. Maybe we could sort that out, John,' he added, turning to my father as the bikes were taken out of the van.

Was I imagining it, or did I see a spark of annoyance in Dad's eyes?

'Actually, their brothers and I have been talking about that already,' he replied.

I noticed a firmness in his voice, as I think did Clive, for the subject was quickly changed.

* * *

There was little difference in how the first day was spent there. The same bedroom and what appeared to be the same sheep in the field outside of our window. What I couldn't understand was why there weren't a lot more of them. The lambs would have grown by now, wouldn't they? And yet it looked as though there were the same amount of big sheep in the fields as there had been the previous year and about the same number of lambs frolicking as well.

Maybe the farmer had other fields we hadn't seen yet? I

resolved to ask him about them when we went over there.

When I had got the explanation a day later, I wished I hadn't asked.

That evening, we sat around watching a film. Naturally, Clive had the very latest VCR machine and a cupboard full of recently released videos. Not that we were asked what we fancied watching. If we had, we would never have picked the film they chose.

I can't remember the title or the names of the actors, but if I try hard enough to bring a picture of it into my head, I can see a couple kissing a lot and our parents seemingly unable to take their eyes off the TV screen. Considering Dad liked war movies and Westerns, he must have been putting on a pretty good act. There were several bowls of different snacks on the table. Phil and I concentrated more on helping ourselves to them than we did the soppy film.

We were none too bothered to begin with when Clive casually sat between us to watch the film – after all, we were not on our own with him, were we? It was a chilly night and the fire was blazing away. As he said, it might have been spring, but Scotland seemed to think the moment teatime arrived, it was still very much winter.

'Are you two warm enough?' he asked and without waiting for an answer, he pulled a thick blanket over us. 'Keep you warm,' was the reason he gave. Hardly the correct one, I was to discover, when his hand slipped underneath and started to stroke my leg. I wished then that I was not wearing shorts. Phil was the lucky one there, he had insisted on wearing his long, thick trousers.

Why did Mum and Dad not look over to where we were sitting?

I felt Clive's hand inch up a little higher.

Couldn't they see what he was doing?

But no, their gaze was fixed firmly on the screen.

I felt a chill of loneliness then. These were my parents and sitting beside me was the man who could do no wrong, feeling confident enough that almost in full view of three other adults, he could run his hands over me.

Were we invisible to them? For that was how I was beginning to feel. And as for Maureen, there she was, not a hair out of place, sitting ramrod straight in her chair without a single glance in our direction.

Did she have any idea what he was up to?

I saw Phil's worried little face looking over at me.

Was he touching him too?

No doubt my brother was shivering more at the thought of what might happen later than feeling cold. Just when I was thinking the same, Clive's hand reached the part of me he wanted to touch. A hand found my penis and gave it a little stroke. I froze, I could hardly breathe. Silently, I begged our parents to look at the clock, see it was past our bedtime and tell us to take ourselves off to bed.

Just when I thought I would make them see that Phil and I were still there by jumping up and saying 'I need to go to the lavatory,' Dad lifted his eyes from the screen and checked his watch.

'Good heavens, just look at the time! You two should have been in bed by now,' was all he said.

No, he hadn't noticed a thing. No one had considered either that maybe Phil and I were unlikely to enjoy sitting in a room where we could not talk while they watched a film that was definitely not for our age group. At least in our room we could play music and chat as much as we wanted. Though all the time until sleep finally overtook us, our ears were on full alert for footsteps approaching.

* * *

Phil and I decided that as there was nothing planned for the next day, we would try and take ourselves off to the farm. We were hoping that we could slip out after breakfast and avoid Clive. Silly us, there he was at the table, smiling away.

'Morning, boys. Sleep well?'

No doubt he had a good idea that instead of sleeping peacefully, we had lain in our beds dreading the sound of his footsteps and the door knob turning.

'Yes,' I replied, 'as soon as my head hit the pillow, I was away.'

And Phil, getting the message, chimed in with a hearty, 'Me too.'

Clive's response was to look amused while Mum asked if we had some idea about how we wanted to spend the morning.

'We'd like to visit the farm, go and see the animals again,' I replied with my fingers just about crossed behind my back.

Please don't jump up from the table and say you're coming with us, the voice inside my head kept repeating.

But I needn't have worried. Looking up at us, another warm smile came our way.

'Wish I could come as well, but you know my business doesn't always leave me alone. Got to make a few calls. You'll be able to find your way there and back, won't you?' he said.

'Yes, it's not far.'

'Well, enjoy yourselves then, boys.'

What a relief! No Clive walking beside us or stopping to play his dirty games with us on the way back. For a whole morning, we were to be free of him. No one was going to be bothered how long we were out as long as we showed up in time for lunch.

We found the same path leading to the farm that we had walked the year before. On the way there, Phil noticed a family of squirrels and after putting a finger to his lips, he pointed up at them. There they were, fluffy little beady-eyed creatures, chasing each other up the trees and along the branches. For that short time as we stood there watching their antics, any anxieties about Clive drifted away. As we wandered up to the farm, we were carefree and innocent.

What we didn't know was that he had phoned ahead and asked the farmer if it was alright for us to pay a visit – it was Mum who let that slip later. It certainly put another feather in our uncle's cap. At our age we had not even thought of the farmer not being there when we arrived. We were just looking forward to seeing him and the farm again.

'Hope his wife gives us some of that milk, Phil – the stuff Mum gets from the shop doesn't taste the same, does it?'

Our wish was granted as we walked into the yard and

there was the farmer smiling away the moment he caught sight of us. I'm sure he must have noticed that Phil's leg was dragging badly, but he made no comment. His black and white collie, Bess, was seated by his side. Her ears and muzzle twitched as we appeared, but he signalled to her and she settled down. The only movements she made were to snap at flies buzzing near her head and to give us a tail wag as we got closer.

'You two have certainly grown,' were his first words of greeting.

Phil's and my face split into wide beams when he asked us if we wanted a ride on his tractor.

'I can see by your grins that the answer's yes. But after that long walk, I think you need a little refreshment,' he told us.

No sooner had he spoken the words than his wife came out carrying a tray with two glasses of milk and some homemade scones with butter, jam and cream on the top. We completely forgot that it was not so long ago that we had consumed a large breakfast as we tucked in.

After the last crumb was swallowed and sticky fingers licked clean, we climbed onto the tractor and were driven around the fields.

'There's the bull, he's huge!' gasped Phil, pointing his finger in its direction.

'Ay, he's getting old, that one. I have a nice little bullock set aside in the other field. He's only a baby now, but it won't take long till he's as big as his father. He'll keep the line going, he'll father some and in a few years, he'll be a grandad.'

It was when we passed the lambs in the field with their

mothers that I asked the questions about the sheep that had been puzzling me.

The farmer drew breath. I think he wanted to try and make the explanation as tactful as he could. Not that he was really able to.

'Well, those lambs get sold,' he told me. 'There's lorries coming tomorrow to collect some of these too.'

'Who are they sold to?'

Clearly not wanting to explain how an abattoir worked, he asked us a question instead: 'Look, boys, you eat meat, don't you?'

'Yes.'

'And where do you think it comes from?'

'Supermarkets.'

'Yes,' he said with a grin, 'all wrapped up in plastic, I know. But it all has a name, doesn't it? There's chicken, I expect you often have that at the weekend. Now they weren't born in the supermarket, were they? When they were little, they ran around a farm just like mine. Then there's beef, isn't there?'

'Yes,' I said cautiously.

'Well, you must know that comes from cows, don't you?'

I suppose we did. It was not something we had given much thought to, any more than when we ate bacon, we thought of pigs.

'And there's lamb, you must have eaten that?'

That was almost too much to take in. Our view of country life, where all the animals lived happily and did little apart from munch grass and look after their offspring, was beginning to fade.

'My own wee boys didn't like hearing that either when they were your age,' he told us gently. 'But it's us farmers who provide the food that gets on your tables. Without us, there wouldn't be any. And if people didn't eat meat, there would be no animals on farms.'

Not wanting to answer more questions about the wellbeing of animals, he changed the subject as smoothly as he could. He talked a bit more about his bull and how the cows had given us the fresh milk and the cream and butter we had just eaten with the scones.

Later that day, I heard the distant rumble of lorries. I might have heard them before, but then I hadn't known why there were coming. It was the desolate sound of anguished bleating as the sheep searched frantically for their missing young that kept us awake that night.

* * *

The following morning, I felt Clive's eyes on us and I'm sure he saw that we were tired. A little smirk appeared on his face when we walked into the kitchen. There was a discussion about our day – there was a beauty spot he wanted to show us all, followed by lunch out.

'And there's a great pub there. Really good food and a garden so if we wrap up well, we can eat outside. And,' he added, smiling over at Phil and me, 'there's a part of the garden where there's a slide and a couple of swings so you two don't have to sit and listen to the grown-ups talking all the time, do you?'

There's not much to say about our drive or the place we went for lunch. My mind was elsewhere. Having felt those looks coming in our direction, I didn't like them. I just knew that he was planning to come to our room that night. In fact, I was pretty certain that nothing was going to stop him.

I was right.

I met Phil's gaze when we heard the soft padding of his feet approaching our door. All I could think then was which one of us would he start on first? When I saw the door knob turning, I just felt sick. In he walked, as though he was a welcome visitor in our room.

'You two look pretty comfy,' he observed as he plonked himself down on the edge of my bed. The smile he gave me was the 'nice uncle' one and for a second or two, I thought maybe he would stick to his bargain, that him touching me in the living room was as far as he would go.

I was as wrong as it was possible to be.

He was so eager for us to get out of our beds and onto that rug that he practically pulled me out by my arm. Phil, seeing Clive's impatience, didn't wait for the same thing to happen to him and got out of bed hastily.

'Now that you're a little older, there's no excuse for you getting all upset, is there? This is what big boys do all the time and that's what you both want to be, isn't it, big boys and not babies? So, lie down on the mat and we'll have some fun.'

Without saying a word, we obeyed and just waited to see what it was he was going to do to us. He leant down and before we could protest or wriggle away, his fingers clutched hold of our pyjama bottoms. With one tug, he pulled them down to our ankles.

My cheeks burnt, as did my brother's. We had reached the age where we didn't even want to be seen in the bath so imagine how we felt when Clive did that. It was more than being embarrassed, it was a mixture of fear and shame.

But if we thought that was bad, what he planned to do next was even worse.

'Now, boys, can you see my hands? Where are they?'

We just looked at him blankly, wondering what he meant.

'You're not very observant, are you? They are behind my back. Now, where are yours?'

Still without speaking, I moved one of mine.

What was he up to now?

'Yes, at your front, aren't they? So, what I'm going to do is give you your first lesson in how you can have fun on your own. Now, both of you put your hands on those little things you call willies.'

Still wondering where this was going, we lowered our hands nervously and placed them on our penises.

'Good! Feels nice, doesn't it?'

The only thing we were feeling was fear.

'Now, wrap your fingers round them and do to yourselves what I've done to you. Move those hands of yours up and down and see what happens.'

This was even worse than before. Our faces must have been flooded with the red tide of humiliation. We always slept with a night light on in our room – how I wished we had switched it off.

'There you go! Now, I'll count to ten and I'd better see those hands getting busy by then. You'll like it, see if you don't. I told you, that's what big boys do all the time. Your brothers and even your dad do it. I'm showing you how to be grown-up.'

Of course, Clive wasn't trying to show us how we could enjoy playing with ourselves. He wanted to humiliate us to such an extent that his control over us became even stronger. Our self-respect, which is just as important to children as it is to adults, was slowly being erased. Only a few months earlier, we had stood up to him and now he wanted to make sure that didn't happen again.

And he succeeded. After just that one night, we had no strength left to fight him. By the end of that holiday, we had no self-respect and no ability to resist. By then, we felt so dirty and so ashamed that we wanted to crawl into a hole and stay there.

Clive must have considered that visit a great success for he came to our room most nights after that. We did as he instructed us to do. Any protests we wanted to make had long since dried up in our throats.

As an adult, I have seen those war films where the humiliation of a prisoner is used as a form of torture. Taking away their last scraps of dignity just about destroys them and we were a long way off from being men. And that was what Clive worked on over the holiday: turning us into his puppets, where we would do his bidding every time he pulled our strings.

32

Ryan

By the time we all left Scotland, Phil and I were convinced there was nothing we could do about Clive. We didn't even talk to each other about it. He had managed to place so many doubts and fears in our minds, we believed there was no one we could turn to.

The adult me now understands some of the many reasons why children don't talk and why they let their abuser control them for so long. Shame is a large part of it, as is a degree of blackmail. I've read about some of the threats that convicted child abusers have used on fearful small children. The worst one I saw, although I'm sure there must be others even more damaging, was where a man molested his neighbours' children – he told them he would kill both of their mothers if they spoke out about him.

'Slit your throats' were the actual words used.

And those two terrified little girls had kept quiet for years.

But Clive was smarter than that. Hadn't he inveigled himself into our family and acted as though Dad was his best friend? He'd gone to a lot of trouble to ensnare not just Phil and me, but Mum and Dad too.

'Your parents couldn't afford holidays without me,' he told us.

Also, 'It's because of me that your mum is friendly again with her sister and you've seen how happy that makes her, haven't you?'

When I asked why they hadn't been friends before, his answer was if I didn't already know, then I'd better ask Warren. Wondering what he meant by that, I tucked the comment into the back of my mind to ask my brother when we were alone.

There were other intimidating warnings thrown in our direction:

'I think your father would kill himself if he lost me as a friend.'

And the one that I think all abusers must use: 'No one would believe you, they would just think you were trying to cause trouble. Then it would be you they would be angry with, not me.'

And the one that, I guess, we feared most:

'Imagine what all of that could do to your poor mother. Make her really ill, wouldn't it? And you know what might happen then...?' And the smirk that appeared on his face was enough to remind me of the warning he had given us in the ice-cream shop.

Yes, those threats were enough to convince our young brains that we had already left it too late to go to our brothers for help.

* * *

Over the next couple of years, I began to feel that the verbal cruelty that came in Phil's direction was almost worse than those awful acts that Clive made us a party to. It was as though he despised people with any kind of disability. Or maybe he was just reinforcing the picture of just how bad our lives would be if we ended up living with him.

On one of those nightmare weekends in Cambridge he showed just how explosive his temper could be – something that up until then he had always managed to control. It was when Phil tried to stand up for himself. The evening before, Clive had announced that he had to visit his shop after breakfast: 'Need to be there, it's where all my accounts are,' was all he said.

It's where you have a bloody rug on the storeroom floor and a lock on the door was the thought that ran angrily through my head then. For since the last Scottish trip, this became his new way of getting us alone in private.

I felt that tinge of fear creeping up from my stomach to my throat the moment I heard the word 'shop'. At first, he took us both with him, but for some time he had only taken me. To think that once upon a time my chest had puffed up with pride when he invited me there – what a contrast to how I felt just a couple of years on.

Later that evening, when we were in our room, he paid Phil and me a visit. We must have looked stunned – he had never risked coming in before everyone else was in bed.

'Oh, relax, I'm not staying!' he told us nonchalantly. 'Just want to fill you in about tomorrow, Phil. I know I always take Ryan to the shop with me. I realise that must look like favouritism to you, which is very unfair, isn't it?'

No answer came his way as we both waited to see what he had up his sleeve this time.

'Oh, come on, Phil! I've seen you watching Ryan getting in the car with me. I know you must have felt left out. You always looked sad, which told me that you wanted to come as well. Tomorrow, you'll have your wish. I've decided that you can come with me this time instead of Ryan.'

I watched as Phil clenched his fists tightly, got off the bed and stood as straight as he could before uttering the sentence that took even me a little aback: 'I don't want to come with you.' For once, his words came out clearly.

'And why's that, Phil? Feeling lazy, are we?'

'You know why.'

'No, I don't. And nor will your mother, will she? It's not me you'll have to explain to about not wishing to help me in the shop, is it? I hope for your sake that you have a good enough excuse to convince her that you're not just being an ungrateful, wilful child.'

Judging by the complacent expression on Clive's face, he was only too aware that Phil had not thought of one. He gave him a few seconds to reply, then laughed dismissively.

'I knew it! You haven't thought of one, have you? I'll tell you something, you can rest assured your mother won't like it if you upset me. I must say, I do wonder sometimes how she copes. I doubt if she could without these breaks that Maureen and I give her. They're pretty important to her, aren't they?

'Let's face it, she has a lot to put up with, hasn't she? Especially with you, Phil. I mean, you still can't walk properly, can you? She must be worried that you're going to stay like that for the rest of your life. And then what happens when you leave school? You'll be around her feet all day, won't you?'

'I won't! I'll be working.'

'Oh, yes? Who do you think will employ you, eh? I can just picture it now, you dragging your leg into the interview room. And if that wasn't bad enough, the person interviewing you not being able to understand a word you say. You think they would offer you a job after that pathetic performance? I don't think so! No, you'll be at home alright. Expecting her to wait on you hand and foot, and she knows it! What a life has she got to look forward to, hey?'

Every one of those words, like poisoned darts, flew across the room inflicting pain, until Phil could take it no longer. He was just about crumbling under them. But still he had a small spark of courage left, which stopped him giving up completely. His mouth opened as he tried to force himself to speak. If I could, I would have called out, 'Phil, don't,' for I knew what was going to happen. Those gulping sounds he made when stressed would be all Clive would hear and I had seen his reaction to them before.

Expressing empathy was an act that Clive was inclined to drop when we were alone with him. He just glared at Phil, who was trying his best to get the right words out, and lost any patience he might have had.

'Oh, for heaven's sake, just shut up, will you? Don't open your mouth again until you can speak properly. Those grating sounds of yours just hurt my ears.'

Phil's face turned a bright pink as he pressed his knuckle into his eyes, desperately trying to stop the tears of anguish from falling. He looked at me despairingly before wrapping his arms around his head and slid his back down the wall until he could perch on his heels. He had nothing left to say, not to me and not to Clive. His efforts had just exhausted him and he knew then that he had no choice: he would be going to the shop.

Clive stood still for a moment, gazing at my twin with something approaching naked contempt. It was that expression more than anything that made me want to hurl myself at him and beat him on the chest as hard as I could. To my shame, I did nothing – I just waited for him to leave.

He must have read my mind, for a mocking smile came in my direction.

'Goodnight, boys. And, Phil, I'll see you in the morning.'

With that, he left.

* * *

Several years later, I was asked why no one had noticed for we must have been showing signs of shock and distress. Truth is, I've discovered, children are often more resilient than adults think. Plus, Clive had spent time getting us to gradually accept those small acts of abuse of his until he believed he was safe in asking for more and more. We might have hated those episodes, but gradually, we were able to compartmentalise. There were good days, the ones where he was not around, and bad days when he was.

We tried the best we could to make the most of the good ones.

That was our way of surviving.

33

Ryan

Morning was much the same as usual. Mum came into our room all breezy and bright, telling us breakfast would soon be ready as she drew back the curtains. 'I'm cooking this morning,' she said. 'Maureen's having a lie-in. So, scrambled eggs and bacon alright for you two?'

To tell the truth, we hardly had an appetite, not that we could tell her that, so we just said yes and did our best to look enthusiastic as if we could hardly wait to eat it. We got dressed as quickly as we could, brushed our teeth, ran a comb through our hair and got down to the kitchen as fast as we could.

We were hoping that if Maureen was still asleep, maybe Clive would be too. A wish that was not granted for there he was at the table, dressed in his weekend casuals, yellow V-neck jumper and chinos, newspaper propped up in front of him and a cheerful smile on his face as he chatted away to Mum and Dad.

'Morning, boys! Sun's out, looks like it's going to be a lovely day.'

Not that he waited for our replies, he just carried on talking about his shop and saying he wished he did not have to go to it.

Not as much as we did, I thought.

'Still, I only have to be there for a couple of hours at most, then we can all go and do something together.'

'Oh, Clive, you work so hard,' Mum sympathised as she passed him and Dad their breakfast.

'Well, lucky one of the boys can help me. I can get my paperwork done and Phil can let me know if anyone comes in.'

A bit unlikely that, I thought, *as the door would be locked*.

'It makes all the difference, knowing I can work safely in the back room.'

Clearly, he had already told Mum which one of us was going with him. And there was me thinking he might just change his mind and at least take both of us with him. However bad it was that he did it, it was not so frightening when the two of us were together.

He hadn't. I could tell from the way his mouth curled up into a smug smile as he slathered marmalade on his toast that he hadn't given it a second thought.

Our breakfasts came and were placed in front of us. Looking up at Mum, Clive urged, 'Come on, Audrey, sit down,' as he picked up the coffee pot and poured cups for all of the adults.

'You might have to bring a warm jumper, Phil. The shop can get a bit cold until the heater's been on for a while,' he said, turning to him. The 'caring uncle' smile was back in place, where it would stay until he was out of Mum's sight.

For me, the worst part of that day was when it was time for Phil to leave. He had his jumper slung over his arm as he climbed meekly into the back seat of Clive's car. 'Easier with his seat belt if he sits there' was the reason given each time we were taken somewhere in the car.

As they drove off, Phil turned so he could look at me out of the back window. Seeing his pale little face, I wanted to run alongside the car and pull him out. I knew what was going to happen when they reached the shop. Exactly the same as he had done to me the time before when we had come for a weekend.

That morning, as the minutes ticked by, images of every movement that Clive would be making flashed into my head. I could picture this as if I was watching a video of the events playing out. First, he would pull up in front of the shop. He would open the car door for Phil and offer him his hand to help him climb out, just in case someone he knew was looking. Then Phil would stand at Clive's side as the front door to the business was unlocked. Inside, he would shiver a little, for the shop was cold nearly all year round. Clive would reassure him that it would soon be warm as he bent down to switch on the wall heater.

Next, he would go alone into that small back room, with only a small window facing a wall so no one could see in. He'd switch on the second heater and come and collect my brother. I could almost hear his smooth tones saying, 'Now, Phil, let's go into the other room and get comfortable, shall we?' Not that this was a suggestion, it was a command. One that Phil would be only too aware of.

As he was of what Clive had planned once they were both in there.

He would see the rug positioned on the floor as he went in and know why it was there, though how Clive could describe lying on it while he grabbed hold of parts of our bodies as 'making us comfortable' hardly made sense. Once the door between the shop and that room closed, the 'benevolent uncle' mask was removed and Phil would see the coldness in the eyes of the real Clive.

I shuddered when I pictured Clive's next movements. First, he would place a roll of kitchen towel near the rug, then tell my brother to lie down. 'Hands at your side' would be his first instruction and then in one fast swoop, he would bend down, grab hold of the bottom of Phil's trousers and repeat what he had done to us in Scotland, pulling them and his tiny pair of briefs down to his ankles.

Humiliation is a powerful weapon, one that he had come to enjoy using. Clive's next command would be for Phil to take hold of his own penis and rub it up and down. I had never told my brother exactly what went on in the room when I was with Clive at the office. Maybe I should have, but did I really want to make his sleep even more tortured?

Clive would stand over him, slowly unbutton his waistband and flies and watch with amusement as Phil's eyes widened with fear. Then he would crouch over him, his bad breath fanning Phil's face as he grabbed hold of his small right hand. He would pull it to where that ugly red thing was poking out of the gap of his trousers, wrap Phil's fingers around it and with his hand on top of Phil's, start to move it up and down and progressively faster. All Phil would be hearing then was Clive's fetid breathing growing heavier and faster, eventually turning to grunts and groans. Suddenly Clive would shudder and Phil's hand would be knocked aside as Clive reached for the kitchen towel.

'You can play with yourself if you want to,' he would tell him. 'No? Well then, pull your trousers up. Think it's time I had some coffee.'

As Phil was struggling back into his clothes, he would make a quick phone call for coffee, cake and cola to be delivered. He'd tell him I normally collected it when I was there but that he was too useless and would spill everything.

Oh, there would be a few business calls made while Phil sat in the shop with his cola and cake. He would hear his uncle chatting away as though he hadn't a care in the world.

But then perhaps he hadn't.

34

Phil

Before Ryan and I reached our teens, we somehow found a way to cope. Apart from my meltdown in London, I think we managed to hide much of what troubled us. Only Mum knew about the bedwetting and the nightmares, something I doubt she shared with Dad. Nor since that first time did she say anything about Ryan washing the urine out of his bottom sheets. I helped him with that, but she must have known what we were doing.

But then Mum was pretty good at keeping a poker face. If she noticed that we hardly looked excited when told Clive was arriving at the weekend, she made no comment. Not that she would have seen how the skin on the back of my neck prickled with fear the moment I heard the news. Neither of our parents seemed to notice that there was no more excited chatter when we were getting ready for a weekend visit to Clive's. We hardly said a word on those journeys, but luckily for both Ryan and me, our visits to Cambridge lessened a little over the next few years. One reason was that with mock

GCEs on the horizon, Leighton had to study even harder than before. We barely saw him in the evenings and as soon as our evening meal was finished, he would disappear back into his room, where he assured us he would be working quietly.

On Fridays, his satchel was just about bulging with weekend projects, not that it stopped his football – 'Just have to get up earlier to fit it in,' he told us. Then there were the family outings where our elder brothers brought along their girlfriends, or should I say future wives, to introduce to us all. Apart from that, there were visits to our grandparents, which Phil and I still loved for they made such a fuss of us. Gran, her face creased into a huge smile, would hug us tightly before telling us how much we had grown.

Within a few minutes a large pot of tea was made. We were now allowed proper cups and it was not just sweetened milk anymore, but best of all, out would come Gran's homemade fruit cake. She knew it was our favourite and made sure there was a freshly baked one waiting for us on each visit.

To add to my parents' calendar of visits and events that could only happen at weekends was the announcement of Ian's wedding. We hadn't seen much of him for some time and as Mum said, 'Now I know the reason why.' Helping to organise the reception, not to mention making sure we all had decent outfits for the big day, took up more of her time and the family's spare cash. Then, as another year slid by, there was getting both Ryan and me ready to leave the junior school and begin the next term at senior school.

The amount of homework we were bringing home had gradually increased too. Now it was not just Leighton who had to work flat out at the weekend. Not that we were complaining – it had given us a really good excuse not to go to Cambridge.

One Friday, as we were walking back from school, Ryan laughingly said, 'Our teacher looked as though she could hardly believe it when you thanked her for giving us all that homework!'

Naturally, Clive did not think that was too difficult to overcome. He told Dad that he quite understood and 'was very pleased the boys were being so diligent'. He would let us use his study while we were there.

'Be a bit more peaceful than sitting at the kitchen table, won't it?' said Dad half-jokingly.

Not being able to find another excuse, we had to put up with a few more visits and silently thanked Ian for announcing his wedding and our other brothers for wanting to meet up a little more often as they too headed towards marriage.

Clive sometimes managed to bring Maureen up to see Mum, which meant them staying with us for a couple of nights. The one advantage of him coming to our house was that although he came into our room, he never stayed long. Those visits were also never as bad as when we were at his house in Scotland or worst of all, at the shop. There, he felt far safer than he must have done in any other place.

No one could walk in on him there. And I doubt if anyone could have even heard us yelling, had we screamed out any protests. Even so, he was pretty confident in his own house, but in ours, he had definitely become far more cautious.

I think the reason was that Leighton was now a pretty

knowledgeable teenager. One that I sensed was far from enthralled by Clive's charm. And if I had sensed it, I guess Clive had too. Leighton was the one person who might have been at least curious and probably even suspicious about why he was in our room. I would not have put it past him to demand to know what he was doing there.

We were surely a little too old for Clive to say he was tucking us in or reading us a bedtime story? Looking back, I'm pretty sure he only risked his nightly visit when Leighton was at Warren's.

35

Ryan

Even when I was still at junior school, I was aware of just how much our parents looked forward to their time with Clive. It was not only his and Maureen's company they enjoyed, it was all the little treats he gave us as well. Afternoons on the river, dinners at his favourite restaurant or at the hotel where he and Maureen were staying, but the biggest treat of all was our three-week holiday in Scotland.

For a couple who needed to look at the price of everything they bought, and had to put money aside for both birthdays and Christmas, my parents must have thought that Clive had transformed their lives. Little did they know that Phil and I were the hidden price they paid.

Once Christmas was over and a new year had been greeted, the main topic of conversation seemed to focus on the Easter holidays and the impending trip to Scotland. We knew from the expectant glances thrown our way that we were meant to chime in and show our enthusiasm. As they were pretty wrapped up in their own plans, the fact that we had hardly anything to add seemed to go unnoticed.

Over the next few years, Phil and I had to try hard not show our real feelings about the holiday. Did we succeed? I suppose we must have, for our parents always seemed to believe we were just as excited about going there as they were. Now, the memories of them have run into each other, so it's hard to say what happened on each of those trips. That is apart from the last one before we moved up to our senior school.

It's not so much what we did there that springs to mind, it's what those holidays did to us.

36

Ryan

Over all those hours leading up to that trip to Scotland, Phil and I not only had to listen to our parents bringing up memories of the last holiday, but also look at bundles of photos as well. As nearly all of them had a smiling Clive standing next to one of us, a hand placed around a shoulder, we really could have done without them being strewn all over the coffee table.

Just one glance was enough to be reminded of his coming into our room.

Once we were in his holiday home, nothing would stop him continuing to do what he wanted with us. Of that, we were in no doubt.

And we were right.

Every excuse he could find to spend time with us, he took. Not just content with coming into our rooms, he seemed to take even more pleasure in touching us outside as well. A walk in the countryside would be good for Phil's leg, he decided. He was most probably right, but being groped in the fresh Scottish air wasn't.

Mum's leg was growing steadily worse, which made her look at him gratefully when he suggested taking us out for 'a spin' and a walk. Sometimes she even made up a picnic to take with us.

Now, all these years later, I can't honestly say that every minute Clive spent with us was all bad. Through some of those walks, I came to enjoy the wildness of the Scottish scenery. When we stopped at some of the old grey stone pubs he so enjoyed frequenting, I found that I too liked the atmosphere there. Chilled drinks were given to Phil and me, while the friendly locals seemed to take a delight in suggesting other walks, where we would see more interesting sights. Not that I could understand everything they said, but I still enjoyed the sound of their voices. As it appears did Dad, for there were a few times when he and Clive nipped out for a pub lunch. I'd guess it had been washed down with a generous amount of beer judging by their jovial mood when they returned. Dad would tell us all about the people he had met there and repeat the names of the places they had suggested we visit.

So, no, I can't say that every day in Scotland was a miserable one for Phil and me. There were times when we actually had fun, like when Clive and Dad took us fishing. And there were quite a few evenings when we did normal things that families on holiday do – had barbecues outside, played board games and Clive even sorted out a few films that Phil and I could enjoy watching.

It's so easy to win children over, if only for a short time.

To me now, I feel it's sad that those memories of our holidays in Scotland are not mainly good ones, for they really should have been. Ones where Phil and I could, over a couple of beers, reminisce happily about our times there. But those bright, cheerful parts have more or less been eclipsed by the darkness that Clive created.

Before we went to senior school, we were still resilient enough to be able to push thoughts of Clive to the backs of our minds. Both Phil and I had school friends who lived nearby and often a whole group of us would take our bikes and cycle out of the village. Our mothers were only too happy to make up picnics for us to take with us. Cycling and spending as much time as possible outside was good for children. Of course, all of our parents had at different times sat us down to give us a few warnings: we knew not to talk to strangers and never, ever accept a lift in a car.

Even though it was not so long ago, this was still an era when families had not accepted that it was seldom strangers who were a danger to children. There were occasions when Phil came along with my bunch of friends but more often than not, he spent time with his own group. Not that the easing of our reliance on each other caused us to drift apart. In fact, it was just the opposite – it gave us more to chat about.

Up to a point, we were happy-go-lucky boys. We were not trapped in overcrowded areas where taking our bikes out for the day would have been impossible, we had plenty of friends and brothers whom we thought the world of. It was when we left junior school and began our first term at the senior school that our lives became less easy. Or should I say it was becoming aware of other boys' reactions to what Clive made us do that began to affect us? As did having to hide so much, which gradually made us feel we did not fit into any group.

37

Ryan

The first few weeks at senior school felt strange to me. I was no longer one of the older boys who newbies looked up to, instead it was Phil and I who were the newbies. Which meant we were targets for teasing unless we stood up for ourselves.

Not that Phil really had to. In the years he had been at junior school he'd won the respect of almost all of his classmates. Even small children could see how hard he had worked to improve his walking and speech. The ones who tried to bully him then had stopped a long time ago and the older boys in senior school were pretty patient with him. One boy had tried to mock Phil's speech only to be put down by another group, who had been at our junior school.

No one else tried after that.

Within a few weeks of being there it was not the teasing that bothered us, it was the smutty talk and jokes we overheard in the playground. Most of them came from the older boys' mouths, but it didn't take long for the younger ones to copy them. To us, the worst insults we heard were those aimed at boys who did not look masculine enough: 'poofs', 'queers', 'fairies', 'faggots' and a few more that I can't bring myself to repeat here. Did 11-year-olds really understand what they meant? We certainly didn't at that age, so I doubt it. All we knew was that no one liked to be called one of those words. A boy only needed to be bad at sport or not be able to jump over the horse in the gym for one of them to be hurled at him. Even the gym master struggled to keep a straight face when he heard them and no reprimands were given out.

I realised just how bad being called any of those names was when a group of boys were chanting them at a slim boy of around thirteen. I had noticed him quite often in the playground. He had such startlingly white blond hair and eyebrows that were almost invisible and so I suppose he looked different. But I don't think that was the reason they were ganging up on him. Then I wondered why he did not, as Phil had done, just grin as they teased him. Maybe if that boy had laughed a little with them, they would have left him alone. On the other hand, from what I had seen, he did not appear to show much interest in being friendly with his classmates. I'd see him walk alone into the playground on our breaks, prop himself up against a wall and open a book, turning the pages with his long, delicate fingers. This time though, unable to ignore the insults, his face turned a bright crimson and I heard unkind laughter from the boys and giggling from behind the hands of the girls.

'Seeing your boyfriend tonight then, are you?' one yelled and now nearly everyone in the playground was paying attention. The blond boy must have felt completely trapped when so many heads were turned towards him. Boys were nudging each other as the mocking continued and not one person offered him any support.

It was the appearance of a couple of the more senior boys, one of whom I recognised as being a friend of Leighton's, that put an end to it. They marched over to the ring of laughing bullies who had begun it. I've no idea what was said to them, but it was enough to make them disperse in all directions.

The following morning, the headmaster gave the assembly a strong warning about bullying. He said it was the weapon of cowards and that it would not be tolerated in his school.

Phil and I didn't realise what the words that had been shouted actually meant. Leighton explained a little of it to us, that there are some men who prefer the company of their own sex. 'And so what if they do?' was his opinion. But by then, we had witnessed how the majority reacted.

That was when our fear of people finding out about us really started to increase.

Then, any boy being labelled 'gay' or 'queer', as boys I knew called them, was heading towards unmerciful bullying. Things have changed dramatically for today's generation, as it had to a certain extent, in mine. But back in the eighties, it had not changed enough.

38

Ryan

Looking back at the memories I have of that time, it almost seems that our voices began to break, we both shot up in height and fine hair begun to sprout everywhere the moment we walked through those senior school gates.

But it was not those fine wisps of hair growing on my body, or how my voice alternated between being squeaky one minute and deep and almost gravelly the next that bothered me. I was OK with those signs and we had seen them in Leighton and understood that we were going through puberty. It was the other embarrassing signs which Clive told us proved two things: that we were on our way to adulthood, but more to the point, we were kidding ourselves when we refused to admit that we enjoyed what he was getting us to take part in. It was this that made him laugh at us and I wanted to put my hands over my ears to block out those mocking words – they placed something deeper than shame in my head.

It was on one of our visits to his house that it happened.

Clive had snuck into our room almost as soon as everyone was in bed. Or in Maureen's case, she was most probably relaxing in a bubble bath. He was already in his dressing gown when he came in, which told me he was not going to stay long. Over the years, I'd worked out a little of his and Maureen's routine. She would tell him she was going to have a bath and he would respond by saying that he had to make a couple of phone calls before taking a quick shower. That gave him roughly thirty minutes to spend with us.

At least that was not so bad as a whole morning, which is what happened in that shop of his.

He stood just inside the door for a few seconds, trying to make us wonder which one of us he was going to choose. But I knew from the way his eyes darted in my direction it was going to be me. It only took him a few more seconds to be at my bedside, his hand under my covers and his fingers wrapped round that part of me he liked so much. I felt it growing hard, which was bad enough, but that night, that was not all that happened.

I could feel his breath on my face, hear him whispering in my ear as his fingers moved steadily up and down my penis, then began to move faster. Something strange was happening to my body. I felt I had no control left over it as it began to shudder as at the same time a weird sensation shot from the base of my body to the top of my head.

There is no other word for what had happened: I had just orgasmed and ejaculated.

I can't remember now if I was old enough to understand exactly what that meant. Had Clive told me the right words, or was it the whispered conversations I heard at school that explained what had just happened? I mean, boys talk, boast about how they manage to satisfy themselves and how they make sure their mothers don't see the stains on their sheets. Some boys mentioned their 'wet dreams' as well – 'Saves us having to do anything,' one commented amid peals of laughter from his mates.

Laughter that I just about managed to join in with.

Other times, it is their own hands that they describe bringing them to satisfaction. Yes, boys talk and some boast, but what was clear though was that it was their own hands and not someone else's that they were talking about. And then after their voices began to break and the beginning of facial hair was showing, it was girls that they started to look at. Girls who only a short time earlier had been called 'pests' now swayed their hips and flicked their hair.

I guess their hormones were kicking in as well.

I too made comments about one or two of those girls – I didn't want my classmates thinking I was not interested in the opposite sex. Girls, I had decided, were best left alone. Hadn't I heard my brothers say they can look inside our heads and see what's going on in them? And in mine there was one big tangled mess.

At night when I lay in bed, vivid images of Clive and what we had done filled my head. I could hear his voice telling me I had lied to him and to myself, that I was just refusing to admit how much I enjoyed it. For hadn't he made me groan and gasp when I reached satisfaction? If that was true, then what did it make me?

I hid those dark thoughts that kept crawling into my mind. I didn't even talk to Phil about them, but they gave me even more reason to look as masculine as I possibly could. I'd seen boys in the playground who worked hard at their lessons, scored high marks and showed little interest in sports being teased.

'Bloody fairy, are you then?' was a fairly friendly insult.

Friendly it might have been, but no one was going to be given an excuse to aim insults at me.

I copied some of the older boys' confident, swaggering walk, loosened my tie and got hold of some hair gel. That was the beginning of my act, the one of being someone who didn't give a shit. An act that I worked at perfecting right up until I entered my twenties.

Even today, I struggle to explain just what effect the disgusting things Clive whispered gloatingly in my ear had on me. The shame I had felt when I was seven was nothing compared to how I felt during my teens. Shame, I have learnt over the years, is an emotion that often turns to anger and then the anger turns inward against the person who feels it.

Which just about sums up what happened to me.

It had not taken long to turn me into the kind of teenager who, with hands in their pockets and a sullen expression on their face, is the one to be avoided. The vibes given out are of someone who has no respect for authority. In fact, his expression says he has little time for anyone. He's the one who pinches cigarettes from his brothers and holds them in two fingers as he smokes them in doorways. The one who resents others' happiness. The one who blamed the world and everyone in it for not being understood. Deep down, what he really feels is lost and alone.

Yes, that was me at thirteen.

By then, I had little interest in schoolwork, I just wanted to leave school as soon as I could. Have my own money. Then I would not have to scurrilously search my brothers' pockets for enough loose change to buy a packet of cigarettes. The world would change for me if I was independent, wouldn't it?

House rules would not apply to me once I was no longer at school. Or perhaps I could get my own place, now that would be cool. Not that I gave any thought as to who would pay my bills, check there was enough food in the fridge and make sure I had clean shirts to wear. Even more to the point, I hadn't a clue what kind of job I would be able to apply for if I dropped out.

Did my parents try and talk to me? They did, especially after the headmaster called them in and told them he was worried about my progress. Or lack of it was more likely to have been the reason he wanted to talk to them. I know the importance of sitting exams was brought up. Mum shouted at me enough about that: without qualifications, what future did I think I would have?

Clive no doubt had been asked to talk to me after my parents had seen my school report. I doubt it was flattering. The slightest criticism of my work or a question as to why I hadn't completed my homework was enough to make me argue with the teachers and my way of voicing my opinion was enough to have me more than once removed from the classroom for talking back. On more than one occasion I had been called into the headmaster's office, where he asked me for an explanation for what he considered down-right rudeness.

Clive was back to being the 'friendly uncle'. He told me that if I worked a little harder, in a few years, he could help me with employment – 'I've got a lot of contacts, Ryan, just tell me what you have in mind. Come on, lad, think for a moment ... what would you like to do when you leave school?'

To which I gave him my stock answer, 'I dunno.'

The strange thing is I believe Clive really did want to help me. But haven't I said it was as though two people lived quite comfortably in his head? There was a part of him that could be kind and thoughtful. That was the Clive I had always been so fond of. Then there was the other side. It took me a long time to ask myself a question: if there really was such a good side to him, how come it never tried to force the bad part out?

And the answer?

Clearly, he had no intention of doing any such thing. All he wanted was to camouflage his real perverse self under layers of charm and generosity.

The second question I have never been given the answer to is this: was it only his chosen victims who saw it?

Phil

When I was little, Ryan was the strong one, the feisty one, the one who ever since we were toddlers, had tried to protect me. When I could hardly cope with Clive's presence in our life, it was Ryan I leaned on then. Without him, I knew I would never have managed. When I was feeling a little down, he would try and distract me, pull funny faces to make me laugh or tell me a little bit of gossip he had inadvertently picked up.

He was pretty good at overhearing things that were not meant for his ears, that was for sure. When Ryan finally came to see that Clive was not the person he had believed him to be, he was pretty devastated. It didn't have the same effect on me, because I had never really been taken in by him. I don't think everyone else saw him in the same light that my parents did either. But Ryan had really looked up to him, perhaps seen him as a bit of a role model, and maybe he believed that Clive really did care for him.

It's not easy, is it, for a 7-year-old to be let down so badly?

Not that anyone other than me seemed aware of it. But then we didn't have to use words to know what was going on in each other's heads. Yes, when I look back, I can see that Clive damaged our lives in so many ways. It seemed no sooner had we managed to get over one blow than another one was swung in our direction.

I think it must have been around that time that Ryan and I started making plans for what we were going to do when we were grown-up. Leave home and get our own flat together was one thing we decided on. Can't remember much more, though I hope our dreams were bigger than that.

It was when we went to senior school that I began to see that Ryan was beginning to change. That cocky, cheerful personality of his became subdued, that grin of his that made me giggle was gradually replaced by a dominant, sullen expression – I could feel the growing anger in him.

I knew it was partly caused by fear. Not so much fear of what Clive was planning to do the next time we were under one roof, but fear of himself. He wanted reassurance that he was never going to be the same as his uncle. For that was one of the little seeds Clive had planted in his mind. There were others as well, ones that ate away at him.

If only then he could have talked to someone. But to whom? He was scared of losing the love of those who were important to him.

For the first couple of years, teachers did show concern and asked if anything was troubling him, to which he always replied with an abrupt 'No'. By the time he was around thirteen, they no longer asked.

I don't know if Clive thought I was asleep when after he had been all over Ryan's body, I had no choice but to listen to what he kept telling him. I might not have understood the expressions 'brainwashing' or 'gaslighting' then, but I do now. And that was what he was doing alright. If it wasn't that, he was certainly playing with Ryan's mind. Inserting doubts and fears into his brain as deeply as he could. For he did not want them removed, just the opposite: he wanted them to grow.

He was trying to make us doubt our sexuality, to make us believe that we enjoyed what it was he did. That we were not so innocent as we would like to believe. That was rich, coming from a married man who was the father of two grown-up sons.

So, what label would he have placed on himself? 'Just a super-intelligent businessman who is smarter than all the rest', I expect. I suppose that part was true, but what about his sexuality? Not that we thought about it much when we were children. Though by the time we were around thirteen, we knew what his label would be. And I think that is part of the reason he wanted to make us believe that we were a party to it.

While Clive was whispering sweet nothings to Ryan, he ignored me. My body development was a little behind my brother. Remember how those baby teeth came late? Well, so too did sprouting hair and my voice breaking. From Clive's point of view that was rather disappointing. Not because he was growing tired of smooth young bodies, but because my body was not ready to ejaculate. Which meant he couldn't go on and on at me about how he had proof that I enjoyed those acts. Because I didn't, and I made sure he knew it.

The only good thing about hearing those words he poured into Ryan's ears was that it helped me barricade my own mind against them and so there was no emotional blackmail for him to throw in my direction. He could try all he liked, once that part of my body he grabbed hold of let me down by not ejaculating. But finally, it did. Oh, how he crowed with triumph. 'I knew you wanted it,' became his grubby little mantra despite my having disappointed him for so long. I wonder now if in some perverse way he wanted to believe that. After all, he repeated it enough times. I suppose if he could, then he could also believe he really was that benevolent uncle who played the part so well. After all, how many perverts have ever stood in the dock and told the prosecutor, 'You've got it bang to rights there, my man. I'm really what you say, a nasty worm of a man who doesn't care one iota about the harm I've done to those children.'

What I was becoming more aware of though during that time was the effect his words were having on Ryan. At school, not only do boys talk, they ask questions as well.

Ones that made both our faces turn bright red, much to everyone's amusement.

Since Clive had begun his games with us – or should I use the right words now? – since he had abused us, we had both felt shame. Once we entered our teens, that shame grew much stronger. Not only that, when he succeeded in making us ejaculate, the shame was more than we could bear. It raised questions that we were by no means mature enough to answer. And out of the two of us, I could see it was having a worse effect on Ryan than me. After all, I had overcome teasing and name-calling when I was small. In a way, that had toughened me up a little. Up to a point I could separate my body's response to his actions from my mind. Even if that part of me between my legs gave him the wrong impression, the important part of me, between my ears, loathed what he did to me.

Ryan just became even more withdrawn and surlier. Mum and Dad believed he was being a difficult teenager. Neither of them seemed to understand that he was a very troubled one. There was still some bedwetting, as well as those nightmares that he denied having, but neither raised any questions. They just thought that ticking him off and forbidding him to leave the house until his homework was completed was enough. When his school report arrived, which, from the expressions on their faces I guess was hardly complimentary, they just said how disappointed they were in him. I knew they were both puzzled at his behaviour and were just hoping he would grow out of it. The older boys had all been easy teenagers so they seemed to accept that there was bound to be one who wasn't.

I knew that Clive felt he hadn't gained complete control over our thoughts. So, what did he do? He just bided his time and waited until we were a little older when, like most boys of our age, we were beginning to notice girls.

* * *

It was at one of those family barbecues Dad had arranged when he knew Clive and Maureen were staying the night with us. I was wanting a little quiet to escape the sound of Clive's laughter and had slipped down the side of the house. I have no idea how he knew where I was, maybe he had been watching me more closely that I realised. I was leaning against the wall that divided our garden from the neighbours' when suddenly there he was, a smug grin of triumph on his face.

'Waiting for me, were you, Phil?' he asked, as barely waiting for me to reply, his hands reached out to grope my groin.

That evening, I just wished my older brothers would come looking for me and catch him. I was so tired of this secret we had been living with for so long, tired of what it was doing to us and tired of hearing what a good person Clive was. If my brothers caught him then surely his 'benevolent uncle' act would be finished, alongside his presence in all of our lives?

'See, you like it, Phil. That's why you slipped away, wasn't it?'

The combination of his hand down my trousers and his mocking voice gave me such a surge of adrenalin-fuelled anger that I gathered as much saliva as my mouth could hold and was so very tempted to spit it straight into his leering face. But I forced myself to repress this urge and swallowed hard. There was little I could do; I was not strong enough to push him away. I was able to come up with the words that would make him think it was not a good idea to have his hand where it was.

'Someone might come looking for us,' I stated as calmly as I could.

Thankfully, that sentence penetrated his brain.

'A little too much to drink' was his excuse that time. Must have been more than a little to make up that excuse was the thought that should have stayed in my mind.

'If you say so,' I said, but then I realised that he must have heard my contempt for him in my voice.

His face flushed and the look he gave me was venomous – Clive was not a man who liked to lose control over his victims.

'Well, Phil, you *are* thinking on your feet! Getting a bit of practice in for when you're older, were you? I know what you'll be getting up to in a few years' time, even if you're not facing up to it.'

He paused, waiting for me to ask exactly what he meant. I didn't.

'You'll be creeping down to those lavatories at the backs of parks, where boys like you go to jerk each other off. Or you might be able to travel to my neck of the woods, or London, there's plenty of bars for your sort there. Anyway, from what I've heard, guys aren't that fussy about who they have a one-night stand with, so even you'll do alright. Mind you, judging from tonight, I guess you'll be more likely to creep down a few dark alleys!'

I could feel those treacherous tears trying to force themselves out.

Don't let them, I told myself as I pressed my nails as hard as I could into the palms of my hand. *Block him out, don't listen. Stand up to him. Just how disgusting can this man get? Go on, show him that you don't believe a word he says.*

So, I dredged up as much courage as I could, pulled my shoulders back and looked him straight in the eyes.

'You're wrong,' I told him. 'That's not me, I'm never going to be like you. I like girls, not boys.'

I must say he looked rather taken back. I'd definitely scored a point and should have left it there. But I didn't. *Just how stupid was I*, I asked myself later, *to give away my small, personal secret?*

'There's a girl in my class, she's really nice. She comes and talks to me on our breaks. I like her ...'

Talk about playing into his hands. I knew I shouldn't have said it the moment he burst out laughing.

'Oh, come on, Phil! Think about it. You say she talks to you? Well, one of you would have to – I doubt she understands a word you say. Still, for your sake, I hope she's a nice girl who just feels sorry for you. I doubt if any other girls have sought out your company, have they? I just hope for your sake it's not a dare. You know the sort of thing girls do, don't you? "Let's see how long it takes the Spaz to ask you out?" Well, kids are cruel, aren't they? I expect you know that by now. So, I hope for your sake, it's her pity for you that's making her friendly.'

I felt a lump forming in the back of my throat, a lump full of solidified tears, so I bit my lip. Clive wasn't going to make me look more pitiful than he had just told me I was. But he hadn't finished, he was on a roll and nothing was going to stop him.

'You've got to face facts, with that leg of yours dragging behind you, not to mention your arm that's almost useless, pretty girls are not going to want to be seen out with you. And if your looks aren't bad enough, your speech would finish off any interest. Can you imagine what it would be like if she took you home and her parents couldn't understand a word you said? No, you've not given it any thought, have you? Well, *I* have and trust me, there wouldn't be another invitation. Everyone would be so embarrassed. No, Phil, you can forget all about girls. Trust me, they won't be thinking about you. Well, not the way you'd like them to.'

It was then that I heard Ryan's voice.

'They're looking for you, Clive. Don't want them finding you down here, do we? Whatever might they think?' And I knew from the firmness in his voice that my brother had heard every word that had been said.

'I'd better get back before they send out a search party then,' was all Clive said as he brushed past my brother and made a fast exit back to the party.

I closed my eyes as I leant against the wall, though what I wanted was to thump it until my hands bled.

Because I believed him, didn't I? Every single word of what he just said had made complete sense to me.

40

Phil

I have to say my teachers at senior school went out of their way to help me with my learning. Because of my problems with both my arm and my speech, I was given a laptop and a dictaphone. Trying to answer a question that was being asked of the class was still difficult for me to get the words out and for the teacher to understand them. Now I could quietly answer the questions being put to the class into the dictaphone and check them later. Once I was shown how it all worked, I felt a whole new world had opened up for me – especially when I was shown how spellcheck could be used!

It was at the beginning of my final year when the headmaster called me into his office to talk about my future. Had I got any plans for what I wanted to do once I left school? Remembering that evening when Clive had thrown my disabilities into my face by saying that no one would ever employ me, I told the headmaster that if I could, I would work at just about anything.

'I know there's not much I can do, but I don't want to be a burden to Mum and Dad,' I blurted out.

'Phil, I don't think you realise it, but you've done very well. I've never seen someone as determined as you have been. You should be proud of yourself. You're never going to be a burden to anyone so banish that thought immediately, OK?'

'Yes, sir,' I said. I could tell by the warmth of his smile that he meant every word and I felt myself beginning to relax. The thought that perhaps Clive had been wrong flashed through my mind.

'Now I've asked around and I think I've found something that you would really fit into. The local college is looking for someone they can train to work in the Reprographic unit. It's where they do all their photocopying, lamination of charts and flyers and business cards. Now I expect you have heard of the YTS scheme, the government initiative so young people leaving school can still be taught some extra skills?'

I had, so I just nodded at him.

'Well, Phil, the college will find some work for you four days a week and on the fifth day, you'll attend a course at the college. Then if you do well, which I'm certain you will, you will be asked to join them full-time. How does that sound to you?'

Sound? I could hardly believe my ears. I could feel my mouth stretching into the widest grin it had done for ages.

Seeing it, he laughed.

'Don't have to answer, Phil. The words "I like it" are written all over your face.'

I managed to stutter out a thank you several times, I seem to remember. Shame I couldn't dance, because that's what I felt like doing when I left his office.

I could hardly wait to tell Ryan, whose face also lit up at my news. 'Well done,' he said, giving me a hug. He was eager to get home and break the news.

'Hey, Mum, Phil's got something he wants to tell you,' my brother said as soon as we walked into the house.

'Well then, Phil, what is it?' Mum asked with a hopeful look on her face which changed to one of relief when I told her.

'You mean you have a job to go to as soon as you leave school? Well, that's just wonderful news, Phil! Your dad's going to be so pleased too.'

And he was; he could hardly wipe the grin off his face either.

After supper had been eaten and Ryan had cleared up, I could hear Mum on the phone to Maureen, telling her sister all about the job I had lined up when I left school.

'Oh, they want to meet him, of course, but if the Head says he has it, he has ...'

I felt so proud to hear her enthusing about me but part of me really wished it was Clive she was telling all about it. I would have liked to think of him having to eat his words.

41

Ryan

Over the last few months before school ended, Phil and I were able to come up with a couple of good excuses why we could not join them all in Cambridge. But no matter how we tried, we couldn't manage to get out of going when Clive invited us for the last time. As we had both managed to find work, he told Mum he wanted to take us all out to celebrate.

'No excuses accepted,' was the message he had asked her to pass on to us. 'So bring something smart with you, I think we can guess where he's taking us all,' she added.

Yes, we could and so we packed our best jeans and a couple of freshly ironed shirts.

When we arrived, Clive was full of congratulations for both of us. Not that the job I had managed to get in the motorway cafe was that important. Even if I was to be given the grand title of 'assistant grill chef'. But then, that was my uncle with his nice side on show. What can I say about the evening? The early part of it was pleasant enough. He had booked us into the usual restaurant, where the manager was all smiles. It was hard to think that the very first time we went there we were so small, we had to sit on cushions.

But then that was almost a decade ago.

'I think the boys can have a small beer each,' he said to my parents when we were looking at the menu. To our surprise, they agreed. Just one, we were told. Still, we did feel we were being treated a little bit like adults.

While Clive appeared to be celebrating our future, Phil and I were celebrating the fact that this was the last time we would be sitting in this restaurant with him. We were no longer school boys, independence was just around the corner. We were entering the adult world, weren't we? We had jobs lined up and our own money would be coming in.

Our parents would no longer feel that we had to visit Cambridge with them. No doubt they thought they would have an even better time without us being there. I wondered just how many invitations they would get once Clive accepted that we were no longer up for visiting – not Cambridge and certainly not Scotland.

What didn't enter my head was that he was already fully aware that this was the last time too. Nor had I taken into account that, self-absorbed as he was, he would want to show it was going to be his decision, not ours. In the restaurant he was all smiles and charm, there was nothing about him that would have told us what he had planned. And there were Phil and I thinking that finally we were the winners.

If I was asked what are the emotions that stay the longest in our heads, the ones that pop up and torment us years after they were placed there, the answer I would give would be guilt and shame. Fear can be driven away, loneliness remedied, even feelings of low self-esteem can be built up, but those two demons dig their tentacles in and no matter how hard we try, they refuse to budge. Over the years they might grow weaker, they might even slumber a little, until revitalised. And then they return to remind us of why they are still there.

Those two were Clive's farewell present to me.

He made sure that they were lodged firmly in my head before he left my side. Even all these years later, the memory of that night, where the whimpers, the gasps and a frightened voice painted the picture of every single movement that was taking place. Not in my bed, but the one just a couple of feet away from mine; a picture so firmly etched in my mind that it is impossible to erase. Other memories I have made disappear, but that one will never leave me.

Phil and I were both in our beds, not really bothered all that much about Clive. As we were leaving in the morning, we thought he would wait to visit our room until the next time we visited. Not that there was going to be one, for we had made a pact that this was to be the very last time.

Although he had not left us alone every time we met up, we had noticed that over the last year as our voices deepened and the hair on our limbs had become much thicker, his interest in us seemed to have waned. We had also put it down to him getting older; we supposed his age must be slowing him down a little. He must have been around fifty then. To us, that was one step away from being ancient.

Now I know that what really aroused him was the

pleading in a child's high-pitched voice, the softness of their hairless bodies and the fear in their eyes.

As I put my light out, I heard him padding down the corridor. Just the sound of his footsteps was enough to strip me of any bravado I felt and make the hairs on the back of my neck stand up. I heard the soft click of the door handle, knew it was him and what he wanted.

He's not going to touch me this time, absolutely no way, I decided.

So, what did I do? Jump out of bed and push him back through the door, or raise my fist and punch him where it hurts? No, I did none of those things. Instead, I curled up as tightly as I could and closed my eyes firmly.

I heard his voice whispering my name, smelt that musty cologne of his and felt his hand on my shoulder.

'Come on, Ryan, sit up! I know you're not asleep,' he said, as his hand shook my shoulder. 'You can't fool me.'

It was only then that I realised that I had grown enough in the last couple of years to be far too heavy to be pulled from my bed easily. Nor would he have been able to turn me into a position where he could place his hands where he wanted them. Now he only had words to use as a tool and they were not working.

I could almost feel his frustration.

Was he, I wonder now, becoming a little wary of me by then? After all, I might not have been quite as tall as him, but I was younger and had filled out a lot. But then those thoughts didn't enter my head, there were still strong remnants of his control over me that blocked them.

'Well, it's a good thing you have a twin who is friendlier,' he told me and with that, he crossed over to my brother's bed.

I heard Phil nearly sobbing out the words 'Please don't,' followed by the rustle of his bedclothes and the creak of bed springs.

Did Phil, who was powerless to push him off, plead for me to act and stop him? His voice might not have, but his mind did.

I knew that, just as I knew everything Clive did to him that night.

It was when the whimpers stopped, but not Clive's voice, which kept giving him instructions, that the picture appearing behind my eyes and in my head told me in very graphic detail the reason my brother was no longer able to speak. For hadn't Clive, on one visit to us, grabbed my head and pulled it down to make me do something so disgusting that I still cannot find the words to describe it?

'We've finished now, Ryan,' I heard him say. 'It's OK for you to wake up now. Phil can tell you all about what you missed when I've gone. Oh, I've left you some tissues to get rid of the mess. Don't want your mum thinking you two have been playing with each other, do we?'

And then he leant down to where I was, his mouth almost touching my ear.

'You're a coward, Ryan. Pretending to be asleep. I knew you weren't and I now know something else about you as well. You can't fool me! You've enjoyed our little sessions, I've seen your body arch and heard you groan. So, go on fooling yourself. Deep down, you know the truth.'

As he spoke it was as though my body was paralysed. Oh, how I wanted to jump up and rain punches down on him, scream at him so everyone would hear, but not one limb moved.

'Want to fight me, Ryan, don't you? But you haven't the guts for it, have you? Anyhow, don't you think you've left it a bit late? Now, here's the news you've been waiting for. I won't be visiting your rooms again, can't stand the smell of you. I think you should bathe a little more often.'

And with that, he was gone.

After he left the room, I rushed to the bathroom and vomited repeatedly. I cried then, the tears running down my cheeks just wouldn't stop. Even those racking sobs seemed to shame me more.

It was not me he had defiled this time, was it, not me he had hurt?

He had only made me feel spineless. He'd shown me to be a coward.

I had to face Phil, I had to go over to him.

His body was still trembling and his teeth were chattering although it was not at all cold.

'He's gone now, hasn't he, Ryan? I mean, he won't be coming back, will he?'

'No, Phil, he won't.'

Oh, I tried to say how sorry I was. Not that my tears or my words were nearly enough. It was Phil who comforted me then and told me there was little I could have done.

'He won't touch us again,' he whispered. 'He doesn't like our bodies anymore.'

'He told you that?'

'Yes. It's over, Ryan. We're free.'

But could we ever be free? I was not so sure.

42

Ryan

My final months of schooling were really pretty boring. It was clear to everyone that I was not going to get good exam results so no one held out much hope of me finding a decent job. Naturally, the YTS scheme offered to Phil was mentioned to me more than once. 'Is there something you would like to train for?' I was asked, more by my brothers than my parents.

My answer was always the same: 'I can't think of anything.'

'Well, when you do, we can talk about it,' was their standard response although they tried to encourage me by following up with: 'Don't worry, Ryan, it's never too late to learn something new. Lots of people leave school not knowing what they want to do and then, when they find the right niche, they go on to become very successful.'

Mum and Dad's way of dealing with me was to express their disappointment.

'You're not thinking of your future,' was the most

frequently repeated remark followed by, 'You'll regret it when you're older and wish you could improve your life. You only get one chance.'

If that was their way of trying to inspire me, it didn't work. The two messages certainly didn't motivate me to explore options.

When I applied for the job at the motorway cafe, now known as Little Chef, and was accepted, my family all looked more relieved than happy. It might not have been what they had wished for me, but at least I would be working.

What I hadn't been expecting was that once I began to work on the grill and in the frying area, I found myself really enjoying it. Even though very little of the food was made on the premises, for even the chips and salads were delivered in large plastic bags, I did try to make it appear as appetising as possible when it went out on the plate. Though when my friends asked what I liked most about the job, I told them it was easy to work with a hangover.

Yes, in my opinion I really had perfected my tough guy image and my friends all seemed to buy into it.

I suppose with my detached attitude, hands thrust deep into my jean pockets and a sullen expression, it was pretty amazing that I suddenly seemed to have a girlfriend. Not only that, it was she who had come on to me. Now that had to be pretty good for my ego.

Not that I would ever have admitted it, but I always felt a bit awkward around girls. I was never quite sure what it was they expected. Up until then there had been a bit of snogging at the back of the school pavilion and later at the pub, and I might even have taken a bit of advantage and slid my hand up a jumper and fumbled around a bit, but that was as far as it got. When friends asked if I was seeing anyone, my answer was a shrug and some muttering that so far no one had caught my eye.

Truth was, I was a bit scared about having any sort of relationship. I knew from listening to my brothers over the years what girlfriends expected of you. That you would spend time together, having deep conversations and discovering what films and music you both liked. And then there would be the deeper conversations as we got to know each other better, ones where we talked about our family and our childhood. It was that which frightened me.

I had such a big dirty secret that I wanted to keep hidden. And hadn't I overheard one of my brothers saying that girls like to confess their secrets and then wait expectantly to hear what their new boyfriend was going to reveal? Wouldn't someone who was trying to get close to me work out that I was hiding something? And then that would be the end of trust, because girlfriends, I had heard, expected complete honesty.

OK, I was still a teenager when all these worries were circulating in my head. Even though our school was mixed, girls still remained a bit of a mystery to me.

I had downed a couple of pints when I met Kate and there is nothing like a few drinks to send inhibitions flying out of the window. I was standing at the bar with a group of guys I knew, while she was sitting with her girlfriends at a table near the window. My mates noticed them and nudged each other as the girls took it in turns to come up to the bar and order another trayful of cocktails, but then it was happy hour and everyone was making the most of it.

Kate was the petite, dark-haired girl, wearing a snug-looking jumper and a brief miniskirt over a pair of black leggings, who, one of my mates whispered, was sneaking looks at me. Not believing him, I glanced over to their table just as she stood up and picked up the tray. I saw large eyes circled with thick eyeliner, long glossy brown hair which, once back with her friends, she flicked every time she laughed. And she seemed to laugh a lot.

'You're imagining it,' was all I said to him, before I ordered another beer.

A few minutes before happy hour ended, she was back at the bar again and placed herself next to me.

'Same again?' the barman asked.

'No, just another piña colada for me, that was a bit of an office do we were having and the others have to get off now. Actually, make it two of those, seeing as happy hour is nearly over.'

'So, what's your name then?' she asked once her drinks were in front of her.

I was a bit startled at this direct approach and I could hear my mates making comments as they waited to see what I was going to do. Still, I managed to blurt my name out as I tried my best to appear nonchalant, but I could feel a blush moving up my neck.

She laughed a little then, because I was clearly not well versed in the art of chatting up.

'You can call me Kate if you like,' she said.

'Can I buy you another drink?'

Where those words came from, I had no idea. They seemed to surprise her as much as they did me. I just hoped that she wasn't going to ask for another expensive cocktail.

She grinned at me. 'Still have two and happy hour's finished now. Tell you what, I'll have a glass of white wine later if you're staying.'

We sat at the bar and a couple of drinks later, my face was aching with the number of times Kate had made me laugh. Now this you might have guessed was not something I was really known for.

One of my mates nudged me. 'Hide that beer and order a Coke quickly, the bloody fuzz are coming through the door!'

The barman, hearing the warning, quick as a flash made my beer disappear at the same time as the police burst through the doors, shouting at everyone not to move.

'Bloody drugs bust! Haven't they got anything better to do?' the barman muttered as picking up a cloth to wipe the bar, he slid a Coke in my direction.

'Here, have that one on me.'

Kate looked a bit scared at the sight of so many bodies dressed in blue. She turned round to me and said, 'Just put your arms round my shoulders and look all butch and protective.' As I duly obliged, I saw her hand drop a small package down her front.

'No problem,' I said as I drew her close to me while watching what was happening around me. The police seemed to enjoy the fact that people looked afraid. I saw youths made to stand as they were frisked and girls' handbags being opened and searched.

A few people were marched outside, one was a pretty blonde who looked as though she was going to burst into tears. I saw one officer calling out to another as he held up a small plastic bag – it looked to me as though it was full of pills. That resulted in three men being almost dragged out of the premises by several hefty-looking policemen.

'They might be searching everyone,' Kate whispered quietly, 'but they know who they're looking for.'

'Right, you too!' boomed a voice.

Looking up, I saw it belonged to the woman I'd seen walk in with the police and giving instructions. As she was not in uniform, I guessed she was a pretty senior officer.

The young constable standing next to her asked me to empty my pockets. Luckily, the most suspicious thing I had in them was a packet of cigarettes, which he politely gave back.

There was nothing of interest in Kate's bag either when he asked her to open it. Glancing down into it, he told her it was fine and then he walked away, leaving the stern-faced blonde woman still standing by my elbow. Bright, inquisitive blue eyes studied me thoughtfully through tortoiseshell-rimmed glasses.

'What's your name, son?' she asked.

'Ryan,' I replied.

'Ryan who?'

'Fisher.'

'And your age?'

'Nineteen.'

'Really? I doubt you have any proof on you, like a driving licence?'

'Eh, no, not taken my test yet.'

'Of course you haven't, though I suppose you're old enough to take lessons. Still, I would like to see proof of your age. I could ask you for your address and pay your dad a visit. I'm sure he can remember your date of birth. Or wouldn't you like me to do that?'

'Eh, no.'

A question she had been smart enough to throw at me, for no doubt she guessed what my answer would be. Plus, the tide of red creeping up my neck would have confirmed her suspicions.

'Still, at least your voice has broken, so it's not all bad.'

And I realised that as stern as she sounded, there was some amusement in her eyes. 'Oh, don't think I'm fooled by that can of Coke,' she added, throwing the barman a penetrating glance. 'You reek of beer, goodness knows what would happen if I asked you to blow into a bag.

'I'll tell you what, Ryan. Next time I catch you in a pub knocking back pints of lager, you better be celebrating your eighteenth! Until then, stick to those nice cans of Coke. Do you understand?'

What could I say apart from a yes?

'Good.'

'Oh, and James,' she said, turning to the barman, 'you'd better not serve him any alcohol when I leave. Still, I know you wouldn't consciously serve drinks to anyone under eighteen, would you?'

'Of course I wouldn't.'

'Good to hear.' And with one more stern glance, she moved over to the few officers who were still inside and then they all left.

My face was burning, I was so embarrassed. Surely Kate would walk off now, I thought, but no, she didn't. Instead, hanging on to my arm, she invited me back to her flat – 'We can pick up some beer from the off licence on the way, so are you coming?'

I don't know if it was the thought of extending my time with her or the temptation of carrying on drinking that put a smile back on my face. Most probably a bit of both. I certainly didn't have to think about it for too long before I agreed.

Kate kept her arm tucked in mine as we walked to her local shop that was stocked with just about everything, including a good selection of alcohol. Carrying a couple of bags full of beers and nibbles, we then walked the few yards to her flat, which was on the ground floor of a fairly small grey-bricked terraced house. The front door had seen better days and the windows could have done with some paint, but inside, she had made it look warm and cosy. Hockney prints hung on the walls, there was a bright rug with huge, thick, comfortable floor cushions piled on it and wedged against the wall was a TV and a decent-looking sound system. On went the music, a gentle bluesy number, as we collapsed onto those floor cushions.

'Fancy a smoke?' she asked, putting her hand down her top and bringing out the small packet she had slipped down there earlier. 'I know a bit about that inspector. She's not really interested in finding dope, it's the dealers she wants to catch. They're selling stuff to the kids that's a lot worse than a bit of weed,' she told me as she crumbled part of the small block that she had removed from her bra. She pulled out some cigarette papers, expertly mixed some tobacco with the weed and rolled it in a machine, then inserted a small tip into it, before lighting it. After placing it in her mouth, she inhaled deeply.

'It's good stuff,' she said, giving me a grin as with smoke whirling round her head, she passed it over to me. 'Take the deepest drag you can,' she told me.

I did and within seconds, I felt almost as though I was drifting away into a world of bright colours, where I could hear every note of music more clearly, smell the musky scent coming from a dish of potpourri and feel the softness of the cushions beneath me.

'Sure this isn't your first time?'

'Of course not,' I said, lying through my teeth.

'Come on now, you can tell me the truth. Anyhow, how old are you really?'

'Seventeen.'

'Ah, so the inspector guessed right then. Not that she was that bothered. She was just playing with you, having a bit of fun.'

While we were sprawled on the cushions, smoking weed and taking swigs of beer, we talked a bit about our families. Which is when I discovered that she knew Vicky, Warren's girlfriend.

'Yeah, I've met Leighton too,' she told me. 'Had no idea you were his brother when I saw you in the pub.'

I wondered how well she knew him.

'I don't really know him well, just when I was having a drink with Vicky one evening, he came in with Warren. That's all.' And another grin came in my direction.

Must say I was relieved by that titbit of information – had she been dating my brother that would have been far too weird.

I was tempted to stay longer, maybe even the whole night, but I had to get to the cafe in the morning. It did take some determination to sober up and pull myself together, but I was chilled enough to make a date to see her on the Sunday, my day off.

* * *

That night, I stayed at Leighton's. He had given me a key some time ago. He didn't say why he thought I needed one, he just accepted that there might be times when I needed a bolthole. 'We all need our own space,' he had said more than once. And once the company he was working for gave him his first decent promotion, he had managed to rent a small Victorian house.

The key had been handed over to me nearly at the same time as he was given his. Without asking questions or making comments, he accepted that the atmosphere at home had grown rather chilly. My parents disapproved of my way of life. As far as they were concerned, I was mixing with the wrong sort, coming in late and they guessed that I was drinking and smoking – 'I can smell it on your clothes, bad enough that you come home smelling of food and deep-fat frying, but even that isn't enough to hide the smell of beer and cigarettes,' muttered Mum crossly as she insisted all my clothes went straight in the wash when I came home each night.

'You'll be lucky if you hold your job down,' she told me more than once when I'd slept through my alarm and had to run to get my lift to work. 'What would you do if your dad or I didn't wake you?'

Phil, much to my surprise, decided around then to move in with a friend. As I was planning to spend so much time at Kate's, I was pleased for him. He told me it was partly because he had no wish to be around when Clive and Maureen visited. Mum and Dad got annoyed if we made excuses when we knew he was coming. Not only that, my brother felt uncomfortable when Mum criticised me to him. He felt his anger boiling up inside him when she did. He was also aware of my growing resentment towards our parents. A resentment that I was unable to suppress, even though I did try. For I could not help myself for blaming Mum more than Dad for not noticing the effect Clive had on us. Weren't there times when, even if Dad didn't, Mum must have seen how troubled Phil and I were? And yet she had never asked the right questions. Why was I not concentrating at school, why had I no interest in my career and why, even if my bedwetting had ceased, did I still have intense nightmares, sometimes waking the whole household? Surely there would have been concerns, so then why was it that she had never asked me?

Phil and I managed, depending on my shifts, to meet up at least a couple of times a week. The closeness between us was still there but when we were together, I could see that he, like me, was drinking too much. When he was still taking his course, I did point out that it was important that he was fresh and bright each morning. Not that I was a good example.

'Helps us sleep, Ryan, doesn't it?' he said more than once.

I was relieved for his sake that once he moved in with Trevor, a friend he had made at work, he cut down on his drinking. Perhaps he had moved out because he wanted to work on controlling his habit – he certainly managed that well before I did.

He was happy in his work, made new friends there and I expect it was mixing with them that also helped him cut back on his drinking, for none of them were serious drinkers. They accepted him and his limitations, but his speech was difficult to follow at the best of times so a slurring Phil would have lost friends and he so wanted to fit in.

He was over the moon when he finished his course and was offered the full-time job he had been promised. We went out together to celebrate, as we had when I picked up my first pay packet.

Although I had no idea what I wanted from a career, I had no intention of spending my days at the Jobcentre or sitting around at home watching daytime TV, and while I feigned disinterest, I had been getting worried that might just happen. When I got the job at the Little Chef, I was pretty relieved. It was not difficult work they had told me, wouldn't take more than a day or two to learn everything I needed to know; in fact, it had only taken me a few hours. The money wasn't bad either as we were paid extra for night shifts and almost double when we worked on a bank holiday. I also got on well with the people there for they were a pretty cheerful bunch and the customers were friendly as well. They just wanted a quick break with a coffee and something to eat, and then get on their way, so there were few complaints.

What no one had told me, though I should have been able to work it out for myself, was that frying bacon and eggs in the morning and hamburgers the rest of the day could not remain interesting for long. Occasionally a customer ordered something different, such as a salad, then we had to pull out an assortment of leaves from a plastic bag and get out some tuna from a tin, or a pre-cooked chicken breast. But it was OK. I had money for what I wanted the most – cigarettes and nights out in the pub – and I got on well with all my workmates. It was just that I was beginning to get an urge to do something a bit more creative. Like, actually cook something from scratch that was not just a boiled, fried or scrambled egg. This seed of ambition was taking shape and I brought it up when Kate and I were perched on a couple of bar stools, later that evening. She had chosen a small pub that she said the police never showed any interest in.

Hair gelled, a new leather jacket with its collar turned up, hands in pockets, I looked pretty cool. Or so I kept telling myself as, glancing in shop windows, I admired my reflection as I made my way to what was my first proper date. While I was quaffing down my beer and Kate was delicately sipping white wine, I brought up in conversation that I was becoming frustrated with my job. I was expecting her to joke a little or tell me I should have stayed at school longer if I wanted a more challenging career. Instead, she gave my arm a squeeze.

'Doesn't surprise me that you'd like to do more,' was her response. 'Look, maybe you're really cut out to be a chef – a proper one in a full-on restaurant, I mean. Have you thought of that?'

'Well, no,' I said but suddenly the idea really appealed to me. 'Wouldn't I need to go to college?'

'Not necessarily, there are places that will take on people and train them as they go along. Mind you, they spend a lot of their time in the kitchen, peeling potatoes and chopping vegetables into tiny little squares. Tell you what, why not hang on where you are for a bit so you get a good reference? That's the most important thing when you start having a look around.'

I tucked this suggestion away in my head. It sounded promising and I was going to have a real think about it later. But looking at Kate, dressed in her snug-fitting trousers and an off-the-shoulder top, I had other things on my mind just then. It felt so natural to be sitting with her and chatting away. Apart from thinking she was attractive, I really liked her. Hard to believe that I'd only known her for a matter of hours and already felt so relaxed in her company. She too appeared to feel the same, but wouldn't that all change if she knew everything about me?

Better keep that very quiet, I decided. Which I might have succeeded in doing if we hadn't gone back to her place and watched that film. It was after a couple more drinks and a conversation about films we liked that the suggestion came up. We had both agreed that love stories were not for us, but good mystery ones were.

'There's one on tonight that sounds great. You know what, why don't we get some fish and chips to take back and drop into the off licence round the corner from me and get a few beers? Then in case it's too scary, we can always snuggle up together, can't we?'

I wasn't sure exactly what she had in mind, snogging perhaps or maybe even a bit more. The thought of a bit more made my skin tingle and I felt my face flushing.

That was until she dropped a bombshell.

'Hope you like kids,' she said. 'Got to get back and let my little girl's sitter go.'

Those pictures in my head of just what we might get up to were blown straight out. I managed to ask her a couple of questions, like how old her daughter was and her name. It turned out Suzy was three. And before I could ask, no, there was no husband, never had been, just a boyfriend who had disappeared.

'I was in my last year at school,' she explained, 'so like you, I didn't exactly stay on to do all my exams. But I've done a few evening courses. You could also do that, Ryan, study part-time? Sorry, I should have told you about Suzy,' she said when I went a bit silent.

I could hardly comment, could I? Having a 3-year-old was nothing compared to what I was covering up.

'Oh, don't worry, she'll be asleep when we get back. Well,

she'd better be,' she added.

'So, where was she the other night?'

'At Mum's. I can't afford to send her to nursery school and I've got a part-time job. Do some admin and secretarial work for a small recruitment firm, sort out their accounts and stuff like that. When we met, I was out with the sales team having a quick drink after a good month. Mum always has her on the days I work.'

Oh God, I thought, *imagine if she knew about me. She might think I was the wrong person to be around children, mightn't she?*

It was Clive who shouldn't be around children, not you, my inner voice told me. Nothing like an inner argument to make me feel nervous.

'So, what's the matter? You look a bit glum,' she said, perhaps thinking I was put off after learning about her daughter. Hoping to salvage the moment, I quickly wrapped an arm around her shoulders.

'Nothing, just thinking of having to work early tomorrow,' I said, drowning the last of my pint. 'So, let's go and get those fish and chips, shall we?'

Part Three

Survival

43

Ryan

It was the film that did it, or rather it was the ending that just about finished me. As soon as the babysitter had left and Kate had checked on her daughter, we propped ourselves up on her floor cushions, opened a couple of beers and tucked into our fish supper. On went the TV and as the ads finished, the film title flashed up.

The opening was attention-grabbing, alright. The main character, a senior policewoman, who, with thick blonde hair, a well-fitted uniform and feet tucked into high heels was a lot more glamorous than the one we'd seen on the drugs raid, was looking at a trio of dead bodies. It was clear that the man standing near them was a pathologist and they were in the morgue. The film then moved to where the police officer called her team in. She announced that there was a connection between the murders of those three young women and explained that they were now on a search for a serial killer, one who enjoys strangling young women and one who would do it again unless he was caught.

The first two women were prostitutes, but then, as the film showed a little later, protection for girls on the streets only seems to come from rather nasty pimps. Which appeared to be the reason the police hadn't considered it being the same man. Even worse, they hadn't thought that other young women could be at risk. Whereas the first two murders hadn't woken the press up too much, the third one, of a nice middle-class student, would.

Not only that, the inspector informed her team, her father was a well-known businessman in the area and his daughter was his only child. So, she told her team, the pressure was on and the killer had to be found before there was another body in the morgue. The police investigation questioned all known sex offenders and the film showed interviews with girls working on the streets. None of them had seen anyone acting suspiciously although someone had seen one of the girls getting into a car. Not unusual, but she remembered it and was able to describe both the vehicle and the man inside it. The police kept pinning their hopes on one suspect after the other only to have their hopes dashed.

It was not far from the end when armed police rammed a door down and brought in the most unlikely suspect the police had questioned earlier. He had never been caught kerb crawling, never been caught committing a crime, not even a speeding ticket. He was also highly thought of in the firm of accountants he worked for. Amazing how the police had worked out that he was the one! Even more amazing was how once, when interviewed by the police, with his solicitor by his side, he admitted everything.

Oh, not in a cowardly way, more in a cold, detached one. He even told the police where there were more bodies.

It was those few minutes before the credits came up that cut through my relaxed mood. In the court case, it turned out that the man might have been a killer, but he was also a victim. He'd been in one of those children's homes, where he had been abused from the day he was placed there. His lawyer argued that it was the abuse that had turned the poor little boy he had once been into a murdering psychopath.

'Great film, wasn't it?' said Kate when the credits rolled.

Maybe if I hadn't been slightly stoned I might have held it together. Right up until the last few minutes of the film, nothing had disturbed my feeling of dope-induced calmness. I told myself that the pictures of the crime scenes were not real and the bodies in the morgue were actors playing dead bodies. But the words of the lawyer in the summing-up at the trial cut through my haze of contentment, leaving me shaking. I could hear Kate asking what was the matter, felt her hand on the back of my head, but all I could hear were the words 'repeated systematic abuse'.

'What was it about the film that upset you so much? Come on, Ryan, you can tell me.'

'You won't want to see me again if I do. Especially when you have a kid.'

'Why? Are you a serial killer too?' she asked, prodding me in the side as she tried to make me laugh along with her. 'Come on, just tell me.'

I could hardly find the words to say how I felt about an actor telling the film's audience that today's victims are tomorrow's monsters. It might have been said in a film, but what about all the people watching it? Weren't they going to believe that it goes without saying, if you are abused then you become a danger to others?

I could almost hear Kate's mind ticking away.

'I think we'd better have another drink,' she said and getting up, she went to the kitchen and came back with two cold bottles of beer.

'So, who was it, Ryan?' she asked in a matter-of-fact way.

I might not have uttered a word, but my silence had spoken for me.

44

Ryan

It was as though a dam of pent-up pain had burst, releasing a torrent of words that I just couldn't put a halt to, even if I had wanted. Kate held my hand and encouraged me to stop and take a deep breath every few minutes – 'Slow down a little, Ryan. Come on now, just stop and take a few deep breaths, it will calm you and help you get it all out.'

'I'm sorry, Kate,' I kept saying.

After all, this was hardly turning into the romantic evening she must have envisaged.

'Don't worry about me, you need to get it all out,' she told me soothingly as her fingers entwined with mine.

When finally, I had little left inside me to say, it was as if the flood of words had taken all my strength. Completely drained, I could feel the dampness on my cheeks and Kate's fingers brushing my tears away with great gentleness.

'Just relax here for a moment,' she told me as she went into the kitchen. When less than a minute later she came back in, instead of the ice-cold beer I was expecting, she handed me a warm mug.

'It's a herbal tea,' she told me when she saw me staring at it. 'It's made from chamomile leaves; it will help you relax. Drink that and I'll roll us a joint. A little dope will help as well but best we leave the beers alone for now.'

She made sure I was drinking the tea before she asked me the question that must have been running through her mind while she boiled the kettle.

'Am I really the only person you've told about this?'

'Yes, I tried to tell Mum when I was little, but she didn't seem to hear me.'

'Maybe you were too young to explain what was happening then?'

'Maybe. Anyway, I know now he was grooming us, so apart from touching us a lot, there wasn't that much happening then. Nothing compared to what happened to us later.'

'You mean you and your twin have kept this inside you for all these years? You didn't even talk to your other brothers?'

'No.'

'Was that because your uncle made threats and also worked on making you both feel a deep sense of shame?'

'Yes, Kate, it was.'

She wrapped her arms around me then and I felt something I had not felt for a very long time – comforted.

'Ryan, you've got to start believing that you've got nothing to be ashamed of. You were just an innocent little kid. I know it was that bit in the film at the end that really upset you, but it was all fiction, not fact. Just forget that part of it where they said the villain of the piece had been molested as a child. Like that's a good excuse for going around killing people? Have a look at the real killers who have hit the headlines. Do you remember reading that any one of them had been abused? And you more than most would have picked it up if that had been on the news.'

'Well, no.'

'Thought so.'

'Look at those two bastards, the Moors Murderers. Can't get much more evil than that! So, what was their defence?'

'Don't think they had one.'

'Exactly.'

'And what about the Yorkshire Ripper? Thirteen women killed and if he hadn't been caught, there would have been more. And his defence? Apart from him being nuts, that is, was that his mother had once been unfaithful to his father! I mean, come on, who's going to believe that one? You know what, though? I'm going to write to that director. Tell them they shouldn't put stuff like that in their films. Don't they ever think of the harm that can cause? Pisses me off, it really does. Anyhow, you've got to get rid of these dark thoughts, Ryan,' she told me as she rolled a joint for us to share.

'Tell me a little more about those threats Clive made,' she asked, once I had taken a deep drag.

'They kept changing as we got older,' I said, and then I told her about the one that had really stuck in my mind – that Dad would top himself if he were to lose his best friend.

'Bloody conceited man that Clive, isn't he?'

A response that finally brought a smile to my face.

'True, but I've always believed that Mum would be devastated if she had to face up to what he was up to. It would be bound to wreck her relationship with her sister and having Maureen back in her life has made her so happy. I guess that's more important to her than us.'

That was a piece of information that Kate pounced on and she asked why Maureen hadn't been around earlier. And then I told her something I remembered Clive had told me: 'He said, "Ask Warren, he knows."'

'Maybe you better had then,' she suggested when I told her that. 'Loose ends are always best tied up.'

I half-expected Kate to try and persuade me to talk to all my brothers, but she didn't. Nor did she ask me if I had told her everything, which was a relief. Because I hadn't.

I hadn't been able to tell her the part which shamed me so much.

The fact that I had ejaculated with him.

45

Ryan

I knew I needed to take a step forward in my life but it still took a few weeks for me to mull things over. By that time Kate and I were spending most evenings together. Which when I woke up that morning after breaking down and telling her just about everything, I didn't think would happen. In fact, I wondered if I would ever see her again. I had felt such a mixture of embarrassment and gratitude that morning. She had listened to me, said all the right things and finally pulled a blanket over us as she lay beside me, gently stroking my back until I fell asleep.

It was her calling out my name that made me open my eyes. A strong cup of tea was placed next to me, before she told me that she had put a towel out for me so I could grab a shower.

'You've got enough time to get to work and I've got time to drink my tea. Suzy's not woken up yet, thank goodness!'

The thought that was running through my head then was that no doubt she would be pleased to see the back of me.

Could hardly blame her if she did, could I? And then, just as I was about to walk out through the door on my way to work, she said those magic words, 'You doing anything tonight then?'

Talk about relief! I told her I had nothing planned and couldn't stop smiling at her.

'Right then, come here this evening after work. I'll cook us something, then you can meet Suzy.' And giving me a hug, she just said, 'See you later.' And I, walking on air, made my way to work. Mind you, I did feel a bit of a wimp when I turned up at her door that evening. After all, this was only our second date and no one could say the first one had gone that well! But there was something about Kate that stopped me feeling any embarrassment. Plus, having a miniature version of her chatting away to me was also helpful. There was nothing shy about her 3-year-old.

When the food was placed on the table, I discovered that Kate was not only a good listener, she was a good cook as well. Lasagne and an assortment of salads appeared on the table, along with a couple of beers I had bought on the way.

Once Kate's little chatterbox was tucked up in bed, we did, as I had learnt from my brothers, have one of those boy/girl conversations, where we got to know each other more. Though in our case it had happened the wrong way round – I had spilled my deepest secrets first before all the mundane stuff.

That evening, I learnt that once her daughter started school, Kate was going to study further – she wanted to be financially independent and make a decent living. She said she would feel a lot more confident if, as well as having good references, she also had more qualifications. Her work had been really encouraging and 'Mum's really up for me to do that too,' she enthused. 'I'm so lucky there.'

When, after our first few weeks of getting to know each other more, I told her I had decided to ask Warren about Mum's life before she married my dad, all she said was, 'I think that's a really good idea, Ryan. Well done!'

Kate was not someone who asked too many questions.

*　*　*

When I rang Warren and asked if I could come over and see him the following evening, his response was, 'Sure, no problem.' I suppose I was a bit nervous, for although he had told us about Mum having polio and being off school a lot, he had never really said much about us having different fathers. I just hoped that he wouldn't think I was being a bit too nosy. I guess Warren must have thought I just wanted to find out a bit of family history, because when I asked him what the problem between Mum and Maureen had been, he hardly looked surprised.

'Well, I suppose it was me,' he said with a chuckle. 'You know that I was born a few years before Mum met Dad and that after they married, Dad adopted me?'

'Yes, I know that.'

'And I suppose you worked out there was no previous husband?'

I shrugged.

'I guess so, not really given it much thought.'

'Well, you would have if you'd been born twenty years earlier. Maybe that part of the story needs to be told.'

46

Phil

Since the first day I had walked through the doors of the college, I had been made to feel part of the team. By the end of my very first day, any worries I had about entering a place full of strangers had disappeared. I had felt quite disoriented when I arrived and saw what seemed like hordes of students, rushing purposefully in every direction. But before I could panic at the thought of finding out where I was meant to go, I heard someone calling my name and saw one of the women who had interviewed me walking purposefully in my direction.

'Good to see you, Phil. Thought I'd better meet you on your first day and introduce you to the team you'll be working with.'

That was one worry out of the way. Who would I talk to during my breaks was another one for it was the first time I had been so completely separated from my twin. Even making my way to the college without him by my side had felt strange. And the third one was would I manage the induction course and the requirements of the job? Worries that all disappeared by the end of my first day.

I was taken around the complex and shown the different photocopier machines and how to check them for blockages and fill them with paper. Following this, I attended the induction course, where all the new staff were gathered in the personnel offices. We signed our contracts and they were explained, together with all the rules on campus, fire drills, where to eat and what your hours of work were, even down to what to do when you were sick or wanted leave. It was nothing like as difficult as I had imagined and everyone I met was really friendly. No one there seemed to take any notice of the difficulty I had with my speech or made any comments about my leg. And as for breaks, what I hadn't realised was that although I might have been a student for one day a week, I was working on the other four. Which made me a member of staff. Therefore, I sat with the team and ate in the subsidised canteen.

At the end of those first six months when I was learning as well as working, I finally became a full-time employee. My six-month course was also over and I earned a pass certificate. That was one happy day for me, especially as my workmates were so pleased for me too and they said they were happy that I was definitely one of them now.

One of the team was Trevor, who was quite a lot older than the others. He came up to me later that week and reminded me that I had told him that one of the reasons I was hoping I would be offered a full-time job was because I wanted to get my own place and leave home.

'Mum died a few years ago and left me her house,' he told me. 'So I have more rooms than I need. If you'd like, you can have one. Don't need to pay rent, just want someone I get on with who can chip in with the bills.'

For several reasons, it was an offer I took up. Ryan had a girlfriend now and however close we were, it was time for me to become more independent.

* * *

I had hardly begun working full-time after completing my YTS scheme when I was given a small wage increase. The reason being that I was put in charge of checking all the photocopiers in all the college buildings. My job would be to make sure there was always enough ink for them. It was amazing how fast that got used up and some of the specialist ones needed different colours as well. I was also becoming the person they always asked for to look at a machine if they couldn't clear a blockage. Me, useless Phil, becoming the expert – I couldn't believe it! Wait till I told Ryan and Mum and Dad. Would Mum tell Maureen? I hoped so, especially as Clive had said no one would employ me and that I was useless.

But I felt secure in my job and that the senior people above me wanted me to enjoy being there. More than once, they had told me that if I had any problems, I could go to them. Which was good, only the problems that still lingered were not ones I could take to people at work. I could hardly explain why certain words could cause a panic attack. One of them being 'Scotland' while another was the word 'holiday'. Just hearing them placed Clive back in my memory. There were others, like 'queer' or 'gay', that I hated the sound of – not that my work colleagues ever said the first one.

When my promotion was announced, I could see just how pleased all my workmates were and it also meant that although I joined them most Fridays for a drink after work, they thought we should all go to a new bar which had just opened to celebrate my new status. 'And guess what it's called?' one of the girls said, 'TGIF! You know what that stands for, Phil? Thank God it's Friday!'

It certainly turned out to be the smartest bar I had ever been into. Gone were the wooden benches and stained carpeting, instead it was all sleek and bright and there were even large flower arrangements on the bar and mirrors everywhere. The girls certainly were enthusiastic in their praise – 'They even have a good selection of wines, not like that dodgy plonk some of the pubs sell. Can I get you one to celebrate, Phil?'

It's funny but even the word 'wine' brought back memories I did not wish to be in my head: that of Clive, with his superior smile, sipping from a crystal glass and spouting on about the vintage and the bouquet. I felt my hand shake slightly. *Don't let your past win, remember?* I told myself firmly, *Your life's getting good now.*

'No, I'll stay with lager, thanks,' I said with a smile.

No girl had ever offered me a drink before either.

There were other evenings I looked forward to, meeting up with Ryan being the main one. I was really pleased for him that he had found a girlfriend. Even more pleased when we met in his local bar for a couple of happy hour drinks and she invited me to join them for supper later.

'I call it that because it means less cooking than dinner,' she told me with a smile and I liked her humour straight away.

Ryan hadn't told me that Kate knew anything about our past. He said he wanted me to be relaxed around her and meet little Suzy first. And relaxed I was. During the first few times we met she made me feel that though I might never have a girlfriend, I could have a friend who was a girl. It was a couple of weeks later when it was just Ryan and I meeting up that he told me about that night with Kate.

'Let's just say I had an even bigger meltdown than you had at seven,' he told me.

'So she knows everything about us?'

'Almost everything,' he answered and while I pondered this, he ordered another couple of beers.

'Do you remember Clive saying we should talk to Warren if we wanted to know about Mum and Maureen? Like, why they didn't see each other for so many years?'

'Yes, I think I do, why?'

'Because I have, I just have a feeling we should know. So, I've phoned Warren and asked if I could go round to him tomorrow. Then I thought it actually concerns you as well and that I should take you with me. Are you up for that, Phil?'

'OK, if you think it's a good idea, I'll come.'

47

Ryan

'For you both to understand a few things, you will have to try and stop thinking of Mum as just our mum. Instead, I want you to try and imagine her before any of us came along, when she too was a teenager. She must have had dreams for her future then, but whatever they were, I doubt if any of them came true. Let's face it, the world's not always kind to teenagers, is it?'

Warren paused then and I felt there was something he wanted to ask, but I just shrugged and said, 'I suppose not.'

'Remember Mum was a teenager in the sixties. How much do you two know about that time?'

'A bit, I know there were some really good musicians about and that The Beatles caused an uproar with their long hair and style of singing. Don't think the oldies approved of them one bit, but the young people went mad for them,' I said.

'Yes, it was an exciting time to be young then, so much was changing. That is if you were into the new wave of music, loved dancing and were keen on all the funky fashion being designed for the youth at that time. Teenagers would have given little thought to the vaccine that had been administered in all the schools. Polio was by then more or less the forgotten pandemic. As for Mum, well, she was just Audrey, the girl who wore ugly, built-up shoes and walked with a bad limp.

'Funnily enough, no one says a word about the minidresses being worn today but back then, they certainly caused a fuss. The older generation were scandalised. Teenage girls wanted those latest styles alright! Short hair as well as short skirts were really in. And Mum must have felt that she just didn't fit in. She could only ever wear long skirts and now she wears trousers all the time. So, can you see how left out she must have been feeling?'

Phil looked a bit sad as he pondered these words: 'It must have been much worse for her than it's been for me. I've got you and Ryan and my other brothers, haven't I, Warren? None of you have ever made me feel left out. And now I've got a job I like and they never mention my problems.'

'But she had two sisters! I know Elaine was younger, but what about Maureen?' I wondered.

'I'll get to her a bit later. Now, I might not know much about girls' fashion, but I do know most won't leave the house until they feel good about how they look, so it must have been a bit of a shitty time for Mum, not that she would ever admit it. She once told me that she used to watch a programme called *Top of the Pops*. You know, one of those shows where the latest music is played and the audience dances to the hits. The sad thing is that she was listening to it inside those four walls, instead of in bars and discos with her friends.'

Phil chipped in, sounding quite annoyed: 'Surely her sister could have taken her out, made sure she had a good time? Ryan did with me, introduced me to all his friends and I can't even speak that well.'

Warren looked, if anything, a little amused.

'Ah yes, Maureen … As far as I know, she'd managed to get herself engaged by then. But now, aren't you interested to know how I came about?'

'Mum met a man, I suppose,' Phil and I said almost in unison.

'Yes, she did, but not a very nice one. But I don't think we can blame her for falling for the first boy to pay her some attention. Things were different then. Today, loads of girls want to concentrate on their careers before they even think of getting married. But back then, it seems marriage was what nearly every girl was aiming for. Even having a boyfriend was a status symbol. And as for a ring … well, that really was a big event. So, do you see how important having a boyfriend would have been then? I bet he made such a fuss of her that she walked down the road with her head held high. She would have believed then what she wanted to, that he really cared for her. Well, that was until she told him that I was on the way.'

'So what did he do?' I asked.

Warren gave a dry laugh then, adding, 'What those sort of men always do, took steps – big ones – to get out of the area as fast as he could.'

'And you've never met him?'

'No. Mum never saw him again as far as I know. She's never talked about him and I don't even know his name. I suppose she was so hurt that all she wanted was to wipe him from her memories. The last time I brought it up, she told me that her name on my birth certificate was good enough.'

'And what was down as your father's name, Warren?' Phil asked because he had needed his own birth certificate when he started college and saw that it had both our parents' names.

'Unknown. Because to her, he was.'

'So what happened after that? I mean, she had you and then what?' Phil persisted.

'Well, basically her family threw her out. Elaine told me all about that part. Our grandmother suddenly noticed Mum's swollen stomach. Let's just say she went white with horror while our grandfather's face went just about crimson with rage. Of course, a whole lot of questions were fired at her – did the father know, had he offered to marry her, and if not, what was his name and where did he live? I expect Grandad thought a visit from him would result in a hasty wedding.

'She just told them he had gone, left the area. I don't know if that was true or not, but it seems they thought it was. For once, they accepted there was not going to be a wedding. It only took them forty-eight hours to arrange for Mum to go into a mother-and-baby home run by nuns. Both her parents escorted her there, most probably wanted to make sure she had gone into it. When they turned to leave, their last words were that once the baby had been handed over for adoption, she could return home. They had already made it clear to the nuns that the child was to be adopted.'

'How did she get out of that?' I asked, thinking of Kate and Suzy. She had a loving mum and there was no shame in being an unmarried mother. I started to mull over how the world had changed in just twenty-odd years when Warren continued with the story.

'She just refused to sign the papers, even though they kept asking her to. And every time she told them she was keeping me. Can you imagine the pressure that was put on her? She would have been asked how she, a young, single woman, barely a child herself, was going to manage to support herself and look after a baby.'

'They had a point …'

'They did, but Mum still hoped that her mother would relent. Or she just refused to accept that she wouldn't. After all, she was going to be a grandmother. And while Mum was working away, cleaning and scrubbing in that home, she held on to that belief.'

Warren smiled at us then before saying, 'You know Mum, she never shows much emotion, that's her way of dealing with things. But I still think of something she once told me. Dad was out, Leighton was in bed and you two hadn't arrived yet when she started talking about how it had been in that home. I can almost hear her saying, "Of course I was expected to work, Warren. We all did as we would have done in our own homes – washing, cooking and cleaning. And we had to clean the chapel and polish all the brass. They had high standards, those nuns."

'She went on to tell me a little about the days when I was getting ready to come into the world. That she then only had very light work to do and every few minutes she would stop, press her hand to her enlarged stomach, so she could feel me moving inside her. That, she said, made her even more determined to keep me.

'A week or so earlier, the nuns had started waving those adoption papers around again. More because they couldn't see how Mum would be able to cope. No one in her family had come to the home to visit her, which convinced them that there would be no support coming from them. They kept telling her it was for the baby's sake and that she had to think of my future too. Those nuns must have thought that they were banging their heads against a brick wall as they tried every trick in the book to persuade Mum to sign those papers.

'"You can't make me," she told them. And she was right, they couldn't.'

'So,' I asked, 'how did she manage? Did our grandparents eventually help her, or was it Maureen who stepped in?'

'Neither. My grandmother visited just the once, the day she went into labour and told her she'd better sign those papers or she was never coming back home. They were not going to let the family be disgraced. Remember, status was everything then, especially to people like them. As for Maureen, it's not something that Mum has ever wanted to talk about, but as far as I know, she completely agreed with them. Maybe it was because her wedding had been planned and she didn't want her in-laws hearing any gossip about an illegitimate baby in the family. Clive's family were snobs and he was on the up and up.'

'Poor Mum! So, who did help her?' Phil asked.

'The nuns did in the end. Mum thinks it was the way our grandmother had spoken to her just as she was going into labour that did it. After all, she was really not much more than a child herself. She could stay with them, earn her keep and support her baby by helping out. It was unusual but they knew she was a hard worker. I wonder if they might also have thought her family would eventually relent.'

'They didn't, did they?'

'No, Ryan, they didn't. As far as I know, not one single member of the family ever visited over the whole time she lived in that home.'

'And how was she treated by them – the nuns, I mean? I've heard they can be pretty strict.'

My brother laughed at that.

'They don't admire laziness and our mother's certainly not that. But they were kind to her, alright.'

'So, how did she meet Dad?'

'Has no one ever told you?'

Phil and I leant forward, shaking our heads.

'She was his housekeeper. That was the job the nuns found for her. They had come up with the idea that a live-in job would sort out Mum's problems. They made sure that she learnt some good domestic and cooking skills. And then once I was old enough to go to nursery school, they began to look for suitable positions.

'Dad hadn't long been widowed. He must have found it

hard to cope with his grief as well as his children's. They were still at school, so really young to have lost their mother. I should think the whole family was simply heartbroken. He needed someone to run his home, cook decent meals and be around when his sons returned from school.

'I think it might have been Uncle Barry who persuaded him to look for a live-in housekeeper. "Rather than advertise, ask around at the church," he had suggested. The priest knew our mum and spoke to the Mother Superior and she contacted your dad. Well, you can't find anyone more respectable than Mum, can you? And before you ask, what did Dad think about me coming to live there as well? He was really OK with it. In fact, he was more than just OK. As soon as I came through the door, he leant down and welcomed me to my new home and told me I could play with any of the boys' old toys. Yes, he was really good to me, as he was to Mum, right from the start.

'Though from what I've heard, not all his family were too pleased with the arrangement – well, not at the beginning anyhow. I'm sure they thought she was far too young to run Dad's house and look after his three boys. I think Uncle Barry had a much older woman in mind when he suggested the church route. I know Dad's sister Barbara ('Barb') kept popping round to keep an eye on her and asking what Mum had been feeding the kids, not that she was an expert on nutrition.

'Mum told me that for the first few months of living there it did feel strange. She was used to the hustle and bustle of a city, not the quietness of the countryside. You have to think that when she arrived here there were a lot less shops and houses than there are now, it was just a village then. But gradually, she felt she was fitting in. Dad's niece Linda came round to see her most days and the villagers were a lot friendlier than city people. The only thing that really bothered her was our brothers. She felt that every time they saw her in the kitchen, they must have wished it was their mother they were seeing. And goodness knows how they must have felt when they saw her chatting with Dad or laughing at something on TV together. They must have wished and wished that their own mum was still alive and it was she who was in the house, not Mum. And she just didn't know how to comfort them. They were always polite, but she never really thought she had gained their affection.'

'So, how did they feel about them getting married?'

'They've never told me. Which makes me guess that they were none too happy about it at the time. They were really great with me though, so they would have been careful not to hurt my feelings. But I knew they weren't happy when they realised that Mum had become more than a housekeeper to Dad and that was well before the wedding. However discreet they were, we all knew something was going on. Still, in the end, everything worked out. And I was over the moon about the adoption and all three of Dad's sons told me they were really pleased that I was now their proper brother. As they were when Leighton came along and then a few years later, you two. The house was quite crowded then, so they gradually moved out.'

'So was that when she got friendly with her family again?'

'No, not really. Our grandparents did write to her when she let them know about the wedding so I suppose that was a small step. And her younger sister got in touch.'

'But didn't Maureen?'

'Not for a long time. That's the reason she's always been grateful to Clive – she feels he's the one who got them close again.'

'So,' Phil asked, 'when did Mum start seeing them?'

'Oh, I think it was probably not too long after you two were born.'

48

Ryan

I can't remember exactly how long it was after I had met Kate before Warren invited me over to watch a football match on TV with him at Allen's house. I would have been pretty stupid not to think there might have been another reason behind it, for although I had seen Allen quite a lot when Phil and I were little, the frequency diminished when we were older. Not that we weren't really fond of him but since he had moved out, our older brother had become pretty independent, as had Ian. We were always pleased when we met up with them at big family get-togethers and Ian often joined us when we went to the air shows.

Perhaps Allen wants to catch up a bit, I told myself. After all, I had hardly seen him since I left school. I knew that he and Ian saw Dad in their favourite pub fairly often and there had been quite a few occasions over the years when they had come to the house. Both of them appeared to get on with Mum, brought her flowers if they were coming for a meal and always praised her cooking, but as Warren had said, there was not a great deal of warmth between them.

I wondered on the way over if Warren had invited me because there was something else he wanted to tell me. Anyhow, whatever the real reason, I was none too bothered. Perhaps if I had known what it was then I would have made some sort of excuse and wriggled out of going.

There was just the two of them in Allen's house when I arrived, no sign of any female presence nor his children.

'Gone to visit her mother for a few days,' was his answer when I asked where everyone was.

OK, it was a football match we were going to watch, so a bit of a lads' night, I supposed, though I can't say I wasn't beginning to feel a little suspicious. But they made me welcome, brought out some beers as well as a large platter of dips, cheeses and crisps. Allen wanted to know how I was doing as a chef, then there was some chatter about the teams who were about to battle it out. Then the TV went on. Strange thing is I have no memory of that game, not who was playing nor who won, even though I know it was an important one in the league. Because, just as it began, out of the corner of my eye I caught a look they exchanged, one I had seen before. It was that glance that told me they had something planned and all I could do was wait and see.

More beer was brought out during half-time, more friendly banter about the players' performances and I got the impression they were clearly trying to ensure that I was nice and relaxed.

Well, I wasn't, because somehow, I was beginning to guess the reason I was there.

For the rest of the match, as they shouted for their side to win, I could feel my hands dampen with perspiration. Another round of beers once the final whistle went and the players had finished shaking hands and hugging each other. But before the experts analysed every twist and turn of the game, Allen jumped up and turned the TV off as Warren turned to face me. I could tell straight away that whatever he had planned to say to me was making him nervous.

'Look, Ryan, none of us want to upset you, but we are your older brothers and we really want to help. You know that Vicky and Kate are friends, don't you?'

'Yes,' I told him and immediately, I felt my neck growing warm.

'Well, Vicky told me about a conversation they had. How a few weeks ago you got really upset. And I know it was the film on TV that caused it. Funnily enough, Vicky and I had watched it as well, so we understood why it would have distressed you.'

'Only if Kate had told Vicky everything I had asked her not to,' I said angrily.

With a sinking feeling, I knew there was no point in not admitting that what I had told Kate was true. But it should have been my decision to confide in my brothers, not hers. I clenched my fists as I waited to hear what was coming next.

'And then you told her about what has been troubling you for years. I wonder if deep down, you confided in her because you wanted me to know? That you couldn't manage to keep that locked away any longer?'

I stayed silent. That night when I had broken down so badly was still a bit hazy, but I could remember most of what I had told Kate. I thought of how she had stroked my head and wiped away my tears when I couldn't stop crying.

'And since then you've been seeing a lot of her. Sounds as though she's been good for you,' said Allen.

'Yes, I suppose so,' I said, thinking that after this betrayal, my seeing Kate might be coming to an end.

Allen sat down next to me then. 'Come on, Ryan,' he said. 'I can see you're angry, but don't be. She's done the right thing.'

'She really has,' Warren added. 'She only talked to Vicky because she didn't know what to do. It wasn't just that one night that worried her, you know. When you've stayed over at hers, she's heard just how bad your nightmares are. It's those that really concern her; she feels you need some help. And from what I've heard, I think the same.'

'So, let me get this straight,' I said. 'Kate told Vicky, Vicky told you and you've told Allen. Is that it, or do more people know?'

'Only Ian. He wanted to come here tonight to offer his support as well. He told me to tell you he's totally on your side. He's got some work issues to sort out and then he wants to meet up with you. The three of us have talked it through and there are a few things we want to discuss because what happens next has to be your decision. I know this isn't easy for you, but we need a few things clarified a little, to see if we have all the facts. Must say I never liked that man myself, but I never for one moment thought he would be up to something like this.'

'When did it all begin?' Allen asked, no doubt hoping the answer was going to be 'Oh, just a few months ago.'

For a moment I was silent.

Warren laid a hand on my shoulder as he said, 'I know this is difficult, Ryan, but there's nothing you can't tell us. We just want to help you and Phil, which is why Allen asked when it began.'

'It was the year before we started school,' I replied, 'so we were probably four.'

'Four!' they both exclaimed and I could hear the horror in their voices.

'But didn't you say anything at all to your mother or Dad?' asked Allen.

'I tried to tell Mum when I was little. I said that I didn't like the games he played, but I don't think she understood.'

More glances between brothers.

'He was clever, he used those games he played with us to cover up his touching Phil and me. But there was one day when Mum and Maureen went out that he really frightened us both and after that, he left us alone for a while.'

As I told them about that day a picture flashed into my head of Phil, his face a bright pink as Clive made him almost crawl over to where he was standing.

'Phil was more upset than I was and I suppose Clive thought he might get hysterical unless he stopped. He hardly wanted Mum and his wife to return to find two screaming little boys.'

'So, he ceased molesting you two for a while? So, when did it start up again?' Allen wanted to know.

'The year we turned seven, when we went to Scotland with them,' I said. And then I told them about the Up and Down Game and what he'd done to us.

'We thought we could cope, but it got worse after we were ten,' I added.

'I'm not going to ask you why neither of you came to us,' said Warren. 'It's a known fact that children seldom talk, that's what these bastards count on. The abuser tells them things like no one will believe them and that they would be blamed anyhow. They play on little threats, see the fears that the children they have taken time to groom have and then work on manipulating them. And that's what he did to you two, wasn't it?'

'Yes. And when we grew older, everything got much worse. We both felt completely trapped,' I told them as I felt my body beginning to tremble. 'There was still a bit of me that liked him, that made it even more difficult.'

'And you felt completely bewildered by your conflicting emotions, didn't you?'

'Yes.'

I could sense my brothers were waiting for me to say more. I could see that they were finding what I was telling them distressing, but they needed to know everything to decide exactly what advice they were going to give.

'We knew you were drinking heavily,' Allen told me. 'Dad told Ian and I think he was a bit concerned,' said Allen. 'Mind you, we'd all seen you nicking drinks when you were about thirteen. I remember Dad being furious with you because at one family party, you went around taking swigs out of people's glasses. You thought no one saw you, but everyone did. We all feel guilty now that we didn't notice how troubled you were, but we just thought you were going through a stroppy teenager stage and that you'd grow out of it.'

'But I didn't,' I said then with a slight smile.

'Looks like you're beginning to do OK now, though,' Warren said with a smile.

The fact that they seemed to understand why I had never confided in them helped a little.

I got up and walked around the room a bit and helped myself to some cheese – my way of trying to block some of my thoughts out.

'What we think is that for years, you have been suffering from PTSD,' Warren told me. 'Which means there are certain things – like noises or words, for instance – that trigger memories you wished you didn't have. Which is what that movie did. But that's something you can get help for. Mum and Dad need to know as well. We think it would be best if one of us broke it to them. I've volunteered to go and see them. Won't be easy. I think they'll be devastated but it needs to be done.'

'Trouble is,' said Allen, 'it's their big party in a couple of weeks. The one to celebrate their wedding anniversary.'

'Yes, I know. Mum's busy getting ready for it,' I said.

'So, should Warren wait until that's over? I expect Clive and Maureen have already been invited. No doubt they'll be there. So, what do you think? It's up to you and Phil,' he continued.

'Maybe after, but I must talk to Phil first.'

'Yes, we also thought that it would be better that way.'

Another beer was opened. I felt like downing it in a one go. Apart from seeming shocked when I had said how young we were when the abuse first started, my brothers appeared to be taking it all in their stride.

'It was the shame that got to me,' I said suddenly. It was almost as though everything I had bottled up for so long needed to be released. 'I kept quiet, didn't I, and watched when it was Phil's turn. And poor Phil, he could do nothing to help himself. And then, do you know what he did? He kept telling us that we enjoyed it.' I felt the tears welling as I managed to choke out what I hadn't told Kate.

'Once we were older, he got us to ejaculate. We both did, although we tried not to, and then, do you know what he did? He kept telling us that we had only done that because we wanted him to do it. Do you know what it was like for us once he'd put those thoughts in our heads? No, of course you don't, but *I* do!

'I just kept asking myself if it was true. Because if it was, then what did that make me?' I was shaking so much as I sobbed this out, hardly aware that my voice was getting louder and louder. I felt my legs buckle and the next thing I knew, I was on my knees in front of the coffee table. But before my brothers could think what to say to comfort me, I blurted out the rest.

'I just can't get those thoughts of him out of my head,

it's like having a film on a continuous loop. As it flickers, there he is with that smug smile, flicker and there we are, a few years ago on the floor, pyjamas round our ankles. Flicker again to the picture of him crowing when our bodies let us down. That's what makes me feel so dirty, so ashamed. Then there's the one which makes me feel so guilty, the worst part that's on the spool of film in my head. It's when he came into the room for the last time. I refused him, didn't I? Curled up as tight as I could, kept my eyes shut.

'My hands might have covered my ears, but that didn't stop me from hearing what he was doing. My eyes might have been shut, but that didn't stop me from seeing him. And Phil might not have been able to speak, not with what Clive was making him do, but I could hear him in my head, begging me to make Clive stop.

'Clive called me a coward then. If I had felt shame before, I now feel a mountain of it. Though when he arrived on our sixteenth birthday, I marched up to him when no one was looking and told him what a bastard I thought he was. I told him never to come near Phil nor I again.'

'And how did he respond?' asked Warren.

'He didn't really. I think he was scared that someone would overhear. All he said was, "Just enjoy your birthday, Ryan" and then he walked away. Not that confronting him made me feel much better. Everything he's said and done has made me feel so disgusting!'

As those last words came out, my clenched fist banged down on the coffee table. It was so violent, the empty bottles tumbled to the floor and the crisps jumped out of the bowl with the force of my anger and frustration.

It was Allen who moved first. His arm went around me as my head dropped. Sobs burst from my chest and echoed around the silent room. He helped me back up onto the settee. Both my brothers sat either side of me until my anguish started to diminish.

I was exhausted, my body wanted to sleep, my mind wanted to close down. Most of all, I wanted all those images to disappear.

Nothing more was said that night about what should be done but I knew it was not going to rest there.

49

Phil

I found myself being surprisingly calm when Ryan told me about the meeting with Warren and Allen. For years, we had felt weighed down by those secrets we had hidden from everyone. There were many times when the enormity of our shame just got too much for us. They say twins have a special relationship and we certainly felt each other's pain acutely. Ryan used alcohol to help lessen it, which I did as well for a time. Though I often found that when I woke, with a dry mouth and a headache, the weight of my guilt and shame seemed even heavier.

'Are you saying they're not at all angry about the fact that we've kept quiet about Clive for all these years?'

'They aren't, Phil, not at all. They're just very concerned about how it has damaged us. I think they would like to kill Clive, though!'

I felt more of that weight shifting then. My biggest fear had been that the brothers I loved would have been angry with me or even worse, disgusted.

'And Warren...?' I asked hesitantly.

'I was coming to that. He's the one who's been given the task of telling Mum and Dad.'

'Clive has been banned from visiting, hasn't he?'

'He certainly has. So we'll never have to see him again.'

'It's not been easy, keeping secrets, has it, Ryan?'

'No, it hasn't. And we might just have another one to keep.'

Ryan quickly explained what he meant by that. He explained that our brothers had asked when we wanted our parents to be told – 'We need to consider that there's the big party coming up. So, should they be told before or after? It's up to us.'

'I don't know, Ryan. I think it should be sometime after the party. Mum's been planning it for ages and I think she'd be so upset if it had to be cancelled or if there was a huge family scandal happening. So, I think after it. We've waited this long, a couple of weeks more won't make any difference, will it?'

'You know Clive and Maureen will be coming, don't you?'

For what must have been the first time, I found myself grinning when Clive's name came up.

'Just think, Ryan, we will all know it's the last time he'll be visiting our town. In just a short time, he'll be scared to put a foot in it. Our brothers will make sure of that. They could pay him a nice little visit. Tell him they know everything and that he'd better not come near anyone in the family again. So, while he's sitting there, believing he's the most important guest, he won't have a clue as to what's in store, but the rest of us will.'

Ryan burst out laughing. 'You're right, Phil. The stupid bastard won't have a clue and it'll be us feeling superior for a change.'

'Exactly!'

Ryan placed an arm around my shoulder. 'You really are someone very special, Phil,' he told me, giving me a quick hug. 'And don't you think we'd better go round to Leighton's before the party and fill him in on what's been happening? It's another step towards putting it all behind us.'

'We're going to tell him everything?'

'I think we should. We'll play it by ear anyhow, see how it goes.'

I knew that confiding in Leighton was a big deal for him. Warren was the big brother who had always taken an interest in us. The one who, when I was little, I had felt safe with. Leighton was the one who looked out for us at school, while Ryan always tried to copy him. I was aware that being unable to protect me from Clive had weighed heavily on Ryan, for he took the idea that he was the older twin very seriously. It was as if he felt guilt for being the firstborn. Maybe he thought had things been different, I wouldn't have had that stroke.

'We will want him sitting with us at the party. Clive will just see a barricade of brothers, won't he? Do you think he might guess that his game's up?

Ryan looked pretty cheerful at the thought. 'That would be really great if he did. Mind you, we'd better not be glaring at him for Mum's sake. Anyhow, let's get going. We can pick up some beers on the way, that always makes us even more welcome at Leighton's.'

He was right: Leighton greeted us with a wide smile, especially when he saw the bag of cans.

50

Ryan

Telling Leighton about Clive felt totally different from when I had told Kate and my other brothers. This time I didn't shake or burst into tears, which had to be a step or two in the right direction. And as for Phil, he was pretty stoic when he listened to me telling the secrets of our childhood. But now I come to think of it, he had been that way as a child.

By the time I had finished telling him and answered a few questions, it was Leighton who nearly broke down.

'Oh my God, you two! Why on earth didn't you tell me? The bastard! I never guessed, but I should have done.'

'Why didn't he touch you up too? Was that the reason you never wanted to come to Cambridge with us or join us in Scotland?' I wanted to know.

'Oh, it was nothing like what he's done to you. He was a bit drunk at one of our barbecues and kept telling me how cute I was. Just things like that, but it made me feel uncomfortable.'

'And that was all?'

'No, and I should have told Mum and Dad then, shouldn't I? Then you might have been spared. He managed to corner me later that evening when I was in my pyjamas, grabbed hold of my private parts and said I was going to be a big boy. But he must have forgotten how much football I played and that I was usually the striker. Let's just say my legs were pretty strong then. He really pissed me off, grabbing me like that, so I kicked him hard, told him not to try that again and walked off.

'Look, I thought he was creepy alright, but I just thought he was a bit drunk. It never entered my head that he would have gone further than that. I'm so sorry I did nothing about it, at least I should have warned you two.'

I felt so sorry for Leighton then; I could see how guilty he was feeling. Both Phil and I told him not to get upset. After all, he was only a kid when that happened and as he said, it was only the one time so how would a young boy have known that Clive was a lot more than a drunken groper?

It was a bit later on when the three of us had talked enough about Clive that Leighton voiced something I didn't want to think about:

'Don't you think we should report him to the police?'

An idea that after a bit more discussion, we dismissed. He was family, after all. If we told the police, everyone in the town would know. It was enough that the party would be the last time he set foot in our town. So that would be the end, wouldn't it?

Or so we hoped.

51

Ryan

What none of us had taken into account was Clive's secret vice might not have vanished into thin air: just because he had backed away from Phil and me didn't mean he was not on the lookout for other young victims. To us, at seventeen, he was an old man whose addiction for molesting young boys must have dried up.

Talk about naive.

It was at the party that alarm bells started ringing. Up until then, I had not been taking much notice of Clive – in fact, I had tried to avoid him. Polite hellos and 'How are you doing?' had been exchanged, but that was about all. It was Phil who spotted that familiar expression on Clive's face. He touched my arm to get my attention and I saw his gaze flickering sideways, telling me where to look. Not so much at Clive, but at the child sitting near him. A little boy wearing a short-sleeved blue T-shirt with a brightly coloured motif on the front and a pair of denim shorts. A red baseball cap was perched on his blond curly head and I saw his hand raise up to touch it – it was obviously a piece of clothing that he was very fond of.

Now I was transfixed although I kept my eyes averted. I heard his mother telling Clive that it was his first little boy outfit that he had chosen – 'He looks so cute in it,' she said laughingly. And indeed, he did. I could hear the child's voice piping up and I glanced surreptitiously in their direction.

A shudder ran down my spine when I caught a glimpse of the expression on Clive's face. An expression that went as fast as it had arrived, but it was there when his gaze rested on the boy.

'A credit to you both,' he was saying to the parents.

'Oh, the charm's out,' Phil whispered to me. He had heard him asking where they lived – 'Wouldn't be surprised if he suddenly found he had some business near them.'

In my mind's eye, I could almost see Clive licking his lips at the prospect of such fresh new prey. If it wasn't that child, it would be another that he would begin to groom. Of that, I was certain then.

Sickened, Phil and I went out into the car park to talk and we asked each other what we could do.

'We have to do something to stop him, Ryan, don't we?' my brother told me. 'But what?'

Neither of us wanted to put into words what the only solution was.

52

Ryan

Kate had decided not to come to the party when I asked her. Mainly because she didn't want to clap eyes on Clive. She had lots of questions about it though and when I told her about seeing that fleeting, lascivious expression on my uncle's face when he was looking at the little boy, I thought she was going to erupt.

'Look, Ryan, I'm not telling you what to do, but think how you would feel if that uncle of yours finds some more young victims, which I'm sure he will, because men like him don't stop.'

'I know,' I replied.

'Well, why don't you phone Warren, tell him that you and Phil would like a family pow wow?'

So much for not telling me what to do, I thought.

'Actually, Phil and I have arranged to meet up with Leighton. I didn't tell you, but Clive made a pass at him as well.'

'So, if you decide to take this further, there will be three of you to make statements. Not much chance of him wriggling out of that then.'

I asked Kate if she wanted to come along as well but she said she'd rather not meet up with Leighton as she wanted Phil and I to make our own decisions.

'Look, Ryan, I've a daughter not much younger than you were when Clive began grooming you. If anyone touched her, I'd want to see that person jailed for life. So, it would be hard for me to keep quiet. It's much better if the three of you decide what you want to do. Anyhow, I think it's good for you to be in control of what happens next,' she told me.

* * *

When Phil and I met up with Leighton, it was clear that he had given the subject of Clive a great deal of thought.

'The thing is,' he said, 'Clive's not someone who grabs hold of a child in the street and abuses them. I suppose we should be grateful for that at least. The difference is I believe that he's someone who enjoys the hunt. He's not just on the lookout for a child he can groom, but a whole family that he works on until he has them wrapped around his little finger. And if he chooses right, even if several years later it all comes out, they probably won't report it. Why? Because they don't ever want to admit that they didn't see what was happening right under their noses. They would feel some of the dirt rubbing off on them. You see they would suspect that in the eyes of the police, they were also partially to blame.

'The sort of family he will be on the lookout for would have to be a little naive. But then Clive's a married man and the two of them seem very respectable. Added to that, he can talk about his sons, show photos of his family. He could even show them some nice ones of you two, his nephews.'

Phil and I listened intently to what Leighton was saying and it all made complete sense.

'He's not any of those things that might set off the alert buttons in their heads, he's on the hunt for a couple with a young child who he can impress. Someone not too well-off or super bright, where the husband has a fairly ordinary job. Then gradually he becomes a bit of an uncle figure to their children. It wouldn't take long for everyone to like him and then the dinners out would begin, not too quickly though. He'll tell them he has business in the area and them joining him would be a tax write-off. Which means the couple will not feel embarrassed at eating in a hotel or restaurant that they could not afford themselves.'

'He's got his eye on that young couple you saw him talking to at the party,' I said.

'Yes, who are they?'

'They were visiting one of the neighbours and Mum said of course they were included in the invitation. Warren and Vicky were chatting to them quite a bit too. So, Warren says he will make sure they're warned off. Which only means they would be the ones who got away. But the next one might not. We know that there will be another victim. People like him have to be stopped, for it's not something they will ever decide to do themselves. But what would be the reason for them to do so? Men like Clive have no conscience, no empathy. And somewhere there's a happy little boy, who trusts adults because no one has ever hurt him. A boy whose life will be ruined unless we do something. We have to go to the police, don't we?'

Phil and I looked at each other then nodded our heads.

'Good lads!'

Leighton stood up and came over to put a strong hand on our shoulders. The three of us had made our decision, a decision our older brothers congratulated us on when we all met up a couple of days later.

Warren was the one who would talk to the police first so we would not have to tell a duty sergeant why we were standing in front of him. Of course, I hated the thought of talking to strangers and telling them everything that had been Phil's and my secret for so long. But we had accepted that we had no other choice, that it was the right thing to do.

Warren also had the dismal task of informing our parents. Not just about the crimes that Clive had committed, but that we had decided to go to the police.

Neither Phil nor I were there that night. I was staying at Kate's and Phil, wanting to be near his brothers, bedded down at Leighton's. We were pretty certain that it might be better if we avoided Mum and Dad until after Warren had informed them of everything and outlined our intentions.

As we suspected, it was not something that went easily, as Warren concurred the following evening when we all got together again:

'I went round in the afternoon to talk to Mum on her own. To begin with, she kept saying that she didn't want Dad to know. That it would upset him so much. I had to tell her that if I didn't break the news to him, Allen and Ian would.'

'And did you?' I said.

'Yes' – and I could see that Warren was looking sad. 'Mum was right, he was so upset – I hardly knew what to do.'

'But he believed you?'

'Yes, he did, once it had sunk in. They did suggest us dealing with it within the family, but I told them that would not protect other children.'

'And you explained about us going to the police?'

'Yes, Dad said it was up to you three. But Mum's both upset and angry. She's worried about Maureen and the effect it will have on her. And if she'll blame us if Clive ends up in prison. She said that she had lost her once and didn't want to lose her again. I did try and point out that it would hardly be your fault if Clive ends up inside, that it will be his. Somehow I don't think that got through to her. But I explained that you have both decided that you're going ahead and all us brothers are completely on your side.'

*   *   *

Warren made the appointment with the police and explained exactly what it was all about. He told them that he had no doubts that this was going to be very hard for us and that he wanted it handled sensitively. When he came back after what seemed like hours, he gave us the time of the appointment: 10am the following morning. He assured us they had been briefed and we were to be interviewed by a team specialising in sexual crimes.

I think we both felt numb. It was hard to take in that finally, Clive was going to be stopped.

53

Ryan

Ten o'clock the following morning came and the three of us were there, standing outside the police station, trying to pluck up our last bit of courage to push open the door and enter. The question running through my head, and I'm sure it was the same for my brothers, was just how had we managed to end up outside the police station's stark red building? It was all happening so fast, we could hardly take it in. Just for a few split seconds I was tempted to turn around, take to my heels and run away as fast as I could. Instead, I glanced at my brothers, squared my shoulders and reached out to open that door.

It was Leighton who told the middle-aged duty sergeant what our names were and who we had an appointment with. A friendly, reassuring smile came in our direction.

'That's right, lads, Inspector Medlock is expecting you. Just take a seat while I let her know you've arrived.'

He picked up the phone near his elbow and through the

glass partition we could hear him giving our names as he told whoever was on the other end that we had arrived.

'Someone's coming down to collect you,' he told us. 'Only be a minute or two.'

Sitting on that hard, wooden bench, I felt more than uncomfortable. Blue uniformed officers were scurrying about and sideways glances came in our direction. Of course, paranoia jumped in and I started thinking that everyone there knew all about us and wanted to take a look at the boys who had been abused. I felt that prickling on the back of my neck as those thoughts just about made me squirm with embarrassment.

It might only have been a couple of minutes before a young constable came over and asked us to follow him, but it was long enough for my hands to have become damp, my heart racing.

We followed him into a room which was slightly more comfortable-looking than the ones I had seen on TV. There was a desk, piled high with folders, several chairs with scuffed legs, a filing cabinet and, looking rather out of place, a dusty pot plant.

'Can I get you some drinks?' the constable asked. 'Tea, coffee, water?'

As he left, Inspector Medlock walked in. I felt my heart sink when I remembered where I had seen her before – she was only the inspector who had been in charge of the drugs raid when I first met Kate. The one who had ticked me off. She must have noticed that I looked pretty uneasy when I saw her, for she placed a hand on my shoulder and gave it a slight squeeze before walking round to the other side of the desk.

She introduced herself to us as Inspector Joy Medlock, adding, 'But you can call me Joy.' Smiled again. Gave us all a warm, pleasant smile. She certainly looked very different to the stern-faced officer I had seen arresting people on that raid. She also apologised for the lack of comfort in the room – 'Cutbacks,' she explained with a wry smile, 'but as long as I have a desk, I'm not that bothered.'

She went on to say that although Warren had told her quite a bit about our uncle's actions, she needed to hear it directly from us. She then asked each of us in turn if we were feeling OK to answer all her questions, which would form the main part of our statements.

I found out later that we were all relieved it was a woman we would be talking to – we felt they would be more understanding.

Leighton replied, saying his was hardly going to be a long one, because he was lucky in that it only happened once. When he told her about kicking his uncle hard, she made us laugh by saying it was a pity he hadn't been a bit taller then – 'Just a few inches higher and you might have stopped his dirty antics for good.'

'Ah, here's our coffees, boys,' she said as the constable came back, carrying a tray with packets of biscuits as well as four mugs. She must have been used to teenage boys who crave sugar for she waited until the biscuits were passed around before she spoke again.

'First, I want you to know that we take any kind of abuse

very seriously. There are other officers here who are also extremely experienced in dealing with cases like yours. One of them, Tom Mitchell, will be joining us. Mainly he will be taking notes as we talk, which will be typed out ready for you to sign.'

She went on to tell us that it was her role to keep us informed every step of the way. She then threw a question that I wasn't expecting: 'So why now? What made you decide to report your uncle?'

It was a question that we all gave more or less the same answer to: we wanted him stopped because we believed he would find other young victims. I went on to tell her about Clive's behaviour at the party.

'It was after that,' Phil explained, 'that we talked it over and decided we must come to you.'

'Which is brave of you, I know,' she told us and I could see that the reason we had given had pleased her. But before she asked us anything else, there was a knock on the door and another plain-clothes officer appeared. I think it was then that I started to realise not only was this a serious case, but she had her reasons for not having the second officer in the room from the start. She must have thought that facing two people just might have overwhelmed us.

I remembered what Kate had said about her then: 'It's the dealers she wants to catch. She wants them put away before they turn any more kids into addicts.' And suddenly I found myself smiling at her – a smile that said I was putting my trust in her, she told me later. And that alone was enough to make her want to make sure that Clive was going to be charged.

Over the course of that morning I felt her main concern was to make sure that the case didn't damage us any further. Her first question was not 'What age were you when it started?', but 'How did he have so much access to you?' And gradually she drew us out until I'm sure the one taking notes must have had arm-ache.

More coffees with an assortment of sandwiches were brought in to keep us going so I realised it was lunchtime. We continued until it was probably nearly teatime.

She called a halt then.

'You've done very well, lads. And you two,' she told Phil and me, 'you've been really very brave. We're going to make sure he doesn't touch any more children. The courts will decide on his punishment, but we have a very good case.'

'So you believe everything we've told you? He always told us the police would laugh at us,' I said.

'Yes, Ryan, I do. A 17-year-old boy might occasionally fib about his age, especially if he's in a bar,' she told me with a bit of a grin, 'but they don't lie about this. So, don't even think that. He's going to be charged.

'I'm going to have you all back in a couple of days. Just a few more questions and then we can go through your witness statement and make sure there's nothing left out.'

'When will he be arrested?' Phil asked and I could hear the nervousness in his voice, as could she.

'Once he's charged, he will not be able to contact any of you. And that's going to be pretty soon.'

54

Ryan

I can't remember the exact date when Clive was charged. Everything around that time seemed to happen so fast, it felt almost unreal. Phil and I could hardly get our heads around the fact that he was finally out of our lives for good.

If he's found guilty, that is, was the niggling doubt that kept popping up in my head, for hadn't we been told for so long that we wouldn't be believed if we talked? And now we had.

'He will be, stop doubting it,' my brothers and Kate kept telling us. 'Anyhow, he's out of your lives completely.'

OK, I accepted that never again would I have to see him at a family party or bump into him when he visited Mum and Dad. But if he was not convicted, there would always be that question hanging in the air: had we been telling the truth? And if those worries were not enough, I managed to scrape up another one to fret over: how would people react to Phil and I once they knew?

Small wonder a lot of that time is a bit of a blur for us

both, but I can remember an interview we had with Inspector Joy Medlock around then with great clarity. Not that it went the route I expected police interviews to go. It was more about her wanting to make sure we were coping alright with the process.

At first, we thought she had more questions for us. We had come in to go through and sign our statements, but that hardly warranted the mugs of coffee and biscuits that arrived almost as soon as we sat down. Of course, another doubt immediately sprang up in my mind: had she really believed us? A doubt that was knocked on the head within seconds of her joining us. Her smile alone would have done that, even if the first couple of sentences when she asked us how we were getting on didn't.

As we sipped away at our coffee and munched on biscuits, she made it clear that she wanted to make sure that we were able to handle everything that was happening and the pressure that might be building up.

'I know it's never easy reporting a family member,' she told us. 'Trouble is a high percentage of abusers are either a family friend or a relative. Some are even closer relatives than Clive, which means often a family becomes divided on what should happen.'

'Our brothers have been really great,' I told her before she had a chance to ask.

'And your parents?'

'It's difficult for them,' I replied hesitantly. 'I mean, Dad saw Clive as his best friend and Mum's worried about her sister and losing her friendship.'

'So, you can't talk to them much?'

'No, not really, but seeing as three of my brothers are a lot older then us, well, that kinda helps, if you know what I mean.'

'Yes, I do. They've taken over the supportive adult role, which is something you need in a case like this.'

She wanted to tell us what some of our feelings since the beginning of the abuse up until now were likely to have been. She then reassured us that feeling guilty and ashamed was a completely normal reaction – 'An undeserved one,' she hastened to add.

'That's why being with our brothers has been so good for us,' Phil told her. 'We feel we can tell them anything and not be judged.'

I suppose the difference in talking to Joy was that she was not only trained to put us at our ease but also to ask the right questions, ones that would help us to confide in her about any fears we might have. She led up to that by covering why children don't talk and when we repeated Leighton's summing-up of men like Clive, she told us he had got it spot on.

I have to say, she was really good at wheedling information out of us!

She finally brought up how the type of abuse we had suffered can leave boys very confused – in fact, frightened – about who they really are. She didn't ask us if that was how we felt, either she had the ability to see into our heads and know the answer, or her years of experience had given her great insight.

The main problem for boys is that even before puberty, their penis will grow stiff during abuse. But little boys, still in their nappies sometimes, have erections. The abuser is aware of that and then seizes the opportunity to plant those seeds of guilt in the child's head.

Phil and I found ourselves nodding in agreement to that, for this was one of the main things that made us so full of shame.

'Now what happens when they move into their teenage years seems far worse for them, doesn't it? Worse for the boys he's controlling that is, but good for the abuser. For those teenage hormones have just given him another weapon. One where he could accuse his victims of being very willing participants and no matter how many times they protested, he would keep repeating that they had enjoyed his hands being on them. Hadn't their bodies just told him that?'

Listening to her every word, I found myself nodding in agreement. Glancing at Phil, I saw he was nodding too.

'What's happened to both of you has taken place over a very long time,' she explained at the end, 'so you can't expect to be completely over it in a matter of a few weeks. So, if you feel you would like to talk to someone outside of your family, I can arrange it and I might even suggest it. The one fear I have come across when it's a teenage boy who has been abused is does that mean he's gay?'

I felt myself redden at that last comment.

'The thing I always tell them is that being forced into any kind of sexual act doesn't make anyone gay, what does is liking their own sex. Not that there's anything wrong with feeling that way either.'

She then asked if we had any questions for her.

I told her that we were both dreading the court case. The thought of being cross-examined by a barrister whose job was to tear our statements to shreds was enough to give me more nightmares.

'They're not completely inhuman,' she said with a grin. 'Anyhow, the judge would not allow any aggressive cross-examination towards you. Not that he would stop Clive being given a grilling. If he pleads guilty, that helps reduce his sentence. With the evidence against him, his barrister will almost certainly advise him to do that. So, let's hope he takes that advice. With a guilty plea, you two need not appear.'

We left the station feeling that the load we had carried for so long was almost gone. I was almost light-headed with relief. My hands came out of my pockets, my shoulders straightened and a smile settled on my face.

* * *

Clive's case was heard just three months after we made our statements. He pleaded guilty and received a four-year sentence.

For him, it was the end of his good reputation in the town.

For us, it was the beginning of closure.

55

Ryan

Right up to the day I heard that Clive was finally in prison, it was the adrenalin that kept me going. That buzz of excitement and anticipation was nearly always with me. I was so looking forward to the case being over – then I could move on, couldn't I?

In the meantime, I could enjoy a night out with guys I knew, pub friends really, where large quantities of beer were drunk before I staggered back to Leighton's. Other evenings, it was Kate and I having a good night out and then coming back to smoke the dope she never seemed to have trouble producing.

Phil, on the other hand, remained fairly calm. He was happy in his job and still living at Trevor's. My family were also satisfied that the law was taking its course and they just wanted Phil and I to start to recover from what had happened.

It was when Joy Medlock told us that Clive had pleaded guilty so we wouldn't have to be witnesses and that he had been given a four-year prison sentence that I finally started to relax after all that pent-up energy. The result being that I began to feel lethargic.

The moment my brothers heard the news they insisted we all went out to celebrate. 'Now you can both move on,' they told us. And I did my best to look as enthusiastic as they expected me to be, but I didn't feel it. There was no emotion in me at all when I heard the news, just an emptiness. I worked hard at hiding the numbness that overwhelmed me; not just from my brothers and Kate, but from myself as well. Alcohol and dope helped with that, as did spending time with those who had supported us for weeks. But they had their own lives to go back to now the crisis was over, while I had no plans for the future. I was vaguely aware that instead of making a path forward for myself, I was just allowing the days to slide by. I could also sense that Kate and I were beginning to drift apart. Oh, not in a difficult way, more that she had her ambitions and I still had to identify what mine were. I knew that she had my wellbeing at heart, but was getting frustrated with my lack of initiative.

It was she who found out that Lincoln's extremely popular Tyrwhitt Arms was looking for staff for their pub restaurant. Trainee chefs, she told me, and encouraged me to give them a call and formally apply.

A drop of adrenalin must have remained hidden somewhere because I did just that. One phone call and I had secured an interview, which unbeknownst to me then was going to change my life.

The phone call might have only taken a few minutes; making myself presentable took a lot longer. A quick visit to the barber for a decent haircut was number one on my priority list. Next, what to wear? Well, I only had jeans, so I put on my best pair – after all, I wasn't applying for a job where they would expect me to wear a suit and style was really important, but cleanliness would matter. Nails cut neatly and scrubbed clean, nice close shave and with a freshly ironed shirt and clean shoes, I was ready for my interview.

OK, I was pretty nervous. I suddenly realised that I must have woken up a bit, for I really wanted this job.

I had watched enough on TV to know that there were chefs who had done their training at college and others who had worked their way up from kitchen porter to head chef. With the right training, I was beginning to think that if I worked hard, there was a career waiting for me.

But what was I going to say if they asked me about exams?

To my relief, it seemed what I had achieved at school was not of any interest to them. They were far more interested in asking me why I wanted to leave the motorway cafe. After all, it was pretty easy work and the pay was good.

'I want to do more than grill hamburgers and toss chips in a pan,' was my reply.

And then I screwed up some more courage.

'I want to learn to be a chef, a proper one,' I told them and remembering what Kate once said to me, 'even if it means I spend weeks peeling potatoes and dicing up vegetables.'

Now that made them laugh and the interview immediately became more relaxed.

'Well, Ryan, I think you'll fit right in here,' said Mark, who happened to be the head chef.

And I realised I had just been offered the job.

I started as a trainee under Mark's guidance. He appeared to enjoy encouraging young chefs to improve their skills and when the kitchen wasn't too busy, he would show us some more advanced techniques. He would explain the science as to why things could go wrong with a sauce and how to fix it without starting again. He was a great character and a good mentor and the banter in the kitchen was good for me. I didn't know it then, but I must have been extremely hard to work with at times, especially when I was hungover after a night off, but when I managed to do something right, he was really generous with his praise.

Did he know I was troubled? I guess now they all did. My family often visited the pub and a few years earlier, my mother had a part-time job there. Although details of the trial were not in the local papers as Clive didn't live there, gossip still spread almost as fast by word of mouth as Twitter and WhatsApp do now through tapping fingers. Whatever the reason, Mark persevered in giving me the best training he could. We worked very long hours in the kitchen and when I finished at night, Kate, my family and friends were getting ready for bed, which meant I had to have my nightcaps on my own.

It was after I had been at the restaurant for over a year that Kate sat me down to break the news that she was moving to Manchester.

'I've been offered a really great job in PR. They will

sponsor me finishing my studies part-time and I've found a preschool for Suzy. They have aftercare and in the summer holidays, Suzy will come down to Mum,' she told me.

In a way, I was happy for her. She had been working towards that for some time and I knew it was what she wanted. Yes, I was going to miss her. Of course, she said all the things people do when a relationship has begun to fade away. That we would keep in touch, meet up when she came to visit her mother, that I could come to her when I had a free weekend.

It's just that none of those plans ever seem to happen, do they?

56

Ryan

I just didn't know how lost I must have been feeling until I met Helen. Up until then, it was as though I were divided into two people. One who managed to turn up for work, follow the procedures I had been taught and most of the time please my work colleagues, my head chef and the customers. Then there was the other person. The one who had not stopped feeling worthless, no matter what had been said to me by my brothers, Kate and the police.

So, what did I do to help chase away those dark thoughts?

Put as much alcohol down my throat as I could, that's what.

Over the years, what I have learnt about booze is that it persuades us to believe it's our best friend. For doesn't it give us confidence, make our jokes funnier and our conversation more interesting? But should we consume too much, it turns on us. We wake feeling even more worthless than we did the day before. We wipe away the tears that have formed as we slept and try and push aside those negative thoughts. We shower, comb our hair, brush our teeth and pull on clothes that are fresh and clean. Now, don't we look good enough to play the part of a competent person? In fact, our reflection even manages to convince us that we are. Then we go to our workplaces and survive another day without making one mistake.

When the working day is over though, doesn't our memory betray us? We have forgotten that only a few hours earlier, we swore not to touch another drop? But no, our friend is waiting for us, so we walk a little quicker as we make our way to the pub, the off licence or the late-night shop, where it will be.

That was the place I was in when I first saw Helen.

It was a Saturday night, close to last orders for food, and we were busy cleaning down the kitchen. The bar's late-night licence allowed the function room to be turned into a disco. Us single ones wanted to go to the bar in there, have a drink and let our hair down a bit. All the adrenalin that pumps on a busy night in the kitchen needs to wind down slowly.

I had just finished putting all the rubbish in bags and was making my way to the skip at the back of the pub when I reached the function room's large open doors and I stopped in my tracks, for I could hardly believe my eyes. I was looking at the most beautiful girl I had ever seen; I was simply gobsmacked. I still believe that it was love at first sight.

I don't have to look at a photo to see her as she was then, all I have to do is close my eyes for a second and there she is, with her shoulder-length, light brown hair and those amazing blue eyes of hers, dressed in hip-hugging white trousers and a glittery black top. As I stood there, she was dancing away and I thought she was the most radiant person I had ever seen.

I was going to make sure that I found out who she was alright.

So, why did I wait until I had finished in the kitchen and not simply go and ask her myself? A tiny bit of common sense that I didn't know I possessed told me that approaching a girl on a night out with her friends was not always the best way to go about it. So, I finished taking the rubbish out and asked Mark to pop out so he could see the function room door. I nodded towards where she stood and asked if he could find out who she was.

'You're in luck, Ryan. She works here, she's our new cleaner. Her name's Helen and she's living on the caravan site next door. But be careful, she's had a bit of a rough time. Don't know the whole story, but she's recently been through a messy divorce and come here for a fresh start. She has a little boy, he's about two or three and he comes into the restaurant with her early in the morning and she's finished before your shift starts. So, I'd play it very cool if I was you, the management and the day staff really like her. Hard worker too.'

Cool or not, I couldn't get Helen out of my mind.

In the end, I asked the manager's son who was a friend of mine to try and arrange a date for me with her.

'Tell you what, I'll ask her to meet you in the bar of the restaurant. You can see if you click over a drink and always have dinner if it's going well,' he told me.

To my delight, she agreed. It might have been a bit of a blind date, but meeting in the restaurant where she worked was a pretty safe choice. And how did that first time go? We met in the restaurant bar, which really was a lovely setting. The bar was small, it had discreet patterned carpet and the tables and chairs were of a good quality.

I finished work, had a quick wash in the changing room and then made my way gingerly into the bar to find this beautiful girl I was going to meet properly for the very first time. I was so nervous, but the date did seem to be a great success and I was even more in love now than before.

I still had a lot of growing up to do, but I was convinced this was the start of my new life and I had just met my life partner for the first time. I thought it went well, even though she did drop into conversation that escaping from her husband had been an ordeal she never wanted to go through again and as far as she was concerned, it was her and her little boy Jess against the world.

Another date was set and then a third one.

And to my excitement at the end of the third date she told me that her parents were due to visit and she invited me to join them all for a meal.

'But first, you'd better meet Jess,' she said.

And to me, these were two really big steps forward in our growing relationship.

57

Phil

I was so happy for Ryan when he introduced me to Helen. I just knew straight away that she was not going to disappear from our lives. I also knew that she was going to be really good for him. There was both a calmness and a strength about her.

I hadn't seen my brother looking as relaxed as this in a very long time – in fact, probably never. Though it had taken a few months to get there as I was only too aware of, for he kept me informed of just about every stage of his relationship with Helen. Even though a lot of his free time was being taken up because he was spending it with her, he still made sure that we met up on a regular basis.

I almost began to look forward to hearing about the next stage of his and Helen's relationship, for I had listened to all the details about how he felt from the first time he saw her. That was followed by his description of their first date, where she had told him a little of how she managed to leave her husband.

'And that explains why she doesn't want to dive into another relationship, Phil.'

Not that I ever believed he was going to take much notice of that.

The next big stage was Helen inviting him to meet her parents, which should have pleased him, but instead it appeared to have just the opposite effect. I knew something was amiss as soon as he walked into the bar.

'What's up, Ryan?' I asked once our beers had arrived.

'She's asked me if we could arrange to both have the same day off so I can spend some time getting to know her son, Jess.'

'But that's great!' And then seeing the expression on his face I added, 'Isn't it?'

The problem was, he confided in me, that he had not yet plucked up the courage to tell her about his past. I could see how uptight he was, but I didn't think for one moment that she was going to hold the abuse we had suffered against either of us. My advice was to go ahead and tell her immediately and get it out of his system.

I did feel for him that night when we went our separate ways. For all the bravado that others saw, I knew his fear of rejection was still lingering in his mind. Despite everything Joy Medlock had said to us, maybe he still couldn't get the end of that film out of his head.

When we met the next time, I was pretty relieved by the broad smile on his face that told me everything had gone well.

'You've told her, haven't you? So, go on then, tell me what her response was.'

Ryan told me that Helen was a bit shocked about his reason for telling her: that he thought she should know about him before he met her son. And when she asked why, he had told her that he was so worried she would see him as a threat.

'And what did she say to that?'

'That she was really upset about how the two of us had suffered for so many years, but what I had to try hard to do was to get rid of the blame and the shame I still carried. Phil, she didn't need reassurance about that. She had guessed I was troubled, it intrigued her, but no one had told her the reason.'

'Did she suggest counselling, just as Joy did?'

'Yes, but I'm not going. I don't want to sit talking to some stranger about Clive and us. I'll sort myself out, I know I can do it. She asked a few questions about you, Phil, wanted to know how you were coping. I bet when she knows you a little better, she'll try and get you to go as well.'

He was right about that: it didn't take Helen long to bring the subject up with me after we met.

The difference was I agreed to go.

And did it help?

It did.

It made me understand what had happened to us far more clearly. Looking at things through my adult eyes rather than my child's ones was really enlightening. But my therapist told me that I should also accept that not every bit of damage can be repaired and not everything can be got over. She made me feel that what was important was my acceptance that my flashbacks and bad dreams were a normal reaction to what had happened. And that once I understood that, they would in fact almost certainly begin to lessen over time.

'And if you're frightened of the dark, just leave a night light on.'

It was the word 'normal' that I repeated and repeated to myself every time a flashback or a frightening nightmare invaded my peace.

As for Helen, she certainly made it clear that she was there for me to talk to if ever I needed to unburden myself. Without saying the words, she had taken on the task of not just sorting one person out, but two.

* * *

It was three years after their first date that Ryan and Helen invited me over for a celebration. There I was, thinking it was celebrating a three-year anniversary, and then they told me I was going to be an uncle – Helen was pregnant! How can I describe it? Their joint happiness was just wonderful.

Months later, Harry was born at 10.47pm and weighed a healthy 7lb 3oz – the greatest moment ever! After his son's arrival, Ryan, to our great surprise, agreed to have therapy. Helen had picked the right moment to ask him again. At that stage in his life, anything that she asked for, he was going to say yes to.

58

Ryan

It was when the sixth anniversary of our first date was on the horizon that Helen and I thought of a slightly different way to celebrate: why not have a wedding? Ours, that was.

Money was a bit tight as we had just bought our first house, but we were not going to let a little thing like that stop us from having a wedding to remember. Luckily for us, over the time we had been together, we had made some really good friends. The moment they heard the word 'wedding', help was offered. One, a photographer, told us that his present would be our wedding album. And then the Saturday night DJ from the function room at the pub said as long as he had an invite, he would make sure we had a great evening party. Another friend's parents offered to lend us their Jag so that took care of the wedding car.

Mum and Dad gave us some money as soon as they knew about the wedding. And Helen's parents, Elaine and Ron, generously not only gave us some money towards the big day, but her mum told us she would make our wedding cake and order all the flowers. When I saw the three-tiered cake with tiny flowers decorating it and the figures of a bride and groom on the top, I felt like hugging her. We had built up a good relationship and they had welcomed me into their family like one of their own. We often had family meals together and Ron and I enjoyed a game of snooker.

All the catering was done by the pub and their gift to us was to offer a big discount on the cost of the food and booze and the function room hire charge was free. The waiters and barmen – all close friends, people I had worked with for years – worked for free that night, which really helped, and then our bridesmaids, close friends of Helen, told us they would buy their own dresses. As for the suits for the men, well, they could be hired.

Helen was the one in charge of all the arrangements and watching her with loads of lists, I realised that I hadn't a clue how much work there was in organising a wedding. She had sorted out the colour scheme, which was to be white and burgundy. There were flowers for buttonholes for the men, bride and bridesmaids bouquets and corsages for our mums. Then there were burgundy paper napkins and table decorations.

The first time Helen met my family, it was just Mum on her own. It went well and Mum really liked her. Following that, Helen and three-year-old Jess were invited for dinner at my parents' home and met them and some of my brothers. Again, it went well, even though Jess did ask Mum about her grey hair, which embarrassed Helen, but we all laughed and my family embraced them both.

As the months flew by, my mind was full of little else than our upcoming October wedding and as I worked away in the kitchen, it was a wonder I got the orders right!

Talk about more luck being on our side, there was not a cloud in the sky when the date finally arrived. That alone told me that our wedding day was going to be magical. Helen had arranged to get ready at her parents' hotel, while I, surrounded by all my brothers and my best pals, got dressed in ours. Phil couldn't stop grinning with happiness for me. He was single, but close to Helen and so happy to see us getting married. Clive might have said neither of us would ever get a girlfriend, but Phil must have been thinking, *If Ryan can do it, maybe I can too*. A few drinks were handed around – well, my nerves needed settling was my excuse. Then it was off to the registry office and at 2pm precisely, we took our vows.

The service was wonderful, with a small audience of family and close friends. Helen looked beautiful in her ivory dress – it was stunning, simple and elegant. You could feel the love and contentment in the room; both families had come together and fully approved of our marriage. There were tears and laughter. I, for sure, had to hold back a tear when I first saw Helen. As she got to me, she said, 'Let's do this!' and squeezed my hand tightly. We could sense each other's nerves.

Arriving back at the pub afterwards, we were touched by the effort our work friends had put into decorating the function room. There were balloons and masses of flowers, all in white and burgundy, which they must have done before they prepared the enormous hot and cold finger buffet. They had placed bottles of white and red wine out on the tables as well as cold drinks and jugs of water. After the meal, there would be a cash bar for the rest of the reception, although Dad had already put enough money behind the bar for the first round of drinks to be on him.

When I looked around at members of our families and close friends I saw traditional wedding outfits galore, along with an array of amazing hats. Having all our close friends and family together in one place made our day even more perfect.

The speeches were brilliant and we had such a giggle. My best friend was the best man (and also the son of the pub landlord). He kept the room amused telling some of the most embarrassing moments from my younger years and some of the things I said when I first saw Helen. Helen's dad has a superb sense of humour and had everyone in fits when he told them how he never thought anyone would take his daughter off his hands. Joking apart, you could tell she was the apple of his eye. The mums were given flowers, then our two page boys – Jess and Harry, our younger son – received gifts, as did our bridesmaids. The cake was cut and slices passed around before we posed for more wedding photographs.

By late afternoon, the older guests began to take their leave – 'No, we're not staying for the evening disco, we don't have the stamina!' they told us laughingly. So, most of us opted to watch the weekend's big match – we could hardly knock back wine all day after all!

We had been lent a couple of rooms so that we could

change into suitable clothes for our evening do, which we did before greeting our evening guests. I swapped my shirt for a fresh one and ditched the tie and waistcoat, while Helen wore a shorter, more evening style of dress in the same colour and fabric as her wedding gown. Naturally, she and I were the first couple on the floor, dancing to our favourite song, Roberta Flack's beautiful rendition of 'The First Time Ever I Saw Your Face'. The DJ played from the list of tracks Helen and I had chosen and later that evening, once the kitchen had closed and the last customer had left the bar and restaurant, the staff came in and joined our party, which lasted until the early hours. My new wife looked spectacular as she danced the night away.

I did say I wanted our special day to be magical and it was – it is still one of the most treasured memories of my life. Helen and I reminisce about it often as we leaf through the pages of our wedding album, reliving every moment.

59

Ryan

Twenty Years Later

I have now gone from being a chef to being a full-time foster carer.

So how did that happen?

Let's just say my journey from troubled teenager to being a reasonably together adult was neither short nor particularly easy. Even with all the support from my brothers and Helen, I found I needed extra help. So, I persevered with counselling. Like Phil, in the end I have to admit it really helped me. By the conclusion, I understood that the effects of childhood abuse can linger for a long time – and in some cases, forever.

Once I got to that stage, I began to think I had something to offer others who had suffered. It was around then that Helen and I began to discuss fostering. We knew that we were likely to find that children who came to us would be troubled. Because of my own experience I felt that I could perhaps help those children more than people without my insights into the problems that abuse can generate. Feelings of insecurity were bound to be one of their major fears and that's something I totally understand. Helen also believed that I had something to offer. After all, she had witnessed my pain and helped me in trying to turn my life around. Once we agreed that this was something we both wanted to do, we talked it over with 17-year-old Harry as our son had not left home yet and was at sixth-form college, studying sports chemistry, leisure and business.

'Go for it, Dad,' was his answer.

Professional confidentiality means that I can't talk about the specific reasons why children have been removed from their homes and placed in our care. Let's just say they need to feel understood, loved and secure. It's three years since the first children – two sisters – came to us and two years ago, their younger brother also joined our family. Both Helen and I take immense pleasure in seeing these three siblings gain in confidence.

Phil and I meet up regularly. He's still working at the college where he was given his first job. He has his own circle of friends and is happy and content.

We never saw Clive or Maureen again. On release from prison, Clive returned to his marital home. He died of prostate cancer in a nursing home, aged seventy-two, in 2010. The obituary appeared in my local paper and someone showed it to me.

We did not go to his funeral.

Later, I learnt that Maureen has dementia.

Our father died of bowel cancer in 2015 and all his

family were with him when he passed away. Then, when Mum's health began to deteriorate, Phil moved back to the family home. No, he never married, but he's been a great uncle not just to our two children, but to his other nieces and nephews too.

Compared to many troubled teenagers, I know I've been lucky. Not only had I the support from my brothers, but also the understanding from people I met along the way. Sadly, there are those who do not have the same degree of support so I have offered to do some part-time work for council-run homes. The particular project I'll be working on is a secure unit that houses up to thirty-eight boys, aged between ten and eighteen.

So that's the end of Phil's and my story, although our journey is by no means over. The amazing aspect of writing this book together is that it has brought my brother and I even closer. It has helped chase away those invasive dreams and the occasional bouts of darkness.

For years, we never allowed the name Clive to leave our lips, but now we can.

We've talked at length not just about what happened, but how we felt at the time and when we reflect on it as adults. Both of us appreciate that in writing it down, fragments of the weight we once carried are now falling away. Finally, the invisible chains of our past are broken.

Acknowledgements

We express our sincere gratitude to our brothers, Ian, Allen, Warren and Leighton, and their wonderful partners, for their love, support and encouragement, which has been our saviour and allowed us to live a wonderful and fulfilling life. Our real-life superheroes!

To the police, on the day we first walked into the station, your compassion and professionalism astounded us. Joy, you will forever be in our thoughts.

To Harry, quite often Ryan's reason for carrying on, we thank you for putting up with grumpy Dad over the years and supporting him in our journey.

To Barbara Levy, who we must thank for placing our story in the very capable hands of Bonnier Books.

Toni, we must send our biggest thank you to you, for if it were not for you taking a leap of faith with our story, none of this would have been possible. You have been unbelievably professional throughout this process, which has been an absolute godsend to us. You have made us both feel at ease, even when talking about the very personal things that happened to us. It has been a journey telling you our life story: the good, the bad and real ugly. You have been there for us and have written it with such sensitivity and respect, it is simply perfect.

To any other survivors out there, all we can say is you are not alone. Please seek help if you're having problems or if you need to get things off your chest – we did and it changed our lives. We salute each and every one of you! If we can help any one of you, we will.

To family, friends, the Samaritans, counsellors, doctors and psychologists who have all played such a huge part in our lives, we are grateful.

Thank you everyone.

Ryan and Phil xx